ABOUT THIS PUBLICATION

FOR SERVICE ASSISTANCE

Customer Service
1.704.898.0770

North Carolina General Statues is published by The Muliti-Media Group of Greater Charlotte in Charlotte, North Carolina. Copyright 2015 by the Multi-Media Group of Greater Charlotte. This book or parts thereof may not be reproduced in any form, stored in a retrieval system, or transmitted in any form by any means—electronic, mechanical, photocopy, recording or otherwise—without prior written permission of the publisher, except as provided by United States of America copyright law.

The records required by U.S. Code 2257(a) through (c) and the pertinent regulations 28 C.F.R. Cli. 1, Part 75 with respect to this publication and all materials associated with such records are maintained by The Multi-Media Group of Greater Charlotte, Publisher and available for review by Attorney General.

www.visionbooks.org

Copyright © 2015 by MMGGC
All rights reserved!

TID: 5061451
ISBN (10) digit: 1502913216
ISBN (13) digit: 978-1502913210

123-4-56789-01239-Paperback
123-4-56789-01239-Hardback

First Edition

090520140547

Printed in the United States of America

2015 EDITION

North Carolina Criminal Law And Procedure-Pamphlet # 34

Printed In conjunction with the Administration of the Courts

North Carolina Criminal Law and Procedure
Pamphlet Reference Guide

Chapters	Pamphlet
Chapter 1 Civil Procedure	1
Chapter 1 Civil Procedure (Continue)	2
Chapter 1A Rules of Civil Procedure	2
Chapter 1B Contribution.	2
Chapter 1C Enforcement of Judgments.	2
Chapter 1D Punitive Damages.	2
Chapter 1E Eastern Band of Cherokee Indians.	2
Chapter 1F North Carolina Uniform Interstate Depositions and Discovery Act.	2
Chapter 2 - Clerk of Superior Court [Repealed and Transferred.]	3
Chapter 3 - Commissioners of Affidavits and Deeds [Repealed.]	3
Chapter 4 - Common Law	3
Chapter 5 - Contempt [Repealed.]	3
Chapter 5A - Contempt	3
Chapter 6 - Liability for Court Costs	3
Chapter 7 - Courts [Repealed and Transferred.]	3
Chapter 7A – Judicial Department	3
Chapter 7A – Continuation (Judicial Department)	4
Chapter 7A – Continuation (Judicial Department)	5
Chapter 7B - Juvenile Code	5
Chapter 8 - Evidence	6
Chapter 8A - Interpreters for Deaf Persons [Recodified.]	6
Chapter 8B - Interpreters for Deaf Persons	6
Chapter 8C - Evidence Code	6
Chapter 9 - Jurors	6
Chapter 10 - Notaries [Repealed.]	6
Chapter 10A - Notaries [Recodified.]	6
Chapter 10B - Notaries	6
Chapter 11 - Oaths	6
Chapter 12 - Statutory Construction	6
Chapter 13 - Citizenship Restored	6
Chapter 14 - Criminal Law	7
Chapter 14 –Criminal Law (Continuation)	8
Chapter 15 - Criminal Procedure	9
Chapter 15A - Criminal Procedure Act (Continuation)	10
Chapter 15A - Criminal Procedure Act (Continuation)	11
Chapter 15B - Victims Compensation	11
Chapter 15C - Address Confidentiality Program	11
Chapter 16 - Gaming Contracts and Futures	11
Chapter 17 - Habeas Corpus	11

Chapter 17A - Law-Enforcement Officers [Recodified.]	11
Chapter 17B - North Carolina Criminal Justice Education and Training System [Recodified.] Chapter 17C - North Carolina Criminal Justice Education and Training Standards Commission	11
Chapter 17D - North Carolina Justice Academy	11
Chapter 17E - North Carolina Sheriffs' Education and Training Standards Commission	11
Chapter 18 - Regulation of Intoxicating Liquors [Repealed.]	12
Chapter 18A - Regulation of Intoxicating Liquors [Repealed.]	12
Chapter 18B - Regulation of Alcoholic Beverages	12
Chapter 18C - North Carolina State Lottery	12
Chapter 19 - Offenses against Public Morals	12
Chapter 19A - Protection of Animals	12
Chapter 20 - Motor Vehicles	13
Chapter 20 - Motor Vehicles (Continuation)	14
Chapter 20 - Motor Vehicles (Continuation)	15
Chapter 20 - Motor Vehicles (Continuation)	16
Chapter 21 - Bills of Lading	17
Chapter 22 - Contracts Requiring Writing	17
Chapter 22A - Signatures	17
Chapter 22B - Contracts Against Public Policy	17
Chapter 22C - Payments to Subcontractors	17
Chapter 23 - Debtor and Creditor. r 24 - Interest	17
Chapter 24 – Interest	17
Chapter 25 – Uniform Commercial Code	18
Chapter 25 – Uniform Commercial Code (Continuation)	19
Chapter 25A – Retail Installment Sales Act	20
Chapter 25B - Credit	20
Chapter 25C - Sales of Artwork	20
Chapter 26 - Suretyship	20
Chapter 27 - Warehouse Receipts [Repealed.]	20
Chapter 28 - Administration [Repealed.]	20
Chapter 28A - Administration of Decedents' Estates	20
Chapter 28B - Estates of Absentees in Military Service	20
Chapter 28C - Estates of Missing Persons	20
Chapter 29 - Intestate Succession	21
Chapter 30 - Surviving Spouses	21
Chapter 31 - Wills	21
Chapter 31A - Acts Barring Property Rights	21
Chapter 31B - Renunciation of Property and Renunciation of Fiduciary Powers Act	21
Chapter 31C - Uniform Disposition of Community Property Rights at Death Act	21
Chapter 32 - Fiduciaries	21
Chapter 32A - Powers of Attorney	21
Chapter 33 - Guardian and Ward [Repealed and Recodified.]	21

Chapter 33A - North Carolina Uniform Transfers to Minors Act	21
Chapter 33B - North Carolina Uniform Custodial Trust Act	21
Chapter 34 - Veterans' Guardianship Act	22
Chapter 35 - Sterilization Procedures	22
Chapter 35A - Incompetency and Guardianship	22
Chapter 36 - Trusts and Trustees [Repealed.]	22
Chapter 36A - Trusts and Trustees	22
Chapter 36B - Uniform Management of Institutional Funds Act [Repealed.]	22
Chapter 36C - North Carolina Uniform Trust Code	22
Chapter 36D - North Carolina Community Third Party Trusts, Pooled Trusts	23
Chapter 36E - Uniform Prudent Management of Institutional Funds Act	23
Chapter 37 - Allocation of Principal and Income [Repealed.]	23
Chapter 37A - Uniform Principal and Income Act	23
Chapter 38 - Boundaries	23
Chapter 38A - Landowner Liability	23
Chapter 39 - Conveyances	23
Chapter 39A - Transfer Fee Covenants Prohibited	23
Chapter 40 - Eminent Domain [Repealed.]	23
Chapter 40A - Eminent Domain	23
Chapter 41 - Estates	23
Chapter 41A - State Fair Housing Act	23
Chapter 42 - Landlord and Tenant	23
Chapter 42A - Vacation Rental Act	23
Chapter 43 - Land Registration	23
Chapter 44 - Liens	24
Chapter 44A - Statutory Liens and Charges	24
Chapter 45 - Mortgages and Deeds of Trust	24
Chapter 45A - Good Funds Settlement Act	24
Chapter 46 - Partition	24
Chapter 47 - Probate and Registration	25
Chapter 47A - Unit Ownership	25
Chapter 47B - Real Property Marketable Title Act	25
Chapter 47C - North Carolina Condominium Act	25
Chapter 47D - Notice of Settlement Act [Expired.]	25
Chapter 47E - Residential Property Disclosure Act	25
Chapter 47F - North Carolina Planned Community Act	25
Chapter 47G - Option to Purchase Contracts	25
Chapter 47H - Contracts for Deed	25
Chapter 48 - Adoptions +	26
Chapter 48A - Minors	26
Chapter 49 - Bastardy	26
Chapter 49A - Rights of Children	26
Chapter 50 - Divorce and Alimony	26
Chapter 50A - Uniform Child-Custody Jurisdiction and	

Enforcement Act	26
Chapter 50B - Domestic Violence	26
Chapter 50C - Civil No-Contact Orders	26
Chapter 51 - Marriage	26
Chapter 52 - Powers and Liabilities of Married Persons	27
Chapter 52A - Uniform Reciprocal Enforcement of Support Act [Repealed.]	27
Chapter 52B - Uniform Premarital Agreement Act	27
Chapter 52C - Uniform Interstate Family Support Act	27
Chapter 53 - Banks	27
Chapter 53A - Business Development Corporations and North Carolina Capital Resource Corporations	28
Chapter 53B - Financial Privacy Act	28
Chapter 54 - Cooperative Organizations	28
Chapter 54A - Capital Stock Savings and Loan Associations [Repealed.]	28
Chapter 54B - Savings and Loan Associations	29
Chapter 54C - Savings Banks	29
Chapter 55 - North Carolina Business Corporation Act	30
Chapter 55A - North Carolina Nonprofit Corporation Act	31
Chapter 55B - Professional Corporation Act	31
Chapter 55C - Foreign Trade Zones	31
Chapter 55D - Filings, Names, and Registered Agents for Corporations, Nonprofit Corporations, and Partnerships	31
Chapter 56 - Electric, Telegraph and Power Companies [Repealed.]	31
Chapter 57 - Hospital, Medical and Dental Service Corporations [Recodified.]	31
Chapter 57A - Health Maintenance Organization Act [Recodified.]	31
Chapter 57B - Health Maintenance Organization Act [Recodified.]	31
Chapter 57C - North Carolina Limited Liability Company Act.	31
Chapter 58 - Insurance.	32
Chapter 58 - Insurance (Continuation)	33
Chapter 58 - Insurance (Continuation)	34
Chapter 58 - Insurance (Continuation)	35
Chapter 58 - Insurance (Continuation)	36
Chapter 58 - Insurance (Continuation)	37
Chapter 58 - Insurance (Continuation)	38
Chapter 58A - North Carolina Health Insurance Trust Commission [Recodified.]	38
Chapter 59 - Partnership.	39
Chapter 59B - Uniform Unincorporated Nonprofit Association Act.	39
Chapter 60 - Railroads and Other Carriers [Repealed and Transferred.]	39
Chapter 61 - Religious Societies	39
Chapter 62 - Public Utilities	39

Chapter 62 - Public Utilities (Continuation)	40
Chapter 62A - Public Safety Telephone Service And Wireless Telephone Service	40
Chapter 63 - Aeronautics	40
Chapter 63A - North Carolina Global TransPark Authority	40
Chapter 64 - Aliens	40
Chapter 65 – Cemeteries	40
Chapter 66 - Commerce and Business	41
Chapter 67 - Dogs	41
Chapter 68 - Fences and Stock Law	41
Chapter 69 - Fire Protection	41
Chapter 70 - Indian Antiquities, Archaeological Resources and Unmarked Human Skeletal Remains Protection	42
Chapter 71 - Indians [Repealed.]	42
Chapter 71A - Indians	42
Chapter 72 - Inns, Hotels and Restaurants	42
Chapter 73 - Mills	42
Chapter 74 - Mines and Quarries	42
Chapter 74A - Company Police [Repealed.]	42
Chapter 74B - Private Protective Services Act [Repealed.]	42
Chapter 74C - Private Protective Services	42
Chapter 74D - Alarm Systems	42
Chapter 74E - Company Police Act	42
Chapter 74F - Locksmith Licensing Act	42
Chapter 74G - Campus Police Act	42
Chapter 75 - Monopolies, Trusts and Consumer Protection	42
Chapter 75A - Boating and Water Safety	43
Chapter 75B - Discrimination in Business	43
Chapter 75C - Motion Picture Fair Competition Act	43
Chapter 75D - Racketeer Influenced and Corrupt Organizations	43
Chapter 75E - Unlawful Activities in Connection With Certain Corporate Transactions	43
Chapter 76 - Navigation	43
Chapter 76A - Navigation and Pilotage Commissions	43
Chapter 77 - Rivers, Creeks, and Coastal Waters	43
Chapter 78 - Securities Law [Repealed.]	43
Chapter 78A - North Carolina Securities Act	43
Chapter 78B - Tender Offer Disclosure Act [Repealed.]	43
Chapter 78C - Investment Advisers	43
Chapter 78D - Commodities Act	43
Chapter 79 - Strays [Repealed.]	43
Chapter 80 - Trademarks, Brands, etc.	44
Chapter 81 - Weights and Measures [Recodified.]	44
Chapter 81A - Weights and Measures Act of 1975.	44
Chapter 82 - Wrecks [Repealed.]	44
Chapter 83 - Architects [Recodified.]	44

Chapter 83A - Architects	44
Chapter 84 - Attorneys-at-Law	44
Chapter 84A - Foreign Legal Consultants	44
Chapter 85 - Auctions and Auctioneers [Repealed.]	44
Chapter 85A - Bail Bondsmen and Runners [Recodified.]	44
Chapter 85B - Auctions and Auctioneers	44
Chapter 85C - Bail Bondsmen and Runners [Recodified.]	44
Chapter 86 - Barbers [Recodified.]	44
Chapter 86A - Barbers	44
Chapter 87 - Contractors	44
Chapter 88 - Cosmetic Art [Repealed.]	44
Chapter 88A - Electrolysis Practice Act	44
Chapter 88B - Cosmetic Art	45
Chapter 89 - Engineering and Land Surveying [Recodified.]	45
Chapter 89A - Landscape Architects	45
Chapter 89B - Foresters	45
Chapter 89C - Engineering and Land Surveying	45
Chapter 89D - Landscape Contractors	45
Chapter 89E - Geologists Licensing Act	45
Chapter 89F - North Carolina Soil Scientist Licensing Act	45
Chapter 89G - Irrigation Contractors	45
Chapter 90 - Medicine and Allied Occupations	45
Chapter 90 - Medicine and Allied Occupations (Continuation)	46
Chapter 90 - Medicine and Allied Occupations (Continuation)	47
Chapter 90 - Medicine and Allied Occupations (Continuation)	48
Chapter 90A - Sanitarians and Water and Wastewater Treatment Facility Operators	48
Chapter 90B - Social Worker Certification and Licensure Act	48
Chapter 90C - North Carolina Recreational Therapy Licensure Act	48
Chapter 90D - Interpreters and Transliterators	48
Chapter 91 - Pawnbrokers [Repealed.]	48
Chapter 91A - Pawnbrokers Modernization Act of 1989	48
Chapter 92 - Photographers [Deleted.]	48
Chapter 93 - Certified Public Accountants	48
Chapter 93A - Real Estate License Law	49
Chapter 93B - Occupational Licensing Boards	49
Chapter 93C - Watchmakers [Repealed.]	49
Chapter 93D - North Carolina State Hearing Aid Dealers and Fitters Board.	49
Chapter 93E - North Carolina Appraisers Act	49
Chapter 94 - Apprenticeship	49
Chapter 95 - Department of Labor and Labor Regulations	49
Chapter 95 - Department of Labor and Labor Regulations (Continuation)	50
Chapter 96 - Employment Security	50
Chapter 97 - Workers' Compensation Act	50
Chapter 97 - Workers' Compensation Act (Continuation)	51

Chapter 98 - Burnt and Lost Records	51
Chapter 99 - Libel and Slander	51
Chapter 99A - Civil Remedies for Criminal Actions	51
Chapter 99B - Products Liability	51
Chapter 99C - Actions Relating to Winter Sports Safety and Accidents	51
Chapter 99D - Civil Rights	51
Chapter 99E - Special Liability Provisions	51
Chapter 100 - Monuments, Memorials and Parks	51
Chapter 101 - Names of Persons	51
Chapter 102 - Official Survey Base	51
Chapter 103 - Sundays, Holidays and Special Days	51
Chapter 104 - United States Lands	51
Chapter 104A - Degrees of Kinship	51
Chapter 104B - Hurricanes or Other Acts of Nature	51
Chapter 104C - Atomic Energy, Radioactivity and Ionizing Radiation [Repealed and Recodified.]	51
Chapter 104D - Southern States Energy Compact	51
Chapter 104E - North Carolina Radiation Protection Act	51
Chapter 104F - Southeast Interstate Low-Level Radioactive Waste Management Compact [Repealed]	51
Chapter 104G - North Carolina Low-Level Radioactive Waste Management Authority Act of 1987 [Repealed]	51
Chapter 105 - Taxation	51
Chapter 105 - Taxation (Continuation)	52
Chapter 105 - Taxation (Continuation)	53
Chapter 105 - Taxation (Continuation)	54
Chapter 105A - Setoff Debt Collection Act	55
Chapter 105B - Defaulted Student Loan Recovery Act	55
Chapter 106 - Agriculture	55
Chapter 106 - Agriculture (Continue)	56
Chapter 106 - Agriculture (Continue)	57
Chapter 107 - Agricultural Development Districts [Repealed.]	57
Chapter 108 - Social Services [Repealed and Recodified.]	57
Chapter 108A - Social Services	57
Chapter 108B - Community Action Programs	58
Chapter 108C Medicaid and Health Choice Provider Requirements.	58
Chapter 108D Medicaid Managed Care for Behavioral Health Services.	58
Chapter 109 - Bonds [Recodified.]	58
Chapter 110 - Child Welfare	58
Chapter 111 - Aid to the Blind	58
Chapter 112 - Confederate Homes and Pensions [Repealed.]	58
Chapter 113 - Conservation and Development	58
Chapter 113 - Conservation and Development (Continuation)	59

Chapter 113A - Pollution Control and Environment	59
Chapter 113A - Pollution Control and Environment (Continuation)	60
Chapter 113B - North Carolina Energy Policy Act of 1975	60
Chapter 114 - Department of Justice	60
Chapter 115 - Elementary and Secondary Education [Repealed.]	60
Chapter 115A - Community Colleges, Technical Institutes, and Industrial Education Centers [Repealed.]	60
Chapter 115B - Tuition and Fee Waivers	60
Chapter 115C - Elementary and Secondary Education	60
Chapter 115C - Elementary and Secondary Education (Continuation)	61
Chapter 115C - Elementary and Secondary Education (Continuation)	62
Chapter 115C - Elementary and Secondary Education (Continuation)	63
Chapter 115D - Community Colleges	63
Chapter 115E - Private Educational Facilities Finance Act [Recodified]	63
Chapter 116 - Higher Education	63
Chapter 116 - Higher Education (Continuation)	63
Chapter 116A - Escheats and Abandoned Property [Repealed.]	64
Chapter 116B - Escheats and Abandoned Property	64
Chapter 116C - Continuum of Education Programs	64
Chapter 116D - Higher Education Bonds	64
Chapter 117 - Electrification	64
Chapter 118 - Firemen's and Rescue Squad Workers' Relief and Pension Funds [Recodified.]	64
Chapter 118A - Firemen's Death Benefit Act [Repealed.]	64
Chapter 118B - Members of a Rescue Squad Death Benefit Act [Repealed.]	64
Chapter 119 - Gasoline and Oil Inspection and Regulation	64
Chapter 120 - General Assembly	65
Chapter 120 - General Assembly (Continuation)	66
Chapter 120 - General Assembly (Continuation)	67
Chapter 120C - Lobbying	67
Chapter 121 - Archives and History	67
Chapter 122 - Hospitals for the Mentally Disordered [Repealed.]	67
Chapter 122A - North Carolina Housing Finance Agency	67
Chapter 122B - North Carolina Agricultural Facilities Finance Act [Repealed.]	67
Chapter 122C - Mental Health, Developmental Disabilities, and Substance Abuse Act of 1985	67
Chapter 122C - Mental Health, Developmental Disabilities, and Substance Abuse Act of 1985 (Continuation)	68
Chapter 122D - North Carolina Agricultural Finance Act	68

Chapter 122E - North Carolina Housing Trust and Oil Overcharge Act	68
Chapter 123 - Impeachment	69
Chapter 123A - Industrial Development [Repealed.]	69
Chapter 124 - Internal Improvements	69
Chapter 125 - Libraries	69
Chapter 126 - State Personnel System	69
Chapter 127 - Militia [Repealed.]	69
Chapter 127A - Militia	69
Chapter 127B - Military Affairs	69
Chapter 127C - Advisory Commission on Military Affairs	69
Chapter 128 - Offices and Public Officers	69
Chapter 128 - Offices and Public Officers (Continuation)	70
Chapter 129 - Public Buildings and Grounds	70
Chapter 130 - Public Health [Repealed.]	70
Chapter 130A - Public Health	70
Chapter 130A - Public Health (Continuation)	71
Chapter 130A - Public Health (Continuation)	72
Chapter 130B - Hazardous Waste Management Commission [Repealed.]	72
Chapter 131 - Public Hospitals [Repealed.]	72
Chapter 131A - Health Care Facilities Finance Act	72
Chapter 131B - Licensing of Ambulatory Surgical Facilities [Repealed.]	72
Chapter 131C - Charitable Solicitation Licensure Act [Repealed.]	72
Chapter 131D - Inspection and Licensing of Facilities	72
Chapter 131E - Health Care Facilities and Services	72
Chapter 131E - Health Care Facilities and Services (Continuation)	73
Chapter 131F - Solicitation of Contributions	73
Chapter 132 - Public Records	73
Chapter 133 - Public Works	74
Chapter 134 - Youth Development [Recodified.]	74
Chapter 134A - Youth Services [Repealed.]	74
Chapter 135 - Retirement System for Teachers and State Employees; Social Security; Health Insurance Program for Children	74
Chapter 135 - Retirement System for Teachers and State Employees; Social Security; Health Insurance Program for Children	75
Chapter 136 - Transportation	75
Chapter 136 - Transportation (Continuation)	76
Chapter 137 - Rural Rehabilitation [Repealed.]	76
Chapter 138 - Salaries, Fees and Allowances	76
Chapter 138A - State Government Ethics Act	76
Chapter 139 - Soil and Water Conservation Districts	76

Chapter 140 - State Art Museum; Symphony and Art Societies	76
Chapter 140A - State Awards System	76
Chapter 141 - State Boundaries	76
Chapter 142 - State Debt	76
Chapter 143 - State Departments, Institutions, and Commissions	77
Chapter 143 - State Departments, Institutions, and Commissions (Continuation)	78
Chapter 143 - State Departments, Institutions, and Commissions (Continuation)	79
Chapter 143 - State Departments, Institutions, and Commissions (Continuation)	80
Chapter 143A - State Government Reorganization	80
Chapter 143B - Executive Organization Act of 1973	80
Chapter 143B - Executive Organization Act of 1973 (Continuation)	81
Chapter 143B - Executive Organization Act of 1973 (Continuation)	82
Chapter 143C - State Budget Act	83
Chapter 143D - The State Governmental Accountability and Internal Control Act	83
Chapter 144 - State Flag, Official Governmental Flags, Motto, and Colors	83
Chapter 145 - State Symbols and Other Official Adoptions.	83
Chapter 146 - State Lands	83
Chapter 147 - State Officers	83
Chapter 148 - State Prison System	84
Chapter 149 - State Song and Toast	84
Chapter 150 - Uniform Revocation of Licenses [Repealed.]	84
Chapter 150A - Administrative Procedure Act [Recodified.]	84
Chapter 150B - Administrative Procedure Act	84
Chapter 151 - Constables [Repealed.]	84
Chapter 152 - Coroners	84
Chapter 152A - County Medical Examiner [Repealed.]	84
Chapter 152A - County Medical Examiner [Repealed.] (Continuation)	85
Chapter 153 - Counties and County Commissioners [Repealed.]	85
Chapter 153A - Counties	85
Chapter 153B - Mountain Resources Planning Act	85
Chapter 153C - Uwharrie Regional Resources Act	85
Chapter 154 - County Surveyor [Repealed.]	85
Chapter 155 - County Treasurer [Repealed.]	85
Chapter 156 - Drainage	85
Chapter 156 – Drainage (Continuation)	86

Chapter 157 - Housing Authorities and Projects	86
Chapter 157A - Historic Properties Commissions [Transferred.]	86
Chapter 158 - Local Development	86
Chapter 159 - Local Government Finance	86
Chapter 159 - Local Government Finance (Continuation)	87
Chapter 159A - Pollution Abatement and Industrial Facilities Financing Act [Unconstitutional.]	87
Chapter 159B - Joint Municipal Electric Power and Energy Act	87
Chapter 159C - Industrial and Pollution Control Facilities Financing Act	87
Chapter 159D - The North Carolina Capital Facilities Financing Act	87
Chapter 159E - Registered Public Obligations Act	87
Chapter 159F - North Carolina Energy Development Authority [Repealed.]	87
Chapter 159G - Water Infrastructure	87
Chapter 159H - [Reserved.]	87
Chapter 159I - Solid Waste Management Loan Program and Local Government Special Obligation Bonds	87
Chapter 160 - Municipal Corporations [Repealed And Transferred.]	87
Chapter 160A - Cities and Towns	88
Chapter 160A - Cities and Towns (Continuation)	89
Chapter 160B - Consolidated City-County Act	89
Chapter 160C - Baseball Park Districts [Repealed.]	90
Chapter 161 - Register of Deeds	90
Chapter 162 - Sheriff	90
Chapter 162A - Water and Sewer Systems	90
Chapter 162B Continuity of Local Government in Emergency.	90
Chapter 163 Elections and Election Laws.	90
Chapter 163 Elections and Election Laws. (Continuation)	91
Chapter 164 Concerning the General Statutes of North Carolina.	92
Chapter 165 Veterans.	92
Chapter 166 Civil Preparedness Agencies [Repealed.]	92
Chapter 166A North Carolina Emergency Management Act.	92
Chapter 167 State Civil Air Patrol [Repealed.]	92
Chapter 168 Persons with Disabilities.	92
Chapter 168A Persons With Disabilities Protection Act.	92

§ 58-25-45. Reserve fund; exchange of certificates.

Any order or society entering into such insurance agreements shall maintain on all such contracts the reserve required by the standard of mortality and interest adopted by the order or society for computing contributions as provided in G.S.

58-25-35, and the funds representing the benefit contributions and all accretions thereon shall be kept as separate and distinct funds, independent of the other funds of the order or society, and shall not be liable for nor used for the payment of the debts and obligations of the order or society other than the benefits herein authorized. An order or society may provide that when a child reaches the minimum age for initiation into membership in such order or society, any benefit certificate issued hereunder may be surrendered for cancellation and exchanged for any other form of certificate issued by the order or society: Provided, that such surrender will not reduce the number of lives insured below 500; and upon the issuance of such new certificate any reserve upon the original certificate herein provided for shall be transferred to the credit of the new certificate. Neither the person who originally made application for benefits on account of such child, nor the beneficiary named in such original certificate, nor the person who paid the contributions, shall have any vested right in such new certificate, the free nomination of a beneficiary under the new certificate being left to the child so admitted to benefit membership. (1987, c. 483, s. 2.)

§ 58-25-50. Separation of funds.

An entirely separate financial statement of the business transactions and of assets and liabilities arising therefrom shall be made in its annual report to the Commissioner by an order or society availing itself of the provisions hereof. The separation of assets, funds, and liabilities required hereby shall not be terminated, rescinded, or modified, nor shall the funds be diverted for any use other than as specified in the preceding section, as long as any certificates issued hereunder remain in force, and this requirement shall be recognized and enforced in any liquidation, reinsurance, merger, or other change in the condition or the status of the order or society. (1987, c. 483, s. 2; 1991, c. 720, s. 4.)

§ 58-25-55. Payments to expense or general fund.

Any order or society shall have the right to provide in its laws and the certificate issued hereunder for specified payments on account of the expense or general fund, which payments shall or shall not be mingled with the general fund of the order or society, as its constitution and bylaws may provide. (1987, c. 483, s. 2.)

§ 58-25-60. Continuation of certificates.

In the event of the termination of membership in the order or society by the person responsible for the support of any child on whose account a certificate may have been issued as provided herein, the certificate may be continued for the benefit of the estate of the child, provided the contributions are continued, or for the benefit of any other person responsible for the support and maintenance of such child who shall assume the payment of the required contributions. (1987, c. 483, s. 2.)

§ 58-25-65. Appointment of trustees to hold property.

The lodges of Masons, Odd Fellows, Knights of Pythias, camps of Woodmen of the World, councils of the Junior Order of United American Mechanics, orders of the Elks, Young Men's Christian Associations, Young Women's Christian Associations and other benevolent or fraternal orders and societies may appoint from time to time suitable persons trustees of their bodies or societies, in such manner as they deem proper, which trustees, and their successors, shall have power to receive, purchase, take, and hold property, real and personal, in trust for such society or body. The trustees shall have power, when instructed so to do by resolution adopted by the order, society or body which they represent, to mortgage or sell and convey in fee simple any real or personal property owned by the order, society or body; and the conveyances so made by the trustees shall be effective to pass the property in fee simple to the purchaser or to the mortgagee or trustee for the purposes in such conveyance or mortgage expressed. If there shall be no trustee, then any real or personal property which could be held by such trustees shall vest in and be held by such charitable, benevolent, religious, or fraternal orders and societies, respectively, according to such intent. (1987, c. 483, s. 2.)

§ 58-25-70. Unauthorized wearing of badges, etc.

Any person who fraudulently and willfully wears the badge or button of any fraternal organization or society, either in the identical form or in such near resemblance thereto as to be a colorable imitation thereof, or who fraudulently and willfully uses the name of any such order, society or organization, the titles of its officers, or its insignia, ritual, or ceremonies, unless entitled to wear or use the same under the constitution and bylaws, rules and regulations of such fraternal organization, society, or order, shall be deemed guilty of a Class 3 misdemeanor. (1987, c. 483, s. 2; 1993, c. 539, s. 452; 1994, Ex. Sess., c. 24, s. 14(c).)

§ 58-26-45. Registration as a lien agent.

(a) A title insurance company or title insurance agency authorized to do business in this State that consents to serve as a lien agent upon designation by any owner pursuant to G.S. 44A-11.1 shall register with the Department by providing the following information:

(1) Name of the title insurance company or title insurance agency consenting to serve as a lien agent pursuant to G.S. 44A-11.1.

(2) Physical and mailing address, facsimile number and electronic mail address to which notices may be delivered to the lien agent pursuant to G.S. 44A-11.2.

(3) Telephone number of the lien agent.

(b) Upon receipt of the notice of designation by the owner pursuant to G.S. 44A-11.1, a lien agent shall have the duty to do all of the following:

(1) Provide written notice acknowledging its designation as a lien agent to the owner within three business days of receipt of the owner's written notice of designation, by the same method of delivery used by the owner in delivering the notice of designation to the lien agent.

(2) Receive notices to lien agent delivered by potential lien claimants pursuant to G.S. 44A-11.2.

(3) Maintain a record of the date and time of delivery and the information contained in each notice to lien agent received.

(4) Within three business days of receipt of a notice to lien agent by a potential lien claimant relating to improvements to real property for which the

lien agent has been designated as the lien agent, provide written notice confirming receipt of the notice to the person providing such notice, by the same method used by the potential lien claimant in delivering the notice to lien agent. If the notice is received by email, the acknowledgment sent by the lien agent must include the email received, including the header showing the date and time of receipt.

(5)   Within three business days of receipt of any notice to lien agent by a potential lien claimant relating to improved real property for which the lien agent has not been designated as the lien agent, provide written notice to the potential lien claimant that it is not the designated lien agent for the improved property, by the same method used by the potential lien claimant in delivering the notice to lien agent.

(6),   (6a) Repealed by Session Laws 2013-117, s. 3, effective June 22, 2013, and applicable to improvements to real property affected hereby for which the first furnishing of labor or materials at the site of the improvements is on or after that date.

(7)   Provide written notice of the potential lien claimants having delivered notice to lien agent pursuant to G.S. 44A-11.2, including the information relating to any contractor identified by the owner pursuant to G.S. 44A-11.2(g), and relating to any design professional identified by the owner pursuant to G.S. 44A-11.2(h), within one business day of receiving a request from any of the following persons or their authorized agents:

a.   An owner of the improved property.

b.   A title insurance company or title insurance agency issuing a policy of title insurance on the improved property.

c.   A contracted purchaser of the improved property.

d.   A potential lien claimant.

e.   A closing attorney, lender, or settlement agent as defined in G.S. 45A-3(15) involved in a transaction involving the improved property.

In responding to a request pursuant to this subdivision, the lien agent shall include the information provided by each potential lien claimant pursuant to G.S.

44A-11.2(i)(1) and G.S. 44A-11.2(i)(2) and, if specifically requested, a copy of each notice to lien agent received by the lien agent.

(8) Transfer all notices received and other documentation thereof to any successor lien agent designated by the owner upon termination under G.S. 44A-11.1(d).

(c) A registered lien agent may revoke its consent and be removed from the list of lien agents by providing written notification of its revocation of consent to the Department of Insurance and to all owners by whom the lien agent has been designated pursuant to G.S. 44A-11.1 at least 30 days in advance of the effective date of its revocation of consent.

(d) For services rendered pursuant to each designation as a lien agent for improvements to real property comprising one- or two-family dwellings, a lien agent shall collect a fee of twenty-five dollars ($25.00) from the owner. For services rendered pursuant to each designation as a lien agent for all other improvements to real property, the lien agent shall collect a fee of fifty dollars ($50.00) from the owner.

(e) The Department shall publish on its Web site a current list of lien agents registered pursuant to this section. (2012-158, s. 3; 2013-16, s. 7; 2013-117, s. 3.)

Article 26.

Real Estate Title Insurance Companies.

§ 58-26-1. Purpose of organization; formation; insuring closing services; premium rates; combined premiums for lenders' coverages.

(a) Companies may be formed in the manner provided in this Article for the purpose of furnishing information in relation to titles to real estate and of insuring owners and others interested therein against loss by reason of encumbrances and defective title; provided, however, that no such information shall be so furnished nor shall such insurance be so issued as to North Carolina real property unless and until the title insurance company has obtained the opinion of an attorney, licensed to practice law in North Carolina and not an employee or agent of the company, who has conducted or caused to be conducted under the attorney's direct supervision a reasonable examination of the title. The company shall cause to be made a determination of insurability of title in accordance with sound underwriting practices for title insurance companies. A company may also insure the proper performance of services necessary to conduct a real estate closing performed by an approved attorney licensed to practice in North Carolina. Provided, however, nothing in this section shall be construed to prohibit or preclude a title insurance company from insuring proper performance by its issuing agents.

(b)   Repealed by Session Laws 2002-187, s. 7.1.

(b1)   Domestic and foreign title insurance companies are subject to the same capital, surplus, and investment requirements that govern the formation and operation of domestic stock casualty companies. Domestic title insurance companies are subject to the same deposit requirements that govern the operation of other domestic casualty companies in this State. Foreign or alien title insurance companies are subject to an initial deposit pursuant to G.S. 58-26-31(b), based on the forecasted statutory premium reserve and the supplemental reserve for the first full year of operation in this State, but not less than two hundred thousand dollars ($200,000).

(c)   This Article shall not be interpreted so as to imply the repeal or amendment of any of the provisions of Chapter 84 of the General Statutes of North Carolina nor of any other provisions of common law or statutory law governing the practice of law.

(d)   The premium rates charged for insuring against loss by reason of encumbrances and defective title and for insuring real estate closing services shall be based on the purchase price of the real estate being conveyed or the loan amount and shall not be established as flat fees. If a title insurer has also issued title insurance protecting a lender or owner against loss by reason of encumbrances and defective title, the insurer shall charge one undivided premium for the combination of the title insurance and the closing services insurance.

(e)   If the premium stated upon a policy of title insurance has been understated or overstated due to inadvertence, mistake, or miscalculation of the closing attorney or his employees, and the incident is not purposeful or part of a pattern, the Commissioner of Insurance shall not be required to impose a civil penalty or other sanction for the inadvertence, mistake, or miscalculation. (1899, c. 54, s. 38; 1901, c. 391, s. 3; Rev., s. 4745; C.S., s. 6395; 1923, c. 71; 1973, c. 128; 1985, c. 666, s. 43; 1987, c. 625, ss. 1-3; 1993, c. 129, s. 1; c. 504, s. 15; 2002-187, ss. 7.1, 7.2.)

§ 58-26-5. Certificate of authority to do business.

Before any such company may issue any policy or make any contract or guarantee of insurance, it shall file with the Commissioner a certified copy of the record or the certificate of its organization in the office of the Secretary of State, and obtain from the Commissioner his certificate that it has complied with the laws applicable to it and that it is authorized to do business. (1899, c. 54, s. 38; 1901, c. 391, s. 3; Rev., s. 4745; C.S., s. 6396; 1991, c. 720, s. 4.)

§ 58-26-10. Financial statements and licenses required.

Title insurance companies are subject to G.S. 58-2-131, 58-2-132, 58-2-133, 58-2-134, 58-2-165, 58-2-180, and 58-6-5. The Commissioner may require title insurance companies to separately report their experience in insuring titles and in insuring closing services. The license to do business in this State issued to a title insurance company shall continue in full force and effect, subject to timely payment of the annual license continuation fee in accordance with G.S. 58-6-7 and subject to any other applicable provisions of the insurance laws of this State. The Commissioner shall annually license the agents of title insurance companies. (1899, c. 54, s. 38; 1901, c. 391, s. 3; Rev., s. 4745; C.S., s. 6397; 1987, c. 625, ss. 4, 5; 1991, c. 720, s. 4; 1993, c. 504, s. 17; 1999-132, s. 11.5; 2003-212, s. 26(h).)

§ 58-26-15. Limitation of risk.

No real estate title insurance company shall guarantee or insure in any one risk on real property located in North Carolina more than forty percent (40%) of its combined capital and surplus without first having the approval of the Commissioner, which approval shall be endorsed upon the policy. (1945, c. 386; 1967, c. 936; 1993, c. 504, s. 18.)

§ 58-26-20. Statutory premium reserve.

Every domestic title insurance company shall, in addition to other reserves, establish and maintain a reserve to be known as the "statutory premium reserve" for title insurance, which shall at all times and for all purposes be considered and constitute a reserve liability of the title insurance company in determining its financial condition. (1969, c. 897; 1973, c. 1035, s. 1; 1993, c. 504, s. 19; 2002-187, s. 7.3.)

§ 58-26-25. Amount of unearned [statutory] premium reserve.

(a)   The statutory premium reserve of every domestic title insurance company shall consist of the aggregate of:

(1)   The amount of the unearned premium reserve held as of December 31, 1998.

(2)   The amount of all additions required to be made to such reserve by this section, less the reduction of the aggregate amount required by this section.

(b)   A domestic title insurance company on and after January 1, 1999, shall reserve initially as a statutory premium reserve a sum equal to ten percent (10%) of the following items set forth in the title insurer's most recent annual statement on file with the Commissioner:

(1)   Direct premiums written.

(2)   Premiums for reinsurance assumed less premiums for reinsurance ceded during the year.

(c)   The aggregate of the amounts set aside in statutory premium reserves in any calendar year, under subsection (b) of this section, shall be reduced annually at the end of each calendar year following the year in which the policy is issued, over a period of 20 years, pursuant to the following: twenty percent (20%) the first year; ten percent (10%) for years two and three; five percent

(5%) for years four through 10; three percent (3%) for years 11 through 15; and two percent (2%) for years 16 through 20.

(d)   The entire amount of the unearned premium reserve held as of December 31, 1998, shall be accorded a fresh start and shall be released from said reserve and restored to net profits in accordance with the percentages set forth in subsection (c) of this section.

(e)   A supplemental reserve shall be established in accordance with the instructions of the annual statement required by G.S. 58-2-165 and G.S. 58-26-10 consisting of the reserves necessary, when taken in combination with the reserves required by subsections (a) through (d) of this section to cover the company's liabilities with respect to all losses, claims, and loss adjustment expenses.

(f)   Each title insurer subject to the provisions of this Article shall file with its annual statement required by G.S. 58-2-165 and G.S. 58-26-10 a certification of a member in good standing of the American Academy of Actuaries. The actuarial certification required of a title insurer must conform to the annual statement instructions for title insurers of the National Association of Insurance Commissioners. (1969, c. 897; 1973, c. 1035, ss. 2-4; 1999-383, s. 1; 2002-187, ss. 7.4, 7.5, 7.6.)

§ 58-26-30: Repealed by Session Laws 2002-187, s. 7.7, effective October 31, 2002.

§ 58-26-31. Statutory premium reserve held in trust or as a deposit.

(a)   Each domestic title insurance company shall withdraw from use funds to be used by the Commissioner in the event of the insurer's insolvency, the funds being equal to the statutory premium reserve and the supplemental reserve pursuant to G.S. 58-26-25. The amount shall be held in a trust account, as approved by the Commissioner. The trust account will be held in favor of the holders of title policies in the event of the insolvency of the insurer, and is not subject to G.S. 41-15. Nothing in this section precludes the insurer from investing the reserve in investments authorized by law for that insurer, and the income from the invested reserve shall be included in the general income of the insurer to be used by the insurer for any lawful purpose.

(b) Each foreign or alien title insurance company shall withdraw from use funds to be used by the Commissioner in the event of the insurer's insolvency, the funds being equal to the statutory premium reserve and the supplemental reserve as calculated under G.S. 58-26-25 for North Carolina risks. The Commissioner shall hold the funds as a deposit in accordance with G.S. 58-5-20. Annually, the company shall file a statement of actuarial opinion consistent with the annual statement instructions for North Carolina risks, issued by a qualified actuary, in support of this deposit.

(c) A title insurance company shall have 30 days after notification by the Commissioner to increase the amounts held on deposit. If the amount held on deposit is greater than the amount required under subsection (b) of this section, the Commissioner shall release the excess within 30 days after a request by the insurer. (2002-187, s. 7.8; 2003-221, s. 2.)

§ 58-26-35. Maintenance of the statutory premium reserve.

If the amount of the assets of a title insurance company held in trust or held by the Commissioner under G.S. 58-26-31 should on any date be less than the amount required to be maintained, and the deficiency is not promptly cured, the title insurance company shall immediately give written notice of the deficiency to the Commissioner and shall not write or assume any title insurance until the deficiency has been eliminated and until it has received written approval from the Commissioner authorizing it to again write and assume title insurance. (1969, c. 897; 2002-187, s. 7.9.)

§ 58-26-40: Repealed by Session Laws 2002-187, s. 7.10, effective October 31, 2002.

Article 25.

Fraternal Orders.

§ 58-25-1. General insurance law not applicable.

Nothing in the general insurance laws, except such as apply to fraternal orders shall be construed to extend to benevolent associations incorporated under the laws of this State that only levy an assessment on the members to create a fund to pay the family of a deceased member and make no profit therefrom, and do not solicit business through agents. (1987, c. 483, s. 2.)

§ 58-25-5. Fraternal orders defined.

Every incorporated association, order, or society doing business in this State on the lodge system, with ritualistic form of work and representative form of government, for the purpose of making provision for the payment of benefits of three hundred dollars ($300.00) or less in case of death, sickness, temporary or permanent physical disability, either as the result of disease, accident, or old age, formed and organized for the sole benefit of its members and their beneficiaries, and not for profit, is hereby declared to be a "fraternal order". Societies and orders which do not make insurance contracts or collect dues or assessments therefor, but simply pay burial or other benefits out of the treasury of their orders, and use their funds for the purpose of building homes or asylums for the purpose of caring for and educating orphan children and aged and infirm people in this State, shall not be considered as "fraternal orders"; and such order or association paying death or disability benefits may also create, maintain, apply, or disburse among its membership a reserve or emergency fund as may be provided in its constitution or bylaws; but no profit or gain may be added to the payments made by a member. (1987, c. 483, s. 2.)

§ 58-25-10. Funds derived from assessments and dues.

The fund from which the payment of benefits, as provided for in G.S. 58-25-5, shall be made, and the fund from which the expenses of such association, order or society shall be defrayed, shall be derived from assessments or dues collected from its members. Such societies or associations shall be governed by the laws of the State governing fraternal orders or societies, and are exempt from the provisions of all general insurance laws of this State, and no law hereafter passed shall apply to such orders or societies unless fraternal orders or societies are designated therein. (1987, c. 483, s. 2.)

§ 58-25-15. Appointment of member as receiver or collector; appointee as agent for order or society; rights of members.

Assessments and dues referred to in G.S. 58-25-5 and G.S. 58-25-10 may be collected, receipted, and remitted by a member or officer of any local or subordinate lodge of any fraternal order or society when so appointed or designated by any grand, district, or subordinate lodge or officer, deputy, or representative of the same, there being no regular licensed agent or deputy of said grand lodge charged with said duties; but any person so collecting said dues or assessments shall be the agent or representative of such fraternal order or society, or any department thereof, and shall bind them by their acts in collecting and remitting said amounts so collected. Under no circumstances, regardless of any agreement, bylaws, contract, or notice, shall said officer or collector be the agent or representative of the individual member from whom any such collection is made; nor shall said member be responsible for the failure of such officer or collector to safely keep, handle, or remit said dues or assessments so collected, in accordance with the rules, regulations, or bylaws of said order or society; nor shall said member, regardless of any rules, regulations, or bylaws to the contrary, forfeit any rights under his certificate of membership in said fraternal order or society by reason of any default or misconduct of any said officer or member so acting. (1987, c. 483, s. 2.)

§ 58-25-20. Meetings of governing body; principal office.

Any such order or society incorporated and organized under the laws of this State may provide for the meeting of its supreme legislative or governing body in any other state, province, or territory wherein such order or society has subordinate lodges, and all business transacted at such meetings is as valid in all respects as if the meetings were held in this State; but the principal business office of such order or society shall always be kept in this State. (1987, c. 483, s. 2.)

§ 58-25-25. Conditions precedent to doing business.

Any such fraternal order, society, or association as defined by this Article, chartered and organized in this State or organized and doing business under the laws of any other state, district, province, or territory, having the qualifications required of domestic societies of like character, upon satisfying the Commissioner that its business is proper and legitimate and so conducted, may be admitted to transact business in this State upon the same conditions as are prescribed by Articles 1 through 64 of this Chapter for admitting and authorizing foreign insurance companies to do business in this State, except that such fraternal orders shall not be required to have the capital required of such insurance companies. Organizers or agents shall be licensed without requiring an examination; provided, organizers or agents who are engaged in or intend to engage in the sale of individual policies of life insurance shall take the examination required of life insurance agents. Those organizers or agents licensed for the sale of insurance pursuant to former G.S. 58-268 as of July 1, 1977, shall be exempt from examination. (1987, c. 483, s. 2; 1991, c. 720, s. 4.)

§ 58-25-30. Certain lodge systems exempt.

The following beneficial orders or societies shall be exempt from the requirements of this Article, and shall not be required to pay any license tax or fees nor make any report to the Commissioner, unless the assessments collected for death benefits by the supreme lodge amount to at least three hundred dollars ($300.00) in one year: Beneficial fraternal orders, or societies incorporated under the laws of this State, which are conducted under the lodge system which have the supreme lodge or governing body located in this State, and which are so organized that the membership consists of members of subordinate lodges; that the subordinate lodges accept for membership only residents of the county in which such subordinate lodge is located; that each subordinate lodge issues certificates, makes assessments, and collects a fund to pay benefits to the widows and orphans of its own deceased members and their families, each lodge independently of the others, for itself and independently of the supreme lodge; that each lodge controls the fund for this purpose; that in addition to the benefits paid by each subordinate lodge to its own members, the supreme lodge provides for an additional benefit for such of the members of the subordinate lodges as are qualified, at the option of the subordinate lodge members; that such organization is not conducted for profit, has no capital stock, and has been in operation for 10 years in this State.

The Commissioner may require the chief or presiding officer, or the secretary, to file annually an affidavit that such organization is entitled to this exemption. (1987, c. 483, s. 2; 1991, c. 720. s. 4.)

§ 58-25-35. Insurance on children.

Any fraternal order or society authorized pursuant to this Article to do business in this State and operating on the lodge plan may provide in its constitution and bylaws, in addition to other benefits provided for therein, for the payment of death or annuity benefits upon the lives of children between the ages of one and 16 years at next birthday, for whose support and maintenance a member of such order or society is responsible. The order or society may at its option organize and operate branches for such children and membership in local lodges, and initiation therein shall not be required of such children, nor shall they have any voice in the management of the order or society. The total benefits payable as above provided shall in no case exceed the following amounts at ages at next birthday at time of death, respectively, as follows: one year, twenty dollars ($20.00); two years, fifty dollars ($50.00); three years, seventy-five dollars ($75.00); four years, one hundred dollars ($100.00); five years, one hundred twenty-five dollars ($125.00); six years, one hundred fifty dollars ($150.00); seven years, two hundred dollars ($200.00); eight years, two hundred fifty dollars ($250.00); nine years, three hundred dollars ($300.00); 10 years, four hundred dollars ($400.00); 11 years, five hundred dollars ($500.00); 12 years, six hundred dollars ($600.00); 13 years, seven hundred dollars ($700.00); 14 years, eight hundred dollars ($800.00); 15 years, nine hundred dollars ($900.00); 16 years, one thousand dollars ($1,000). (1987, c. 483, s. 2.)

§ 58-25-40. Medical examination; certificates and contributions.

No benefit certificate as to any child shall take effect until after medical examination or inspection by a licensed medical practitioner, in accordance with the laws of the order or society, nor shall any such benefit certificate be issued unless the order or society shall simultaneously put in force at least 500 such certificates, on each of which at least one assessment has been paid, nor where the number of lives represented by such certificate falls below 500. The death benefit contributions to be made upon such certificate shall be based upon the "Standard Mortality Table" or the "English Life Table Number Six," and a rate of interest not greater than four percent (4%) per annum, upon a higher standard or upon such mortality, morbidity, and interest standards permitted by the laws of this State for use by life insurance companies; but contributions may be waived or returns may be made from any surplus held in excess of reserve and other liabilities, as provided in the bylaws; and extra contributions shall be made if the reserves hereafter provided for become impaired. (1987, c. 483, s. 2.)

§ 58-25-45. Reserve fund; exchange of certificates.

Any order or society entering into such insurance agreements shall maintain on all such contracts the reserve required by the standard of mortality and interest adopted by the order or society for computing contributions as provided in G.S. 58-25-35, and the funds representing the benefit contributions and all accretions thereon shall be kept as separate and distinct funds, independent of the other funds of the order or society, and shall not be liable for nor used for the payment of the debts and obligations of the order or society other than the benefits herein authorized. An order or society may provide that when a child reaches the minimum age for initiation into membership in such order or society, any benefit certificate issued hereunder may be surrendered for cancellation and exchanged for any other form of certificate issued by the order or society: Provided, that such surrender will not reduce the number of lives insured below 500; and upon the issuance of such new certificate any reserve upon the original certificate herein provided for shall be transferred to the credit of the new certificate. Neither the person who originally made application for benefits on account of such child, nor the beneficiary named in such original certificate, nor the person who paid the contributions, shall have any vested right in such new certificate, the free nomination of a beneficiary under the new certificate being left to the child so admitted to benefit membership. (1987, c. 483, s. 2.)

§ 58-25-50. Separation of funds.

An entirely separate financial statement of the business transactions and of assets and liabilities arising therefrom shall be made in its annual report to the Commissioner by an order or society availing itself of the provisions hereof. The separation of assets, funds, and liabilities required hereby shall not be terminated, rescinded, or modified, nor shall the funds be diverted for any use other than as specified in the preceding section, as long as any certificates issued hereunder remain in force, and this requirement shall be recognized and enforced in any liquidation, reinsurance, merger, or other change in the condition or the status of the order or society. (1987, c. 483, s. 2; 1991, c. 720, s. 4.)

§ 58-25-55. Payments to expense or general fund.

Any order or society shall have the right to provide in its laws and the certificate issued hereunder for specified payments on account of the expense or general fund, which payments shall or shall not be mingled with the general fund of the order or society, as its constitution and bylaws may provide. (1987, c. 483, s. 2.)

§ 58-25-60. Continuation of certificates.

In the event of the termination of membership in the order or society by the person responsible for the support of any child on whose account a certificate may have been issued as provided herein, the certificate may be continued for the benefit of the estate of the child, provided the contributions are continued, or for the benefit of any other person responsible for the support and maintenance of such child who shall assume the payment of the required contributions. (1987, c. 483, s. 2.)

§ 58-25-65. Appointment of trustees to hold property.

The lodges of Masons, Odd Fellows, Knights of Pythias, camps of Woodmen of the World, councils of the Junior Order of United American Mechanics, orders of the Elks, Young Men's Christian Associations, Young Women's Christian Associations and other benevolent or fraternal orders and societies may appoint from time to time suitable persons trustees of their bodies or societies, in such manner as they deem proper, which trustees, and their successors, shall have power to receive, purchase, take, and hold property, real and personal, in trust for such society or body. The trustees shall have power, when instructed so to do by resolution adopted by the order, society or body which they represent, to mortgage or sell and convey in fee simple any real or personal property owned by the order, society or body; and the conveyances so made by the trustees shall be effective to pass the property in fee simple to the purchaser or to the mortgagee or trustee for the purposes in such conveyance or mortgage expressed. If there shall be no trustee, then any real or personal property which could be held by such trustees shall vest in and be held by such charitable, benevolent, religious, or fraternal orders and societies, respectively, according to such intent. (1987, c. 483, s. 2.)

§ 58-25-70. Unauthorized wearing of badges, etc.

Any person who fraudulently and willfully wears the badge or button of any fraternal organization or society, either in the identical form or in such near resemblance thereto as to be a colorable imitation thereof, or who fraudulently and willfully uses the name of any such order, society or organization, the titles of its officers, or its insignia, ritual, or ceremonies, unless entitled to wear or use the same under the constitution and bylaws, rules and regulations of such fraternal organization, society, or order, shall be deemed guilty of a Class 3 misdemeanor. (1987, c. 483, s. 2; 1993, c. 539, s. 452; 1994, Ex. Sess., c. 24, s. 14(c).)

§ 58-26-45. Registration as a lien agent.

(a) A title insurance company or title insurance agency authorized to do business in this State that consents to serve as a lien agent upon designation by any owner pursuant to G.S. 44A-11.1 shall register with the Department by providing the following information:

(1) Name of the title insurance company or title insurance agency consenting to serve as a lien agent pursuant to G.S. 44A-11.1.

(2) Physical and mailing address, facsimile number and electronic mail address to which notices may be delivered to the lien agent pursuant to G.S. 44A-11.2.

(3) Telephone number of the lien agent.

(b) Upon receipt of the notice of designation by the owner pursuant to G.S. 44A-11.1, a lien agent shall have the duty to do all of the following:

(1) Provide written notice acknowledging its designation as a lien agent to the owner within three business days of receipt of the owner's written notice of designation, by the same method of delivery used by the owner in delivering the notice of designation to the lien agent.

(2) Receive notices to lien agent delivered by potential lien claimants pursuant to G.S. 44A-11.2.

(3) Maintain a record of the date and time of delivery and the information contained in each notice to lien agent received.

(4) Within three business days of receipt of a notice to lien agent by a potential lien claimant relating to improvements to real property for which the lien agent has been designated as the lien agent, provide written notice confirming receipt of the notice to the person providing such notice, by the same method used by the potential lien claimant in delivering the notice to lien agent. If the notice is received by email, the acknowledgment sent by the lien agent must include the email received, including the header showing the date and time of receipt.

(5) Within three business days of receipt of any notice to lien agent by a potential lien claimant relating to improved real property for which the lien agent has not been designated as the lien agent, provide written notice to the potential lien claimant that it is not the designated lien agent for the improved property, by the same method used by the potential lien claimant in delivering the notice to lien agent.

(6), (6a) Repealed by Session Laws 2013-117, s. 3, effective June 22, 2013, and applicable to improvements to real property affected hereby for which the first furnishing of labor or materials at the site of the improvements is on or after that date.

(7) Provide written notice of the potential lien claimants having delivered notice to lien agent pursuant to G.S. 44A-11.2, including the information relating to any contractor identified by the owner pursuant to G.S. 44A-11.2(g), and relating to any design professional identified by the owner pursuant to G.S. 44A-

11.2(h), within one business day of receiving a request from any of the following persons or their authorized agents:

a. An owner of the improved property.

b. A title insurance company or title insurance agency issuing a policy of title insurance on the improved property.

c. A contracted purchaser of the improved property.

d. A potential lien claimant.

e. A closing attorney, lender, or settlement agent as defined in G.S. 45A-3(15) involved in a transaction involving the improved property.

In responding to a request pursuant to this subdivision, the lien agent shall include the information provided by each potential lien claimant pursuant to G.S. 44A-11.2(i)(1) and G.S. 44A-11.2(i)(2) and, if specifically requested, a copy of each notice to lien agent received by the lien agent.

(8) Transfer all notices received and other documentation thereof to any successor lien agent designated by the owner upon termination under G.S. 44A-11.1(d).

(c) A registered lien agent may revoke its consent and be removed from the list of lien agents by providing written notification of its revocation of consent to the Department of Insurance and to all owners by whom the lien agent has been designated pursuant to G.S. 44A-11.1 at least 30 days in advance of the effective date of its revocation of consent.

(d) For services rendered pursuant to each designation as a lien agent for improvements to real property comprising one- or two-family dwellings, a lien agent shall collect a fee of twenty-five dollars ($25.00) from the owner. For services rendered pursuant to each designation as a lien agent for all other improvements to real property, the lien agent shall collect a fee of fifty dollars ($50.00) from the owner.

(e) The Department shall publish on its Web site a current list of lien agents registered pursuant to this section. (2012-158, s. 3; 2013-16, s. 7; 2013-117, s. 3.)

Article 27.

Title Insurance Companies and Land Mortgage Companies Issuing Collateral Loan Certificates.

§ 58-27-1. Issuance of collateral loan certificates; security.

Any domestic land mortgage company or title insurance company having a paid-in capital and surplus of at least two hundred thousand dollars ($200,000), may, under the supervision and control of the Commissioner, issue collateral loan certificates, or other certificates of indebtedness secured by the deposit of first mortgages on real estate with the Commissioner, or under his direction, or secured by the deposit with the Commissioner, or under his direction, of collateral trust bonds secured by first mortgages, the principal and interest of which said mortgages is guaranteed by a surety company having assets of at least ten million dollars ($10,000,000), upon a basis not to exceed one hundred dollars ($100.00) for each one hundred dollars ($100.00) of liability under the collateral loan certificates or other certificates of indebtedness outstanding and secured by such first mortgages or collateral trust bonds. (1927, c. 204, s. 1; 1991, c. 720, s. 4.)

§ 58-27-5. Prohibition against payment or receipt of title insurance kickbacks, rebates, commissions and other payments.

(a) No person or entity selling real property, or performing services as a real estate agent, attorney or lender, which services are incident to or a part of any real estate settlement or sale, shall pay or receive, directly or indirectly, any kickback, rebate, commission or other payment in connection with the issuance of title insurance for any real property which is a part of such sale or settlement; nor shall any title insurance company, agency or agent make any such payment.

(b) Any person or entity violating the provisions of this section shall be guilty of a Class 2 misdemeanor which may include a fine of not more than five thousand dollars ($5,000).

(c) No persons or entity shall be in violation of this section solely by reason of ownership of stock in a bona fide title insurance company, agency, or agent. For purposes of this section, and in addition to any other statutory or regulatory requirements, a bona fide title insurance company, agency or agent is defined to be a company, agency or agent that passes upon and makes title insurance underwriting decisions on title risks, including the issuance of title insurance policies, binders and endorsements, and that maintains a separate and distinct staff and office or offices for such purposes. (1973, c. 1336, s. 1; 1985, c. 666, s. 24; 1993, c. 504, s. 41, c. 539, s. 453; 1994, Ex. Sess., c. 24, s. 14(c).)

§ 58-27-10. Licenses.

Any domestic land mortgage company, or title insurance company, wishing to do business under the provisions of this Article upon making written application and submitting proof satisfactory to the Commissioner that its business, capital and other qualifications comply with the provisions of this Article, upon paying to the Commissioner, the sum of five hundred dollars ($500.00) as a license fee and all other fees assessed against such company may be licensed to do business in this State under the provisions of this Article until the first day of the following July, and may have its license renewed for each year thereafter so long as it complies with the provisions of this Article and such rules adopted by the Commissioner. For each such renewal such company shall pay to the Commissioner the sum of one thousand dollars ($1,000), and all other fees assessed against such company and such renewal shall continue in force and effect until a new license be issued or specifically refused, unless revoked for good cause. The Commissioner, or any person appointed by him, shall have the power and authority to make such rules and regulations and examinations not inconsistent with the provisions of this Article, as may be in his discretion necessary or proper to enforce the provisions hereof and secure compliance with the terms of this Article. For any examination made hereunder the Commissioner shall charge the land mortgage companies or title insurance companies examined with the actual expense of such examination. (1927, c. 204, s. 2; 1955, c. 179, s. 3; 1991, c. 720, s. 4; c. 721, s. 1; 1999-435, s. 4.)

§ 58-27-15. Annual statements furnished.

Every such domestic land mortgage company or title insurance company doing business in this State under this Article shall annually file with the Commissioner on or before the first day of March in each year a full and complete sworn statement of its financial condition on the thirty-first day of December next preceding. Such statement shall plainly exhibit all real and contingent assets and liabilities and a complete account of its income and disbursements during the year, and shall also exhibit the amount of real estate mortgages deposited by such land mortgage company or title insurance company for the protection of the certificates issued under this Article. The Commissioner is hereby empowered to require such further information as may be reasonably necessary to satisfy him that the statements contained in the sworn statements are true and correct. (1927, c. 204, s. 3; 1991, c. 720, s. 4.)

Article 28.

Unauthorized Insurers.

§ 58-28-1. Purpose of Article.

It is the purpose of this Article to abate and prevent the practices of unauthorized insurers within the State of North Carolina, and to provide methods for effectively enforcing the laws of this State against such practices. The General Assembly finds that there is within this State a substantial amount of insurance business being transacted by insurers who have not complied with the laws of this State and have not been authorized by the Commissioner to do business. These practices by unauthorized insurers are deemed to be harmful and contrary to public welfare of the citizens of this State. The difficulties which arise from the acts and practices of unauthorized insurers are compounded by the fact that such companies may be licensed in foreign jurisdictions and conduct a long-range business without having personal representatives or agents in proximity to insureds. The General Assembly further declares that it is a subject of vital public interest to the State that unlicensed and unauthorized companies have been and are now engaged in soliciting by way of direct mail and other advertising media, insurance risks within this State, and that such companies enjoy the many benefits and privileges provided by the State as well as the protection afforded to citizens under exercise of the police powers of the State, without themselves being subject to the laws designed to protect the insurance consuming public. The provisions of this Article are in addition to all other statutory provisions of Articles 1 through 64 of this Chapter relating to unauthorized insurers and do not replace, alter, modify or repeal such existing provisions. (1967, c. 909, s. 1; 1987, c. 864, s. 46; 1991, c. 720, s. 4.)

§ 58-28-5. Transacting business without a license prohibited; exceptions.

(a) Except as otherwise provided in this section, it is unlawful for any company to enter into a contract of insurance as an insurer or to transact insurance business in this State as set forth in G.S. 58-28-13 without a license issued by the Commissioner. This section does not apply to the following acts or transactions:

(1) The procuring of a policy of insurance upon a risk within this State where the applicant is unable to procure coverage in the open market with admitted companies and is otherwise in compliance with Article 21 of this Chapter.

(2) Contracts of reinsurance; but not including assumption reinsurance transactions, whereby the reinsuring company succeeds to all of the liabilities of and supplants the ceding company on the insurance contracts that are the subject of the transaction, unless prior approval has been obtained from the Commissioner.

(3) Transactions in this State involving a policy lawfully solicited, written and delivered outside of this State covering only subjects of insurance not resident, located or expressly to be performed in this State at the time of issuance, and which transactions are subsequent to the issuance of such policy.

(4) Transactions in this State involving group life insurance, group annuities, or group, blanket, or franchise accident and health insurance where the master policy for the insurance was lawfully issued and delivered in a state in which the company was authorized to transact business.

(5) Transactions in this State involving all policies of insurance issued before July 1, 1967.

(6) The procuring of contracts of insurance issued to a nuclear insured. As used in this subdivision, "nuclear insured" means a public utility procuring

insurance against radioactive contamination and other risks of direct physical loss at a nuclear electric generating plant.

(7) Insurance independently procured, as specified in subsection (b) of this section.

(8) Insurance on vessels or craft, their cargoes, marine builders' risks, marine protection and indemnity, or other risks commonly insured under marine insurance policies, as distinguished from inland marine insurance policies.

(9) Transactions in this State involving commercial aircraft insurance, meaning insurance against (i) loss of or damage resulting from any cause to commercial aircraft and its equipment, (ii) legal liability of the insured for loss or damage to another person's property resulting from the ownership, maintenance, or use of commercial aircraft, and (iii) loss, damage, or expense incident to a liability claim.

(10) An activity in this State by or on the sole behalf of a captive insurer licensed and subject to regulation in another jurisdiction other than this State that insures solely the risks of the company's parent and affiliated companies or the risks of a controlled unaffiliated business.

(b) Any person in this State may directly procure or directly renew insurance with an eligible surplus lines insurer, as defined in G.S. 58-21-10(3), without the involvement of an agent, broker, or surplus lines licensee, on a risk located or to be performed, in whole or in part, in this State. The person shall, within 30 days after the date the insurance is procured or renewed, file a written report with the Commissioner on forms prescribed by the Commissioner. The report must contain the name and address of the insured; name and address of the insurer; the subject of insurance; a general description of the coverage; the amount of premium currently charged; and any additional information requested by the Commissioner. The report must also contain an affidavit of the insured that states that the full amount or kind of insurance cannot be obtained from insurers that are licensed to do business in this State; and that the insured has made a diligent search among the insurers that are licensed to transact and are actually writing the particular kind and class of insurance in this State. Gross premiums charged for the insurance, less any return premiums, are subject to a tax at the rate of five percent (5%). At the time of filing the report required by this subsection, the insured shall pay the tax to the Commissioner. The Commissioner has the powers specified in G.S. 58-21-90 with respect to the tax levied by this subsection.

(c) This section does not apply to any surviving nonprofit corporation that results from a merger between the nonprofit corporation established by the North Carolina State Bar Council pursuant to Chapter 707 of the 1975 Session Laws of North Carolina and another domestic nonprofit corporation; provided, however, that any such surviving corporation shall register with the North Carolina State Bar Council under G.S. 84-23.1. (1967, c. 909, s. 1; 1971, c. 510, s. 3; 1985, c. 688, s. 2; 1987, c. 727, ss. 4, 5; c. 864, ss. 47, 70; 1991, c. 644, s. 6; 1993, c. 409, s. 26; c. 504, s. 20; 1995, c. 193, s. 30; 1999-219, s. 5.4; 2004-166, s. 4; 2007-305, s. 4; 2008-124, ss. 3.1, 3.2; 2013-116, s. 3.)

§ 58-28-10: Repealed by Session Laws 2008-124, s. 3.5, effective July 28, 2008, and applicable to violations that occur on or after that date.

§ 58-28-12. Transacting insurance business in this State.

Definitions. - As used in this section, G.S. 58-28-13, and G.S. 58-28-14:

(1) "Admitted insurer" means an insurer that is licensed to write insurance in this State.

(2) "Kind of insurance" means one of the types of insurance specified in G.S. 58-7-15.

(3) "Nonadmitted insurer" means an insurer that is not licensed to write insurance in this State.

(4) "Transacting insurance business" or "transact insurance business" means:

a. The making of or proposing to make, as an insurer, an insurance contract.

b. The making of or proposing to make, as guarantor or surety, any contract of guaranty or suretyship as a vocation and not merely incidental to any other legitimate business or activity of the guarantor or surety.

c. The solicitation, taking, or receiving of an application for insurance.

d. The receiving or collection of any premium, commission, membership fees, assessments, dues, or other consideration for a contract of insurance or any part of the contract of insurance.

e. The issuance or delivery in this State of a contract of insurance to a resident of this State or to a person authorized to do business in this State.

f. The solicitation, negotiation, procurement, effectuation, or renewal of a contract of insurance.

g. The dissemination of information as to coverage or rates; forwarding of an application; delivery of a contract of insurance; inspection of a risk; the fixing of rates; the investigation or adjustment of a claim or loss; the transaction of matters after effectuation of a contract of insurance and arising out of the contract; or any other manner of representing or assisting a person or insurer in transacting insurance business with respect to properties, risks, or exposures located or to be performed in this State.

h. The transaction of any kind of insurance business specifically recognized as transacting an insurance business within the meaning of this Chapter.

i. The offering of insurance or the transacting of insurance business.

j. The offering of an agreement or contract which purports to alter, amend, or void coverage of an insurance contract.

k. The transaction of any matters before or after the execution of contracts of insurance in contemplation of or arising out of the execution.

l. The maintaining of any agency or office in this State where any acts in furtherance of an insurance business are transacted, including the execution of contracts of insurance with citizens of this State or any other state.

m. The maintaining of files or records of contracts of insurance in this State. (2008-124, s. 3.4.)

§ 58-28-13. Placement of insurance business.

(a)   An insurer shall not transact insurance business in this State unless it is an admitted insurer, is exempted by this Article, or is otherwise exempted by this Chapter.

(b)   A person shall not transact insurance business or in this State directly or indirectly act as agent for, or otherwise represent or aid on behalf of another, a nonadmitted insurer in the solicitation, negotiation, procurement, or effectuation of insurance, or renewals of insurance; forwarding of applications; delivery of policies or contracts; inspection of risks; fixing of rates; investigation or adjustment of claims or losses; collection or forwarding of premiums; or in any other manner represent or assist the insurer in transacting insurance business.

(c)   A person who represents or aids a nonadmitted insurer in violation of this section is subject to penalties or restitution, or both, as set forth in this section.

(d)   This section does not prohibit employees, officers, directors, or partners of a commercial insured from acting in the capacity of an insurance manager or buyer in placing insurance on behalf of the employer, provided that the person's compensation is not based on buying insurance.

(e)   The venue of an act committed by mail or any other medium is at the point where the matter transmitted by mail or other medium is delivered or issued for delivery or takes effect.

(f)   The remedies prescribed in this section are not exclusive. Penalties may also be assessed under Article 63 of this Chapter or G.S. 58-2-161, or both.

(g)   If the Commissioner finds a violation of this section, the Commissioner may order the payment of a monetary penalty after considering the factors in G.S. 58-28-14; or petition the Superior Court of Wake County for an order directing payment of restitution as provided in subsection (i) of this section; or both. The monetary penalty shall not exceed five thousand dollars ($5,000) for the first offense and shall not exceed ten thousand dollars ($10,000) for each succeeding offense. Each day during which a violation occurs constitutes a separate violation. The clear proceeds of the penalty shall be remitted to the Civil Penalty and Forfeiture Fund in accordance with G.S. 115C-457.2. Payment of the civil penalty under this section shall be in addition to payment of any other penalty for a violation of the criminal laws of this State.

(h)   Upon petition of the Commissioner, the Superior Court of Wake County may order the person who committed a violation specified in this section to make restitution in an amount that would make whole any person harmed by the violation. The petition may be made at any time and also in any appeal of any order issued by the Commissioner.

(i)   Restitution to the Department for extraordinary administrative expenses incurred in the investigation and hearing of the violation may also be ordered by the court in such amount that would reimburse the Department for the expenses.

(j)   Nothing in this section prevents the Commissioner from negotiating a mutually acceptable agreement with any person as to any civil penalty or restitution.

(k)   The Attorney General of the State of North Carolina at the request of and upon information from the Commissioner shall initiate a civil action in behalf of the Commissioner in any county of the State in which a violation under this section occurs to recover the penalty provided. Service of process upon the nonadmitted insurer shall be made under G.S. 58-28-40. (2008-124, s. 3.4.)

§ 58-28-14. Monetary penalty; factors to be considered.

In determining the amount of the penalty under G.S. 58-28-13, the Commissioner shall consider:

(1)   The amount of money that inured to the benefit of the violator as a result of the violation,

(2)   Whether the violation was committed willfully.

(3)   The prior record of the violator in complying or failing to comply with laws, rules, or orders applicable to the violator.

(4)   The failure of the violator to provide timely and complete responses to the Department's inquiries about the violator's insurance activities in North Carolina.

(5) The extent and degree to which the violator marketed its insurance product in this State.

(6) The extent to which the violator's marketing materials, including fax solicitations, Internet Web sites, circulars, or other forms of advertisement or solicitations through any medium, were deceptive or misleading to residents of this State.

(7) The number of residents of this State who enrolled in the violator's insurance plan.

(8) The number of policies and amount of insurance coverage issued by the violator to residents of this State.

(9) The failure of the violator to promptly refund premiums and other consideration paid by residents of this State for insurance coverage issued by the violator upon requests by the residents of this State or the Department.

(10) The extent and degree of harm to residents of this State. In assessing the extent and degree of harm, the Commissioner shall consider, among other things, the amount of premiums and other consideration paid by residents of this State for coverage issued by the violator, the failure of the violator to pay claims made by residents of this State, and number and dollar amount of claims made by residents of this State that the violator has failed to pay.

(11) Whether the violator has a prior record of violating this Article or the unauthorized insurance laws of any other state. "Prior record" includes final administrative orders issued by the Commissioner or insurance regulator of any other state; federal or state criminal convictions, including pleas of guilty or nolo contendere; civil judgments; and written settlement agreements of state administrative proceedings, state or federal criminal proceedings, or civil lawsuits against the violator or any entity of which the violator was either a principal or owner. (2008-124, s. 3.4.)

§ 58-28-15. Validity of acts or contracts of unauthorized company shall not impair obligation of contract as to the company; maintenance of suits; right to defend.

The failure of a company to obtain a license shall not impair the validity of any acts or contracts of the company. Any person or insured holding contracts of insurance of an unauthorized insurer may bring an action in the courts of this State under the provisions of G.S. 58-16-35 for the enforcement of any rights pursuant to the contract of insurance. The failure of the insurance company to obtain a license shall not prevent such company from defending any action at law or suit in equity in any court of this State so long as the said company fully complies with the provisions of G.S. 58-16-35(c), but no company transacting insurance business in this State without a license shall be permitted to maintain an action at law or in equity in any court of this State to enforce any right, claim or demand arising out of the transaction of such business until such company shall have obtained a license. Nor shall an action at law or in equity be maintained in any court of this State by any successor or assignee of such company on any such right, claim or demand originally held by such company until a license shall have been obtained by the company or by a company which has acquired all or substantially all of its assets. Nothing in this section shall be construed to abrogate the conditions of admission into this State nor to impair the authority of the Commissioner with respect to the issuance of licenses. The Commissioner in considering the issuance of a license shall take into consideration the acts or transactions which an unauthorized company has engaged in in this State prior to its application for a license. (1967, c. 909, s. 1; 1991, c. 720, ss. 4, 56; 1999-132, s. 9.1; 2000-140, s. 12.)

§ 58-28-20. Cease and desist orders; judicial review.

(a)   Whenever the Commissioner has reasonable grounds to believe that any person is violating or is about to violate G.S. 58-28-5, 58-28-45, or 58-33-95, the Commissioner may, after notice and opportunity for hearing, make written findings and issue and cause to be served upon the person an order to cease and desist violating G.S. 58-28-5, 58-28-45, or 58-33-95.

(b)   Until the expiration of the time allowed under G.S. 58-2-75 for filing a petition for review, the Commissioner may at any time, upon notice and in a manner the Commissioner considers proper, modify or set aside in whole or in part any order issued by the Commissioner under this section as follows:

(1)   Any time before the expiration of the time allowed for seeking judicial review, if no petition for review has been filed; or

(2)   If a petition for review has been timely filed, until the transcript of the record in the proceeding has been filed with the Court.

(c)   If no petition for judicial review has been filed within the time provided under G.S. 58-2-75, the Commissioner may at any time, after notice and opportunity for hearing, reopen and alter, modify, or set aside, in whole or in part, any order issued by the Commissioner under this section, whenever in the Commissioner's opinion conditions of fact or of law have so changed as to require such action or if the public interest requires.

(d)   Whenever the Commissioner has evidence that any person has or is violating G.S. 58-28-5 or G.S. 58-28-45, or has or is violating any order or requirement of the Commissioner issued by the Commissioner under this Article, and that the interests of policyholders, creditors, or the public may be irreparably harmed by delay, the Commissioner may issue an emergency cease and desist order that shall become effective on the date specified in the order or upon service of a certified copy of the order upon the person ordered to cease and desist, whichever is later. The emergency cease and desist order shall also include a notice of hearing, which shall be conducted as provided under Article 3A of Chapter 150B of the General Statutes. However, the person ordered to cease and desist under this subsection may request and shall be granted an expedited review of the order. The emergency order shall remain in effect prior to and during the proceedings, unless modified by the Commissioner as provided under subsection (b) of this section.

(e)   Any person required to cease and desist violating G.S. 58-28-5 by an order issued after notice and a hearing under subsection (a) or (d) of this section may seek judicial review of that order under G.S. 58-2-75. (1967, c. 909, s. 1; 1987, c. 864, s. 61; 1989, c. 485, s. 14; 1999-294, s. 6; 2005-217, s. 1; 2007-305, ss. 2, 3.)

§ 58-28-25: Repealed by Session Laws 2005-217, s. 2, effective October 1, 2005, and applicable to orders issued on or after that date.

§ 58-28-30. Penalty.

Any person who willfully violates a cease and desist order of the Commissioner under G.S. 58-28-20, after it has become final, and while such order is in effect, is subject to the provisions of G.S. 58-2-70. (1989, c. 485, s. 15.)

§ 58-28-35. Provisions of Article additional to existing law; application.

The powers vested in the Commissioner by this Article are additional to any other powers to enforce any penalties, fines, or forfeitures authorized by law with respect to transacting the business of insurance without authority. This Article applies to all kinds of insurance, including service corporations that would be subject to Article 65 of this Chapter, HMOs that would be subject to Article 67 of this Chapter, MEWAs that would be subject to Article 49 of this Chapter, and self-insured workers' compensation operations that would be subject to Article 47 of this Chapter or Article 4 of Chapter 97 of the General Statutes. (1989, c. 485, s. 15; 1999-244, s. 9.)

§ 58-28-40. Service of process on Secretary of State as agent for unauthorized company.

(a) Any act of entering into a contract of insurance as an insurer or transacting insurance business in this State, as set forth in G.S. 58-28-12 by an unauthorized, foreign or alien company, shall be equivalent to and shall constitute an appointment by such company of the Secretary of State to be its true and lawful attorney upon whom may be served all lawful process in any action or proceeding against it arising out of a violation of G.S. 58-28-5, and any of said acts shall be a signification of its agreement that any such process against it, which is so served, shall be of the same legal force and validity as if in fact served upon the company.

(b) Service of process on the Secretary of State shall be made by the sheriff delivering to and leaving with the Secretary of State duplicate copies of such process, notice or demand. Service shall be deemed complete when the Secretary of State is so served. The Secretary of State shall endorse upon both copies the time of receipt and shall forthwith send one of such copies by registered mail, with return receipt requested, to such insurer at its last known principal place of business as shown on the process, notice or demand served on the Secretary of State. The Commissioner and the Attorney General shall see that such address is included on the process, notice or demand which is served upon the Secretary of State. A copy of the complaint or order of the clerk extending the time for filing the complaint must be mailed to the insurer with the copy of the summons. When a copy of the complaint is not mailed with the summons, the Secretary of State shall mail a copy of the complaint when it is served on him in the same manner as the copy of summons is required to be mailed.

(c)   Upon the return to the Secretary of State of the requested return receipt showing delivery and acceptance of such registered mail, or upon the return of such registered mail showing refusal thereof by such unauthorized insurer, the Secretary of State shall note thereon the date of such return to him and shall attach either the return receipt or such refused mail including the envelope, as the case may be, to the copy of the process, notice or demand theretofore retained by him and shall mail the same to the clerk of the court in which such action or proceeding is pending and in respect of which such process, notice or demand was issued. Such mailing, in addition to the return by the sheriff, shall constitute the due return required by law. The clerk of the court shall thereupon file the same as a paper in such action or proceeding.

(d)   Service made under this section shall have the same legal force and validity as if the service had been made personally in this State. The refusal of any such unauthorized insurer to accept delivery of the registered mail provided for in subsection (b) of this section or the refusal to sign the return receipt shall not affect the validity of such service; and any foreign or alien insurer refusing to accept delivery of such registered mail shall be charged with knowledge of the contents of any process, notice or demand contained therein.

(e)   Whenever service of process is made upon the Secretary of State as herein provided the defendant unauthorized insurer shall have 30 days from the date when the defendant receives or refuses to accept the registered mail containing the copy of the complaint sent as in this section provided in which to appear and answer the complaint in the action or proceeding so instituted. Entries on the defendant's return receipt or the refused registered mail shall be sufficient evidence of such date. If the date of acceptance or refusal to accept the registered mail cannot be determined from the entries on the return receipt or from notations of the postal authorities on the envelope, then the date when the defendant accepted or refused to accept the registered mail shall be deemed to be the date that the return receipt or the registered mail was received back by the Secretary of State.

(f) The court in any action or proceeding in which service is made in the manner provided in the above paragraph may, in its discretion, order such postponement as may be necessary to afford such company reasonable opportunity to defend such action or proceeding.

(g) The Secretary of State shall keep a summarized record of all processes, notices and demands served upon him under this section, and shall record therein the time of such service and his action with reference thereto.

(h) Nothing herein contained shall limit or affect the right to serve any process, notice or demand to be served upon an insurer in any other manner now or hereafter permitted by law.

(i) No judgment by default shall be entered in any such action or proceeding until the expiration of 30 days from the date of the filing of the affidavit of compliance. (1967, c. 909, s. 1; 1987, c. 864, ss. 62-64; 1991, c. 720, s. 4; 2008-124, s. 3.3.)

§ 58-28-45. Unauthorized Insurers; prohibited acts.

(a) No person shall in this State act as agent for any insurer not authorized to transact business in this State, or negotiate for or place or aid in placing insurance coverage in this State for another with any such insurer.

(b) No person shall in this State aid any unauthorized insurer in effecting insurance or in transacting insurance business in this State, either by fixing rates, by adjusting or investigating losses, by inspecting or examining risks, by acting as attorney-in-fact or as attorney for service for process, or otherwise, except as provided in this section or in G.S. 58-16-35.

(c) No person shall make, negotiate for or place, or aid in negotiating or placing any insurance contract in this State for another who is an applicant for insurance covering any property or risk in another state, territory or district of the United States with any insurer not authorized to transact insurance business in the state, territory or district wherein such property or risk or any part thereof is located.

(d) Subsections (a), (b), and (c) of this section do not apply to contracts of reinsurance, or to contracts of insurance made through surplus lines licensees as provided in Article 21 of this Chapter, nor do they apply to any insurer not authorized in this State, or its representatives, in investigating, adjusting losses or otherwise complying in this State with the terms of its insurance contracts made in a state wherein the insurer was authorized; provided, the property or risk insured under such contracts at the time such contract was issued was located in such other state. A motor vehicle used and kept garaged principally in another state shall be deemed to be located in such state.

(e) (1) Repealed by Session Laws 1985, c. 666, s. 40.

(2) Such service of process shall be made by delivering and leaving with the Commissioner or to some person in apparent charge of his office two copies thereof and the payment to him of such fees as may be prescribed by law. The Commissioner shall forthwith mail by registered mail one of the copies of such process to the defendant at its last known principal place of business, and shall keep a record of all such process so served upon him. Such service of process is sufficient provided notice of such service and a copy of the process are sent within 10 days thereafter by registered mail by plaintiff's attorney to the defendant at its last known principal place of business, and the defendant's receipt, or receipt issued by the post office with which the letter is registered, showing the name of the sender of the letter and the name and address of the person to whom the letter is addressed, and the affidavit of plaintiff's attorney showing a compliance herewith are filed with the clerk of the court in which such action is pending on or before the date the defendant is required to appear, or within such further time as the court may allow. However, no plaintiff or complainant shall be entitled to a judgment by default under this subdivision (2) until the expiration of 30 days from the date of the filing of the affidavit of compliance.

(3) Service of process in any such action, suit or proceeding shall be in addition to the manner provided in the preceding subdivision (2) be valid if served upon any person within this State who, in this State on behalf of such insurer, is

a. Soliciting insurance, or

b. Making any contract of insurance or issuing or delivering any policies or written contracts of insurance, or

c. Collecting or receiving any premium for insurance; and a copy of such process is sent within 10 days thereafter by registered mail by plaintiff's attorney to the defendant at the last known principal place of business of the defendant, and the defendant's receipt, or the receipt issued by the post office with which the letter is registered, showing the name of the sender of the letter and the name and address of the person to whom the letter is addressed, and the affidavit of plaintiff's attorney showing a compliance herewith are filed with the clerk of the court in which such action is pending on or before the date the defendant is required to appear, or within such further time as the court may allow.

d. Nothing in this subsection (e) shall limit or abridge the right to serve process, notice or demand upon any insurer in any other manner now or hereafter permitted by law.

(f) No unauthorized insurer shall institute or file, or cause to be instituted or filed, any suit, action or proceeding in this State to enforce any right, claim or demand arising out of the transaction of business in this State until such insurer shall have obtained a license to transact insurance business in this State. Nothing in this subsection shall be construed to require an unauthorized insurance company to obtain a license before instituting or filing, or causing to be instituted or filed, any suit, action or proceeding either in connection with any of its investments in this State or in connection with any contract issued by it at a time when it was authorized to do business in the state where such contract was issued.

(g) (1) Before any unauthorized insurer shall file or cause to be filed any pleading in any action, suit or proceeding instituted against it, such unauthorized insurer shall either

a. File with the clerk of the court in which such action, suit or proceeding is pending a bond with good and sufficient sureties, to be approved by the court, in an amount to be fixed by the court sufficient to secure the payment of any final judgment which may be rendered in such action or

b. Procure a license to transact the business of insurance in this State.

(2) The court in any action, suit or proceeding in which service is made in the manner prescribed in subdivisions (2) and (3) of subsection (e) may order such postponement as may be necessary to afford the defendant reasonable opportunity to comply with the provisions of subdivision (1) of this subsection (g) and to defend such action.

(3) Nothing in subdivision (1) of this subsection (g) shall be construed to prevent an unauthorized insurer from filing a motion to quash a writ or to set aside service thereof made in the manner provided in subdivisions (2) and (3) of subsection (e) on the ground either

a. That no policy or contract of insurance has been issued or delivered to a citizen or resident of this State or to a corporation authorized to do business therein, or

b. That such insurer has not been transacting business in this State, or

c. That the person on whom service was made pursuant to subdivision (3) of subsection (e) was not doing any of the acts enumerated therein.

(h) Except as provided in G.S. 58-33-95, any person violating subsection (a), (b), (c), or (k) of this section shall be guilty of a Class H felony and shall be fined not less than one thousand dollars ($1,000) nor more than five thousand dollars ($5,000). Any person violating subsections (e), (f), and (g) of this section shall be guilty of a Class 1 misdemeanor and shall only be fined not less than one thousand dollars ($1,000) nor more than five thousand dollars ($5,000). For the purposes of the fine imposed by this subsection, each day during which a violation occurs constitutes a separate violation.

(i), (j) Repealed by Session Laws 2007-305, s. 1, effective December 1, 2007, and applicable to offenses or acts committed on or after that date.

(k) No person shall act as an officer, director, or controlling person for a person who is engaged in a violation of subsection (a), (b), or (c) of this section. As used in this subsection, "controlling" has the same meaning as in G.S. 58-19-5(2).

(l) In addition to any other penalties or remedies provided by law, any person who violates this section shall be strictly liable for any losses or unpaid claims if an unauthorized insurer fails to pay in full or in part any claim or loss within the provisions of any insurance contract issued by or on behalf of the unauthorized insurer in violation of this Article. The liability imposed by this subsection shall be joint and several if more than one person violates this section.

(m) A civil action may be filed under this section regardless of whether a criminal action is brought or a criminal conviction is obtained for the act alleged in the civil action. (1899, c. 54, s. 105; Rev., s. 4763; C.S., s. 6424; 1945, c. 386; 1985, c. 666, ss. 20, 40; 1987, c. 864, s. 17; 1993, c. 539, s. 454; 1994, Ex. Sess., c. 24, s. 14(c); 1999-132, s. 9.1; 2004-166, s. 3; 2007-305, s. 1.)

Article 29.

Unauthorized Insurers False Advertising Process Act.

§ 58-29-1. Purpose; construction.

(a) The purpose of this Article is to subject to the jurisdiction of the Commissioner and to the jurisdiction of the courts of this State, insurers not authorized to transact business in this State which place in or send into this State any false advertising designed to induce residents of this State to purchase insurance from insurers not authorized to transact business in this State. The General Assembly declares it is in the interest of the citizens of this State who purchase insurance from insurers which solicit insurance business in this State in the manner set forth in the preceding sentence that such insurers be subject to the provisions of this Article. In furtherance of such interest, the General Assembly in this Article provides a method of substituted service of process upon such insurers and declares in so doing, it exercises its power to protect its residents and also exercises powers and privileges available to the State by virtue of Public Law 15, 79th Congress of the United States, Chapter 20, 1st Session, section 340, which declares that the business of insurance and every person engaged therein shall be subject to the laws of the several states; the authority provided herein to be in addition to any existing powers of this State.

(b) The provisions of this Article shall be liberally construed. (1965, c. 910; 1991, c. 720, s. 4.)

§ 58-29-5. Definitions.

As used in this Article:

(1) "Residents" shall mean and include person, partnership or corporation, domestic, alien or foreign.

(2) "Unfair Trade Practice Act" shall mean Article 63 of this Chapter. (1965, c. 910.)

§ 58-29-10. Unlawful advertising; notice to unauthorized insurer and domiciliary insurance supervisory official.

No unauthorized foreign or alien insurer shall make, issue, circulate or cause to be made, issued or circulated, to residents of this State any estimate, illustration, circular, pamphlet, or letter, or cause to be made in any newspaper, magazine or other publication or over any radio or television station, any announcement or statement to such residents misrepresenting its financial condition or the terms of any contracts issued or to be issued or the benefits or advantages promised thereby, or the dividends or share of the surplus to be received thereon in violation of the Unfair Trade Practice Act, and whenever the Commissioner shall have reason to believe that any such insurer is engaging in such unlawful advertising, it shall be his duty to give notice of such fact by registered mail to such insurer and to the insurance supervisory official of the domiciliary state of such insurer. For the purpose of this section, the domiciliary state of an alien insurer shall be deemed to be the state of entry or the state of the principal office in the United States. (1965, c. 910.)

§ 58-29-15. Action by Commissioner under Unfair Trade Practice Act.

If after 30 days following the giving of the notice mentioned in G.S. 58-29-10 such insurer has failed to cease making, issuing, or circulating such false misrepresentations or causing the same to be made, issued or circulated in this State, and if the Commissioner has reason to believe that a proceeding by him in respect to such matters would be to the interest of the public, and that such insurer is issuing or delivering contracts of insurance to residents of this State or collecting premiums on such contracts or doing any of the acts enumerated in G.S. 58-29-20, he shall take action against such insurer under the Unfair Trade Practice Act. (1965, c. 910.)

§ 58-29-20. Acts appointing Commissioner as attorney for service of statement of charges, notices and process; manner of service; limitation on entry of order or judgment.

(a) Any of the following acts in this State, effected by mail or otherwise, by any such unauthorized foreign or alien insurer:

(1) The issuance or delivery of contracts of insurance to residents of this State,

(2) The solicitation of applications for such contracts,

(3) The collection of premiums, membership fees, assessments or other considerations for such contracts, or

(4) Any other transaction of insurance business,

Is equivalent to and shall constitute an appointment by such insurer of the Commissioner and his successor or successors in office, to be its true and lawful attorney, upon whom may be served all statements of charges, notices and lawful process in any proceeding instituted in respect to the misrepresentations set forth in G.S. 58-29-10 under the provisions of the Unfair Trade Practice Act, or in any action, suit or proceeding for the recovery of any penalty therein provided, and any such act shall be signification of its agreement that such service of statement of charges, notices or process is of the same legal force and validity as personal service of such statement of charges, notices or process in this State, upon such insurer.

(b) Service of a statement of charges and notices under said Unfair Trade Practice Act shall be made by any deputy or employee of the Department delivering to and leaving with the Commissioner or some person in apparent charge of his office, two copies thereof. Service of process issued by any court in any action, suit or proceeding to collect any penalty under said act provided, shall be made by delivering and leaving with the Commissioner, or some person in apparent charge of his office, two copies thereof. The Commissioner shall forthwith cause to be mailed by registered mail one of the copies of such statement of charges, notices or process to the defendant at its last known principal place of business, and shall keep a record of all statements, charges, notices and process so served. Such service of statement of charges, notices or process shall be sufficient provided they shall have been so mailed and the defendant's receipt or receipt issued by the post office with which the letter is registered, showing the name of the sender of the letter and the name and address of the person to whom the letter is addressed, and the affidavit of the person mailing such letter showing a compliance herewith are filed with the Commissioner in the case of any statement of charges or notices, or with the clerk of the court in which such action is pending in the case of any process, on or before the date the defendant is required to appear or within such further time as may be allowed.

(c) Service of statement of charges, notices and process in any such proceeding, action or suit shall in addition to the manner provided in subsection (b) of this section be valid if served upon any person within this State who on behalf of such insurer is

(1) Soliciting insurance, or

(2) Making, issuing or delivering any contract of insurance, or

(3) Collecting or receiving in this State any premium for insurance;

And a copy of such statement of charges, notices or process is sent within 10 days thereafter by registered mail by or on behalf of the Commissioner to the defendant at the last known principal place of business of the defendant, and the defendant's receipt, or the receipt issued by the post office with which the letter is registered, showing the name of the sender of the letter, the name and address of the person to whom the letter is addressed, and the affidavit of the person mailing the same showing a compliance herewith, are filed with the Commissioner in the case of any statement of charges or notices, or with the clerk of the court in which such action is pending in the case of any process, on or before the date the defendant is required to appear or within such further time as the court may allow.

(d) No cease or desist order or default judgment under this section shall be entered until the expiration of 30 days from the date of the filing of the affidavit of compliance.

(e) Service of process and notice under the provisions of this Article shall be in addition to all other methods of service provided by law, and nothing in this Article shall limit or prohibit the right to serve any statement of charges, notices or process upon any insurer in any other manner now or hereafter permitted by law. (1965, c. 910; 1991, c. 720, ss. 4, 5, 57.)

§ 58-29-25. Short title.

This Article may be cited as the Unauthorized Insurers False Advertising Process Act. (1965, c. 910.)

Article 30.

Insurers Supervision, Rehabilitation, and Liquidation.

§ 58-30-1. Construction and purpose.

(a) This Article does not limit powers granted to the Commissioner by any other provision of law. To the extent practicable, the Commissioner may supplement the provisions of this Article with those of Part 2 of Article 38 of Chapter 1 of the General Statutes.

(b) This Article shall be liberally construed to effect the purpose stated in subsection (c) of this section.

(c) The purpose of this Article is to protect the interests of policyholders, claimants, creditors, and the public generally with minimum interference with the normal prerogatives of the owners and managers of insurers, through:

(1) Early detection of any potentially dangerous condition in an insurer, and prompt application of appropriate corrective measures;

(2) Improved methods for rehabilitating insurers, involving the cooperation and management expertise of the insurance industry;

(3) Enhanced efficiency and economy of liquidation, through clarification of the law, to minimize legal uncertainty and litigation;

(4) Equitable apportionment of any unavoidable loss;

(5) Lessening the problems of interstate rehabilitation and liquidation by facilitating cooperation between states in the liquidation process, and by extending the scope of personal jurisdiction over debtors of the insurer outside this State; and

(6) Regulation of the insurance business by the impact of the law relating to delinquency procedures and substantive rules on the entire insurance business. (1989, c. 452, s. 1.)

§ 58-30-5. Persons covered.

The proceedings authorized by this Article may be applied to:

(1) All insurers that are doing, or have done, an insurance business in this State, and against whom claims arising from that business may exist now or in the future.

(2) All insurers that purport to do an insurance business in this State.

(3) All insurers that have insureds resident in this State.

(4) All persons organized or in the process of organizing with the intent to do an insurance business in this State.

(5) All persons subject to Articles 64, 65 and 66, or 67 of this Chapter; except to the extent there is a conflict between the provisions of this Article and the provisions of those Articles, in which case those Articles will govern.

(6) Self-insured group workers' compensation funds subject to Article 47 of this Chapter. (1989, c. 452, s. 1; 1995, c. 471, s. 3; 1995 (Reg. Sess., 1996), c. 582, s. 1; 1999-132, s. 7.2.)

§ 58-30-10. Definitions.

For the purposes of this Article only:

(1) "Alien country" means any other jurisdiction not in any state.

(2) "Ancillary state" means any state other than a domiciliary state.

(3) "Court" means the Superior Court of Wake County.

(4) "Creditor" means a person having any claim, whether matured or unmatured, liquidated or unliquidated, secured or unsecured, absolute, fixed, or contingent.

(5) "Delinquency proceeding" means any proceeding instituted against an insurer for the purpose of supervising, rehabilitating, conserving, or liquidating such insurer.

(6) "Doing business" includes any of the following acts by insurers, whether effected by mail or otherwise:

a. The issuance or delivery of contracts of insurance to persons resident in this State;

b. The solicitation of applications for such contracts, or other negotiations preliminary to the execution of such contracts;

c. The collection of premiums, membership fees, assessments, or other consideration for such contracts;

d. The transaction of matters subsequent to execution of such contracts and arising out of them;

e. Operating as an insurer under a license issued by the Department; or

f. The purchase of contracts of insurance issued to persons in this State by an assumption agreement.

(7) "Domestic guaranty association" means the Postassessment Insurance Guaranty Association in Article 48 of this Chapter, as amended; the North Carolina Self-Insurance Security Association in Article 4 of Chapter 97 of the General Statutes; the Life and Accident and Health Insurance Guaranty Association in Article 62 of this Chapter, as amended; or any other similar entity hereafter created by the General Assembly for the payment of claims of insolvent insurers.

(8) "Domiciliary state" means the state in which an insurer is incorporated or organized; or, in the case of an alien insurer, its state of entry.

(9) "Fair consideration" is given for property or obligation when:

a. In exchange for such property or obligation, as a fair equivalent therefor, and in good faith, property is conveyed or services are rendered or an obligation is incurred or an antecedent debt is satisfied; or

b. Such property or obligation is received in good faith to secure a present advance or antecedent debt in amount not disproportionately small as compared to the value of the property or obligation obtained.

(10) "Foreign guaranty association" means a guaranty association now in existence in or hereafter created by the legislature of any other state.

(11) "Formal delinquency proceeding" means any liquidation or rehabilitation proceeding.

(12) "General assets" means all real, personal, or other property that is not specifically mortgaged, pledged, hypothecated, deposited, or otherwise encumbered for the security or benefit of specified persons or classes of persons. As to specifically encumbered property, "general assets" includes all such property or its proceeds in excess of the amount necessary to discharge the sum or sums secured thereby. Assets that are held in trust and on deposit for the security or benefit of all policyholders in more than one state or all policyholders and creditors in more than one state shall be treated as "general assets". No person shall have a claim against general assets unless that claim is in an amount in excess of fifty dollars ($50.00).

(13) "Insolvency" or "insolvent" means that an insurer is unable to pay its obligations when they are due, or that its admitted assets do not exceed its liabilities plus the greater of (i) any capital and surplus required by law for its organization; or (ii) the total par or stated value of its authorized and issued capital stock. For the purposes of this subdivision, "liabilities" includes reserves required by statute, by Department rules, or by specific requirements imposed by the Commissioner upon a subject company at the time of admission or subsequent thereto, except those reserves that are an allocation of surplus as specified in G.S. 58-65-95.

(14) "Insurer" means any entity that is or should be licensed under Articles 7, 16, 26, 47, 49, 64, 65, or 67 of this Chapter.

(15) "Preferred claim" means any claim with respect to which the provisions of this Article accord priority of payment from the general assets of the insurer.

(16) "Receiver" includes a liquidator, rehabilitator, or conservator, as the context requires.

(17) "Reciprocal state" means any state other than this State in which in substance and effect the provisions of G.S. 58-30-105(a), 58-30-270, 58-30-275, and 58-30-285 through 58-30-295 are in force, and in which provisions are in force requiring that the insurance regulator of that state be the receiver of a delinquent insurer; and in which provisions exist for the avoidance of fraudulent conveyances and preferential transfers.

(18) "Secured claim" means any claim secured by mortgage, trust deed, pledge, deposit as security, escrow, or otherwise; and includes any claim that has become a lien upon specific assets by reason of judicial process. "Secured claim" does not include a special deposit claim or a claim against general assets.

(19) "Special deposit claim" means any claim in excess of fifty dollars ($50.00) secured by a deposit made pursuant to statute for the security or benefit of a limited class or classes of persons, but does not include any claim secured by general assets.

(20) "Transfer" includes the sale and every other and different mode, whether direct or indirect, of disposing of or of parting with property, an interest therein, or the possession thereof; or of voluntarily fixing a lien upon property or an interest therein, whether absolutely or conditionally, by or without judicial proceedings. The retention of a security title to property delivered to a debtor is a transfer suffered by the debtor. (1989, c. 452, s. 1; 1995, c. 471, ss. 4, 5; 1995 (Reg. Sess., 1996), c. 582, s. 2; c. 742, s. 24; 1999-132, ss. 2.1, 7.3, 9.1; 1999-294, s. 11(a), (b); 2000-140, s. 13; 2001-223, ss. 24.2, 24.3; 2001-487, s. 103(a); 2005-400, s. 18; 2007-127, s. 9.)

§ 58-30-12. Duty to report insurer impairment; violations; penalties.

(a) As used in this section:

(1) "Chief executive officer", as used in subsection (b) of this section, means the person, irrespective of title, designated by the board of directors or trustees of an insurer as the person charged with administering and implementing an insurer's policies and procedures.

(2) "Impaired", as used in subsections (b) and (c) of this section, means a financial condition in which the assets of an insurer are less than the sum of the insurer's minimum required capital, minimum required surplus, and all liabilities as determined in accordance with the requirements for the preparation and filing of a financial statement under G.S. 58-2-165 and under other provisions of this Chapter.

(3) "Insolvent", as used in subsection (c) of this section, has the same meaning as set forth in G.S. 58-30-10(13).

(b) Whenever an insurer is impaired, its chief executive officer shall, as soon as is reasonably possible, notify the Commissioner in writing of the impairment and shall at the same time notify in writing all of the members of the board of directors or trustees of the insurer, if the chief executive officer knows or has reason to know of the impairment. An officer, director, or trustee of an insurer shall notify the chief executive officer of the impairment of the insurer if the officer, director, or trustee knows or has reason to know that the insurer is impaired. Any person who knowingly violates this subsection shall, upon conviction, be guilty of a Class 1 misdemeanor.

(c) Any person who willfully:

(1) Conceals any property belonging to an insurer; or

(2) Transfers or conceals in contemplation of a delinquency proceeding the person's own property or property belonging to an insurer; or

(3) Conceals, destroys, mutilates, alters, or makes a false entry in any document that affects or relates to the property of an insurer or withholds any such document from a receiver, trustee, or other officer of a court entitled to its possession; or

(4) Gives, obtains, or receives a thing of value for acting or forbearing to act in any court proceedings;

and any such act results in or contributes to an insurer becoming impaired or insolvent; shall be guilty of a Class H felony. (1991, c. 681, s. 40; 1993, c. 539, s. 455; 1994, Ex. Sess., c. 24, s. 14(c).)

§ 58-30-15. Jurisdiction and venue.

(a)   No delinquency proceeding shall be commenced by anyone other than the Commissioner and no other court has jurisdiction to entertain, hear, or determine any proceeding commenced by any other person.

(b)   Except as provided in this Article, no court of this State has jurisdiction to entertain, hear, or determine any complaint praying for the dissolution, liquidation, rehabilitation, sequestration, conservation, or receivership of any insurer; or praying for an injunction or restraining order or other relief preliminary to, incidental to, or relating to such proceedings.

(c)   In addition to other grounds for jurisdiction provided by the laws of this State, the Court has jurisdiction over a person served pursuant to Chapter 1A of the General Statutes or other applicable provisions of law in an action brought by the receiver of a domestic insurer or an alien insurer domiciled in this State:

(1)   If the person served is obligated to the insurer in any way as an incident to any agency or brokerage arrangement that may exist or has existed between the insurer and the agent or broker, in any action on or incident to the obligation; or

(2)   If the person served is a reinsurer who has at any time entered into a contract of reinsurance with an insurer against which a rehabilitation or liquidation order is in effect when the action is commenced, or is an agent or broker of or for the reinsurer, in any action on or incident to the reinsurance contract; or

(3)   If the person served is or has been an officer, manager, trustee, organizer, promoter, or person in a position of comparable authority or influence, in an insurer against which a rehabilitation or liquidation order is in effect when the action is commenced, in any action resulting from such a relationship with the insurer; or

(4) If the person served is or was, when the delinquency proceeding was begun against the insurer, holding assets in which the receiver claims an interest on behalf of the insurer, in any action concerning the assets; or

(5) If the person served is obligated to the insurer in any way whatsoever, in any action on or incident to the obligation.

(d) All actions authorized in this Article shall be brought in the Superior Court of Wake County.

(e) The provisions of Chapter 150B of the General Statutes do not apply to this Article. (1989, c. 452, s. 1; 1991, c. 681, s. 41.)

§ 58-30-20. Injunctions and orders.

(a) Any receiver appointed in a proceeding under this Article may at any time apply for, and any court of general jurisdiction may grant, such restraining orders, preliminary and permanent injunctions, and other orders as may be deemed to be necessary and proper to prevent:

(1) The transaction of further business;

(2) The transfer of property;

(3) Interference with the receiver or with a proceeding under this Article;

(4) Waste of the insurer's assets;

(5) Dissipation and transfer of bank accounts;

(6) The institution or further prosecution of any actions or proceedings;

(7) The obtaining of preferences, judgments, attachments, garnishments, or liens against the insurer, its assets or its policyholders;

(8) The levying of execution against the insurer, its assets, or its policyholders;

(9) The making of any sale or deed for nonpayment of taxes or assessments that would lessen the value of the assets of the insurer;

(10) The withholding from the receiver of books, accounts, documents, or other records relating to the business of the insurer; or

(11) Any other threatened or contemplated action that might lessen the value of the insurer's assets or prejudice the rights of policyholders, creditors, or shareholders, or the administration of any proceeding under this Article.

(b) The receiver may apply to any court outside of this State for the relief described in subsection (a) of this section. (1989, c. 452, s. 1.)

§ 58-30-22. Powers of Commissioner and receiver to examine or audit books or records.

(a) As used in this section, "person" includes an agent of the insurer; a broker, ceding or assuming reinsurer, or reinsurance intermediary that has done business with the insurer; or any affiliate of the insurer.

(b) In addition to other powers granted under this Chapter, the Commissioner in any supervision proceeding under this Article and a receiver in any delinquency proceeding under this Article has the power to examine or audit the books or records of any person insofar as those books or records relate to the business activities of the insurer that is under supervision or subject to a delinquency proceeding.

(c) Repealed by Session Laws 1995, c. 360, s. 2(a). (1991, c. 681, s. 42; 1995, c. 360, s. 2(a).)

§ 58-30-25. Cooperation of officers, owners and employees.

(a) Any officer, manager, director, trustee, owner, employee, or agent of any insurer, and any other person with authority over or in charge of any segment of the insurer's affairs, shall cooperate with the Commissioner in any proceeding under this Article or any investigation preliminary to the proceeding. As used in this section, "person" includes any person who exercises direct or indirect control over activities of an insurer through any holding company or other affiliate of the insurer. "Cooperate" includes replying promptly in writing to any inquiry from the Commissioner requesting such a reply and making available to the Commissioner any books, accounts, documents, or other records or information or property of or pertaining to the insurer and in his possession, custody, or control.

(b)   No person shall obstruct or interfere with the Commissioner in the conduct of any delinquency proceeding or any investigation preliminary or incidental thereto.

(c)   This section does not abridge otherwise existing legal rights, including the right to resist a petition for any delinquency proceeding or other order.

(d)   Any person described in subsection (a) of this section who fails to cooperate with the Commissioner, or any person who obstructs or interferes with the Commissioner in the conduct of any delinquency proceeding or any investigation preliminary or incidental thereto, or any person who knowingly and willfully violates any order the Commissioner issued validly under this Article is subject to the civil penalty and restitution provisions of G.S. 58-2-70 and is subject further to the revocation or suspension of any licenses issued by the Commissioner. (1989, c. 452, s. 1.)

§ 58-30-30. Bonds.

In any proceeding under this Article, the Commissioner and his deputies shall be responsible on their official bonds for the faithful performance of their duties. (1989, c. 452, s. 1.)

§ 58-30-35. Executory contracts and unexpired leases.

(a)   Except as provided in subsections (b), (c), and (d) of this section, the receiver, subject to the Court's approval, may assume or reject any executory contract or unexpired lease of the insurer.

(b) (1) If there has been a default in an executory contract or unexpired lease of the insurer, the receiver may not assume such contract or lease unless, at the time of assumption of such contract or lease, the receiver:

a. Cures, or provides adequate assurance that the receiver will promptly cure, such default;

b. Compensates, or provides adequate assurance that the receiver will promptly compensate, a party, other than the insurer to such contract or lease, for any actual pecuniary loss to such party resulting from such default; and

c. Provides adequate assurance of future performance under such contract or lease.

(2) Subdivision (1) of this subsection does not apply to a default that is a breach of a provision relating to;

a. The insolvency or financial condition of the insurer at any time before the closing of the case;

b. The commencement of a proceeding under this Article; or

c. The appointment of or taking possession by a receiver in a proceeding under this Article or a custodian before such commencement.

(3) Notwithstanding any other provision of this section, if there has been a default in an unexpired lease of the insurer, other than a default of a kind specified in subdivision (2) of this subsection, the receiver may not require a lessor to provide services or supplies incidental to such lease before assumption of such lease unless the lessor is compensated under the terms of such lease for any services and supplies provided under such lease before assumption of such lease.

(c) The receiver may not assume or assign an executory contract or unexpired lease of the insurer, whether or not such contract or lease prohibits or restricts assignment of rights or delegation of duties, if:

(1) a. Applicable law excuses a party, other than the insurer, to such contract or lease from accepting performance from or rendering performance to the receiver or an assignee of such contract or lease, whether or not such

contract or lease prohibits or restricts assignment of rights or delegation of duties; and

b. Such party does not consent to such assumption or assignment; or

(2) Such contract is a contract to make a loan, or extend other debt financing or financial accommodations, to or for the benefit of the insurer, or to issue a security of the insurer.

(d) (1) In a proceeding under G.S. 58-30-105, if the receiver does not assume or reject an executory contract or unexpired lease of the insurer within 60 days after the order for liquidation, or within such additional time as the Court, for cause, within such 60-day period, fixes, then such contract or lease is deemed to be rejected.

(2) In a proceeding under G.S. 58-30-80 the receiver may assume or reject an executory contract or unexpired lease of the insurer at any time before the order for a plan of rehabilitation, but the Court, on request of any party to such contract or lease, may order the receiver to determine within a specified period of time whether to assume or reject such contract or lease.

(e) (1) Notwithstanding a provision in an executory contract or unexpired lease, or in applicable law, an executory contract or unexpired lease of the insurer may not be terminated or modified, and any right or obligation under such contract or lease may not be terminated or modified, at any time after the commencement of the proceeding solely because of a provision in such contract or lease that is conditioned on:

a. The insolvency or financial condition of the insurer at any time before the closing of the proceeding;

b. The commencement of a proceeding under this Article; or

c. The appointment of or taking possession by a receiver in a proceeding under this Article or a custodian before such commencement.

(2) Subdivision (1) of this subsection does not apply to an executory contract or unexpired lease of the insurer, whether or not such contract or lease prohibits or restricts assignment of rights or delegation of duties, if:

a. Applicable law excused a party, other than the insurer, to such contract or lease from accepting performance from or rendering performance to the receiver or to an assignee of such contract or lease, whether or not such contract or lease prohibits or restricts assignment of rights or delegation of duties and such party does not consent to such assumption or assignment; or

b. Such contract is a contract to make a loan, or extend other debt financing or financial accommodations, to or for the benefit of the insurer, or to issue a security of the insurer.

(f) (1) Except as provided in subsection (c) of this section, notwithstanding a provision in an executory contract or unexpired lease of the insurer, or in applicable law, that prohibits, restricts, or conditions the assignment of such contract or lease, the receiver may assign such contract or lease under subdivision (2) of this subsection.

(2) The receiver may assign an executory contract or unexpired lease of the insurer only if:

a. The receiver assumes such contract or lease in accordance with the provisions of this section; and

b. Adequate assurance of future performance by the assignee of such contract or lease is provided, whether or not there has been a default in such contract or lease.

(3) Notwithstanding a provision in an executory contract or unexpired lease of the insurer, or in applicable law that terminates or modifies, or permits a party other than the insurer to terminate or modify, such contract or lease or a right or obligation under such contract or lease on account of an assignment of such contract or lease, such contract, lease, right, or obligation may not be terminated or modified under such provision because of the assumption or assignment of such contract or lease by the receiver.

(g) Except as provided in subdivisions (h)(2) and (i)(2) of this section, the rejection of an executory contract or unexpired lease of the insurer constitutes a breach of such contract or lease:

(1) If such contract or lease has not been assumed under this section or under a plan of rehabilitation under G.S. 58-30-80, immediately before the date of the filing of the petition; or

(2) If such contract or lease has been assumed under this section or under a plan of rehabilitation under G.S. 58-30-80:

a. If before such rejection the proceeding has not been converted to a proceeding under G.S. 58-30-105 at the time of such rejection; or

b. If before such rejection the case has been converted to a proceeding under G.S. 58-30-105: (i) immediately before the date of such conversion, if such contract or lease was assumed before such conversion; or (ii) at the time of such rejection, if such contract or lease was assumed after such conversion.

(h) (1) If the receiver rejects an unexpired lease of real property of the insurer under which the insurer is the lessor, the lessee under such lease may treat the lease as terminated by such rejection, or, in the alternative, may remain in possession for the balance of the term of such lease and any renewal or extension of such term that is enforceable by such lessee under applicable provision of law outside of this Article.

(2) If such lessee remains in possession, such lessee may offset against the rent reserved under such lease for the balance of the term after the date of the rejection of such lease, and any such renewal or extension, any damages occurring after such date caused by the nonperformance of any obligation of the insurer after such date, but such lessee does not have any rights against the estate on account of any damages arising after such date from such rejection, other than such offset.

(i) (1) If the receiver rejects an executory contract of the insurer for the sale of real property under which the purchaser is in possession, such purchaser may treat such contract as terminated, or, in the alternative, may remain in possession of such real property.

(2) If such purchaser remains in possession:

a. Such purchaser shall continue to make all payments due under such contract but may offset against such payments any damages occurring after the date of the rejection of such contract caused by the nonperformance of any obligation of the insurer after such date, but such purchaser does not have any rights against the estate on account of any damages arising after such date from such rejection, other than such offset; and

b.   The receiver shall deliver title to such purchaser in accordance with the provisions of such contract, but is relieved of all other obligations to perform under such contract.

(j)   A purchaser that treats an executory contract as terminated under subsection (i) of this section, or a party whose executory contract to purchase real property from the insurer is rejected and under which such party is not in possession, has a lien on the interest of the insurer in such property for the recovery of any portion of the purchase price that such purchaser or party has paid.

(k)   Assignment by the receiver to a person of a contract or lease assumed under this section relieves the receiver and the estate from any liability for any breach of such contract or lease occurring after such assignment. (1989, c. 452, s. 1.)

§ 58-30-40. Turnover of property by a custodian.

(a)   As used in this section "custodian" means:

(1)   A receiver or trustee of any of the property of the insurer, appointed in a case or proceeding not under this Article;

(2)   An assignee under a general assignment for the benefit of the insurer's creditors; or

(3)   A trustee, receiver, or agent under applicable law, or under a contract, that is appointed or authorized to take charge of property of the insurer for the purpose of enforcing a lien against such property, or for the purpose of general administration of such property for the benefit of the insurer's creditors.

(b)   A custodian with knowledge of the commencement of a proceeding under this Article may not make any disbursement from, or take any action in the administration of property of the insurer, proceeds of such property, or property of the estate, in the possession, custody, or control of such custodian, except such action as is necessary to preserve such property.

(c)   A custodian shall:

(1)   Deliver to the receiver any property of the insurer transferred to such custodian, or proceeds of such property, that is in such custodian's possession, custody, or control on the date that such custodian acquires knowledge of the commencement of the proceeding; and

(2)   File an accounting of any property of the insurer, or proceeds of such property, that, at any time, came into the possession, custody, or control of such custodian.

(d)   The Court, after notice and a hearing, shall:

(1)   Protect all entities to which a custodian has become obligated with respect to such property;

(2)   Provide for the payment of reasonable compensation for services rendered and costs and expenses incurred by such custodian; and

(3)   Surcharge such custodian, other than an assignee for the benefit of the insurer's creditors that was appointed or took possession more than 120 days before the date of the filing of the petition, for any improper excessive disbursement, other than a disbursement that has been made in accordance with applicable law or approved, after notice and a hearing, by a court of competent jurisdiction before the commencement of the proceeding under this Article.

(e)   The Court may, after notice and a hearing, excuse compliance with subsection (a), (b), or (c) of this section, if the interests of policyholders, creditors, and any equity security holders would be better served by permitting a custodian to continue in possession, custody, or control of such property. (1989, c. 452, s. 1.)

§ 58-30-45. Utility service.

(a)   Except as provided in subsection (b) of this section, a utility may not alter, refuse, or discontinue service to, or discriminate against, the receiver or the insurer solely on the basis that a debt owed by the insurer to such utility for service rendered before an order of rehabilitation or liquidation was not paid when due.

(b)   Such utility may alter, refuse, or discontinue service if neither the receiver nor the insurer, within 20 days after the date of an order of rehabilitation or liquidation, furnishes adequate assurance of payment, in the form of a deposit or other security, for services after such date. On request of a party in interest and after notice and a hearing, the Court may order reasonable modification of the amount of the deposit or other security necessary to provide adequate assurance of payment. (1989, c. 452, s. 1.)

§ 58-30-50. Continuation of delinquency proceedings.

Every proceeding that was commenced under the laws in effect before June 26, 1989, is deemed to have been commenced under this Article for the purpose of conducting the proceeding; except that in the discretion of the Commissioner the proceeding may be continued, in whole or in part, as it would have been continued had this Article not been enacted. (1989, c. 452, s. 1.)

§ 58-30-55. Condition on release from delinquency proceedings.

No insurer that is subject to any delinquency proceedings, whether formal or informal, administrative or judicial, shall:

(1)   Be released from such proceeding, unless such proceeding is converted into a judicial rehabilitation or liquidation proceeding;

(2)   Be permitted to solicit or accept new business or request or accept the restoration of any suspended or revoked license;

(3)   Be returned to the control of its shareholders or private management; or

(4)   Have any of its assets returned to the control of its shareholders or private management;

until all payments of or on account of the insurer's contractual obligations by all guaranty associations, along with all expenses thereof and interest on all such payments and expenses, have been repaid to the guaranty associations or a plan of repayment by the insurer shall have been approved by the guaranty associations. (1989, c. 452, s. 1; 1999-132, s. 9.1; 2000-140, s. 14.)

§ 58-30-60. Commissioner's summary orders and supervision proceedings.

(a)   Whenever the Commissioner has reasonable cause to believe, and determines after a hearing held under subsection (e) of this section, that any domestic insurer has committed or is engaged in, or is about to commit or engage in, any act, practice, or transaction that would subject it to delinquency proceedings under this Article, he may make and serve upon the insurer and any other persons involved, such orders as are reasonably necessary to correct, eliminate, or remedy such conduct, condition, or ground.

(b)   The Commissioner may consider any or all of the following standards to determine whether the continued operation of any licensed insurer is hazardous to its policyholders, creditors, or the general public:

(1)   Adverse findings reported in financial condition and market conduct examination reports, audit reports, and actuarial opinions, reports, or summaries;

(2)   The NAIC Insurance Regulatory Information System and its other financial analysis solvency tools and reports;

(3)   Repealed by Session Laws 2013-199, s. 6, effective July 1, 2013.

(4)   Whether the insurer has made adequate provision, according to presently accepted actuarial standards of practice, for the anticipated cash flows required by the contractual obligations and related expenses of the insurer, when considered in light of the assets held by the insurer with respect to such reserves and related actuarial items, including, but not limited to, the investment earnings on such assets, and the considerations anticipated to be received and retained under such policies and contracts;

(5)   The ability of an assuming reinsurer to perform and whether the insurer's reinsurance program provides sufficient protection for the insurer's remaining surplus, after taking into account the insurer's cash flow and the classes of business written as well as the financial condition of the assuming reinsurer;

(6) Whether an insurer's operating loss in the last 12-month period or any shorter period of time, including, but not limited to, net capital gain or loss, changes in nonadmitted assets, and cash dividends paid to shareholders, is greater than fifty percent (50%) of the insurer's remaining policyholders' surplus in excess of the minimum required;

(6a) Whether the insurer's operating loss in the last 12-month period or any shorter period of time, excluding net capital gains, is greater than twenty percent (20%) of the insurer's remaining policyholders' surplus in excess of the minimum required;

(7) Whether a reinsurer, obligor, or any entity within the insurer's insurance holding company system is insolvent, threatened with insolvency, or delinquent in payment of its monetary or any other obligation and which in the opinion of the Commissioner may affect the solvency of the insurer;

(8) Contingent liabilities, pledges, or guaranties that either individually or collectively involve a total amount that in the Commissioner's opinion may affect an insurer's solvency;

(9) Whether any controlling person of an insurer is delinquent in the transmitting to or payment of net premiums to the insurer;

(10) The age and collectibility of receivables;

(11) Whether the management of an insurer, including officers, directors, or any other person who directly or indirectly controls the operation of the insurer, fails to possess and demonstrate the competence, fitness, or reputation considered by the Commissioner to be necessary to serve the insurer in that position;

(12) Whether the management of an insurer has failed to respond to the Commissioner's inquiries about the condition of the insurer or has furnished false and misleading information in response to an inquiry by the Commissioner;

(12a) Whether the insurer has failed to meet financial and holding company filing requirements in the absence of a reason satisfactory to the Commissioner;

(13) Whether the management of an insurer has filed any false or misleading sworn financial statement, has released a false or misleading financial

statement to a lending institution or to the general public, or has made a false or misleading entry or omitted an entry of material amount in the insurer's books;

(14) Whether the insurer has grown so rapidly and to such an extent that it lacks adequate financial and administrative capacity to meet its obligations in a timely manner;

(15) Whether the insurer has experienced or will experience in the foreseeable future cash flow or liquidity problems;

(16) Whether management has established reserves that do not comply with minimum standards established by State insurance laws, regulations, statutory accounting standards, sound actuarial principles, and standards of practice;

(17) Whether management persistently engages in material under reserving that results in adverse development;

(18) Whether transactions among affiliates, subsidiaries, or controlling persons for which the insurer receives assets or capital gains, or both, do not provide sufficient value, liquidity, or diversity to assure the insurer's ability to meet its outstanding obligations as they mature; or

(19) Any other finding determined by the Commissioner to be hazardous to the insurer's policyholders, creditors, or general public.

To determine an insurer's financial condition under this Article, the Commissioner may: disregard any credit or amount receivable resulting from transactions with a reinsurer that is insolvent, impaired, or otherwise subject to a delinquency proceeding; make appropriate adjustments to asset values attributable to investments in or transactions with parents, subsidiaries, or affiliates of an insurer; refuse to recognize the stated value of accounts receivable if the insurer's ability to collect receivables is highly speculative in view of the age of the account or the financial condition of the debtor; or increase the insurer's liability in an amount equal to any contingent liability, pledge, or guarantee not otherwise included if there is a substantial risk that the insurer will be called upon to meet the obligation undertaken within the next 12-month period.

If upon examination or at any other time the Commissioner has reasonable cause to believe that any domestic insurer is in such condition as to render the continuance of its business hazardous to the public or to holders of its policies or certificates of insurance, or if the domestic insurer gives its consent, then the Commissioner shall upon the Commissioner's determination:

(1) Issue an order notifying the insurer of that determination; and

(2) Furnish to the insurer a written list of the Commissioner's requirements to abate that determination that may include any of the following:

a. A reduction in the total amount of present and potential liability for policy benefits by reinsurance.

b. A reduction, suspension, or limitation of the volume of insurance being accepted or renewed.

c. A reduction in general insurance and commission expenses by specified methods.

d. An increase in the insurer's capital and surplus.

e. A suspension or limitation in the insurer's declaration and payment of dividends to its stockholders or policyholders.

f. The filing of reports in a form acceptable to the Commissioner concerning the market value of its assets.

g. A limitation or withdrawal from certain investments or the discontinuance of certain investment practices to the extent the Commissioner considers necessary.

h. Documentation of the adequacy of premium rates in relation to the risks insured.

i. The filing, in addition to regular annual financial statements, of interim financial reports on the form adopted by the NAIC or on such format prescribed by the Commissioner.

j. The correction of corporate governance practice deficiencies.

k. The adoption and utilization of governance practices acceptable to the Commissioner.

l. The provision of a business plan to the Commissioner in order to continue to transact business in the State.

Notwithstanding any other provision of law limiting the frequency or amount of premium rate adjustments, the Commissioner may adjust rates for any nonlife insurance product written by the insurer that the Commissioner considers necessary to improve the financial condition of the insurer.

(c) If the Commissioner makes a determination to supervise an insurer subject to an order under subsections (a) or (b) of this section, he shall notify the insurer that it is under the supervision of the Commissioner. During the period of supervision, the Commissioner may appoint a supervisor to supervise such insurer. The order appointing a supervisor shall direct the supervisor to enforce orders issued under subsections (a) and (b) of this section and may also require that the insurer may not do any of the following things during the period of supervision, without the prior approval of the Commissioner or his supervisor:

(1) Dispose of, convey, or encumber any of its assets or its business in force;

(2) Withdraw from any of its bank accounts;

(3) Lend any of its funds;

(4) Invest any of its funds;

(5) Transfer any of its property;

(6) Incur any debt, obligation, or liability;

(7) Merge or consolidate with another company; or

(8) Enter into any new reinsurance contract or treaty.

(d) Any insurer subject to an order under this section shall comply with the lawful requirements of the Commissioner and, if placed under supervision, shall comply with the requirements of the Commissioner within such period of time established by the Commissioner. The Commissioner may in his discretion extend the time for compliance beyond such period of time for cause. In the event of such insurer's failure to comply within such period of time, the

Commissioner may institute proceedings under this Article to have a rehabilitator or liquidator appointed, or extend the period of supervision.

(e) The notice of hearing under subsection (a) of this section and any order issued pursuant to that subsection shall be served upon the insurer pursuant to the applicable rules of civil procedure. The notice of hearing shall state the time and place of hearing, and the conduct, condition, or ground upon which the Commissioner would base his order. Unless mutually agreed upon between the Commissioner and the insurer, the hearing shall occur not less than 10 days nor more than 30 days after notice is served and shall be either in Wake County or in some other place designated by the Commissioner. The Commissioner shall hold all hearings under subsection (a) of this section privately unless the insurer requests a public hearing, in which case the hearing shall be public.

(f) Any insurer subject to an order under subsection (b) of this section may request an administrative hearing before the Commissioner or his designee to review that order. Such hearing shall be held as provided in subsection (e) of this section, but the request for a hearing shall not stay the effect of the order. If the Commissioner issues an order under subsection (b) of this section, the insurer may, at any time, waive the hearing and apply for immediate judicial relief by means of any remedy afforded by law without first exhausting its administrative remedies. Subsequent to an administrative hearing, any party to the proceedings whose interests are substantially affected is entitled to judicial review of any order issued by the Commissioner.

(g) During the period of supervision the insurer may request the Commissioner to review any action taken or proposed to be taken by the supervisor, specifying wherein the action complained of is believed not to be in the best interest of the insurer.

(h) If any person violates any supervision order issued under this section that as to him is then still in effect, he shall be liable to pay a civil penalty imposed by the Court not to exceed ten thousand dollars ($10,000). The clear proceeds of civil penalties imposed pursuant to this subsection shall be remitted to the Civil Penalty and Forfeiture Fund in accordance with G.S. 115C-457.2.

(i) The Commissioner may apply for, and any court of general jurisdiction may grant, such restraining orders, preliminary and permanent injunctions, and other orders as may be deemed to be necessary and proper to enforce a supervision order.

(j)   In the event that any person subject to the provisions of this Article, including any person described in G.S. 58-30-25(a), knowingly and willfully violates any valid order of the Commissioner issued under the provisions of this section and, as a result of such violation, the net worth of the insurer is reduced or the insurer suffers loss that it would not otherwise have suffered, said person shall become personally liable to the insurer for the amount of any such reduction or loss. The Commissioner or supervisor is authorized to bring an action on behalf of the insurer in the Court to recover the amount of the reduction or loss together with any costs. (1989, c. 452, s. 1; 1989 (Reg. Sess., 1990), c. 1021, s. 6; 1991, c. 681, s. 43; 1998-215, s. 86; 2013-199, s. 6.)

§ 58-30-62. Administrative supervision of insurers.

(a)   As used in this section, an insurer has "exceeded its powers" when it: has refused to permit examination of its books, papers, accounts, records or affairs by the Commissioner; has in violation of G.S. 58-7-50 removed from this State books, papers, accounts or records necessary for an examination of the insurer; has failed to comply promptly with applicable financial reporting statutes or rules and related Department requests; continues to transact the business of insurance after its license has been revoked or suspended by the Commissioner; by contract or otherwise, has unlawfully, or has in violation of an order of the Commissioner, or has without first having obtained any legally required written approval of the Commissioner, totally reinsured its entire outstanding business or merged or consolidated substantially its entire property or business with another insurer; has engaged in any transaction in which it is not authorized to engage under the laws of this State; has not complied with G.S. 58-7-73; or has refused to comply with a lawful order of the Commissioner. As used in this section, "Commissioner" includes an authorized representative or designee of the Commissioner.

(b)   This section applies to all domestic insurers and any other insurer doing business in this State whose state of domicile has asked the Commissioner to apply the provisions of this section to that insurer.

(c)   An insurer may be subject to administrative supervision by the Commissioner if upon examination or at any other time it appears to the Commissioner that the insurer: has exceeded its powers; has failed to comply with applicable provisions of this Chapter; is conducting its business in a manner that is hazardous to the public or to its insureds; or consents to administrative supervision.

(d) If the Commissioner determines that the conditions set forth in subsection (c) of this section exist, the Commissioner shall: notify the insurer of that determination; furnish to the insurer a written list of the requirements to abate those conditions; and notify the insurer that it is under the supervision of the Commissioner and that the Commissioner is applying and effectuating the provisions of this section.

(e) If placed under administrative supervision, the insurer shall have 60 days, or a different period of time determined by the Commissioner, to comply with the requirements of the Commissioner under this section. If the Commissioner determines after notice and hearing that the conditions giving rise to the supervision still exist at the end of the supervision period specified in this subsection, the Commissioner may extend the period; or if the Commissioner determines that none of the conditions giving rise to the supervision exist, the Commissioner shall release the insurer from supervision.

(f) Notwithstanding any other provision of law and except as set forth in this section, all proceedings, hearings, notices, correspondence, reports, records, and other information in the possession of the Commissioner or the Department relating to the supervision of any insurer are confidential. The Department shall have access to such proceedings, hearings, notices, correspondence, reports, records, or other information as permitted by the Commissioner. The Commissioner may open the proceedings or hearings, or disclose the notices, correspondence, reports, records, or information to a department, agency or instrumentality of this or another state of the United States if the Commissioner determines that the disclosure is necessary or proper for the enforcement of the laws of this or another state of the United States. The Commissioner may open the proceedings or hearings or make public the notices, correspondence, reports, records, or other information if the Commissioner considers that it is in the best interest of the insurer, its insureds or creditors, or the general public. This section does not apply to hearings, notices, correspondence, reports, records, or other information obtained upon the appointment of a receiver for the insurer by a court of competent jurisdiction.

(g) During the period of supervision, the Commissioner shall serve as the administrative supervisor. The Commissioner may provide that the insurer shall not do any of the following during the period of supervision, without the Commissioner's prior approval: dispose of, convey, or encumber any of its assets or its business in force; withdraw from any of its bank accounts; lend or invest any of its funds; transfer any of its property; incur any debt, obligation, or liability; merge or consolidate with another company; establish new premiums or renew any policies; enter into any new reinsurance contract or treaty; terminate, surrender, forfeit, convert, or lapse any insurance coverage, except for nonpayment of premiums due; release, pay, or refund premium deposits, accrued cash, or loan values, unearned premiums, or other reserves on any insurance coverage; make any material change in management; increase salaries or benefits of officers or directors or make preferential payment of bonuses, dividends, or other payments considered preferential; or make any other change in its operations that the Commissioner considers to be material.

(h)   During the period of supervision the insurer may contest an action taken or proposed to be taken by the Commissioner, specifying why the action being complained of would not result in improving the insurer's condition.

(i)   This section does not limit powers granted to the Commissioner by any other provision of law. This section does not preclude the Commissioner from initiating judicial proceedings to place an insurer in a delinquency proceeding under this Article, regardless of whether the Commissioner has previously initiated administrative supervision proceedings under this section or under G.S. 58-30-60 against the insurer. The determination as to actions under this section is in the Commissioner's discretion.

(j)   Notwithstanding any other provision of law, the Commissioner may meet with a supervisor appointed under this section and with the attorney or other representative of the supervisor, without the presence of any other person, at the time of any proceeding or during the pendency of any proceeding held under the authority of this section, to carry out the Commissioner's duties under this section or for the supervisor to carry out the supervisor's duties under this section.

(k)   There is no liability by, and no cause of action of any nature arises against, the Commissioner for any acts or omissions by the Commissioner in the performance of the Commissioner's powers and duties under this section. (1991, c. 681, s. 44; 2002-187, s. 2.10; 2003-212, s. 26(i).)

§ 58-30-65. Court's seizure order.

(a)   The Commissioner may file in the Court a petition alleging, with respect to a domestic insurer:

(1)   That there exist grounds that justify a judicial order for a formal delinquency proceeding against an insurer under this Article;

(2)   That the interests of policyholders, creditors, or the public will be endangered by delay; and

(3)   The contents of an order deemed by the Commissioner to be necessary.

(b)   Upon a filing under subsection (a) of this section, the Court may issue forthwith, ex parte, the requested order, that directs the Commissioner to take possession and control of all or a part of the property, books, accounts, documents, and other records of an insurer, and of the premises occupied by it for transaction of its business, and that, until further order of the Court, enjoins the insurer and its officers, managers, agents, and employees from disposing of its property and from transacting its business except with the written consent of the Commissioner.

(c)   The Court shall specify in the order what its duration shall be, which shall be such time as the Court considers necessary for the Commissioner to ascertain the condition of the insurer. On motion of either party or on its own motion, the Court may from time to time hold such hearings as it considers desirable after such notice as it considers appropriate; and may extend, shorten, or modify the terms of the seizure order. The Court shall vacate the seizure order if the Commissioner fails to commence a formal proceeding under this Article after having a reasonable opportunity to do so. An order of the Court pursuant to a formal proceeding under this Article shall ipso facto vacate the seizure order.

(d)   Entry of a seizure order under this section does not constitute an anticipatory breach of any contract of the insurer.

(e)   An insurer subject to an ex parte order under this section may petition the Court at any time after the issuance of such order for a hearing and review of the order. The Court shall hold such a hearing and review not more than 15 days after the request. A hearing under this subsection may be held privately in chambers, and it shall be so held if the insurer proceeded against so requests.

(f)   If, at any time after the issuance of such an order, it appears to the Court that any person whose interest is or will be substantially affected by the order did not appear at the hearing and has not been served, the Court may order that notice be given. An order that notice be given does not stay the effect of any order previously issued by the Court. (1989, c. 452, s. 1.)

§ 58-30-70. Confidentiality of hearings.

In all proceedings and judicial reviews thereof under G.S. 58-30-60 and G.S. 58-30-65, all records of the insurer, other documents, and all Department files and Court records and papers, insofar as they pertain to or are a part of the record of the proceedings, shall be and remain confidential except as is necessary to obtain compliance therewith, unless the Court, after hearing arguments from the parties in chambers, orders otherwise; or unless the insurer requests that the matter be made public. Until such Court order, all papers filed with the clerk of the Court shall be held by him in a confidential file. (1989, c. 452, s. 1.)

§ 58-30-71. Immunity and indemnification of the receiver and employees.

(a)   For the purposes of this section, the persons entitled to protection under this section are:

(1)   All receivers responsible for the conduct of a delinquency proceeding under this Article, including present and former receivers; and

(2)   Their employees meaning all present and former special deputies and assistant special deputies appointed by the Commissioner, staff assigned to the delinquency proceeding employed by the Attorney General's Office, and all persons whom the Commissioner, special deputies, or assistant special deputies have employed to assist in a delinquency proceeding under this Article. Attorneys, accountants, auditors, and other professional persons or firms, who are retained by the receiver as independent contractors and their employees are not employees of the receiver for purposes of this section.

(b)   The receiver and his employees have official immunity and are immune from suit and liability, both personally and in their official capacities, for any claim for damage to or loss of property or personal injury or other civil liability caused by or resulting from any alleged act, error, or omission of the receiver or any employee arising out of or by reason of their duties or employment; provided that nothing in this section holds the receiver or any employee immune from suit or liability for any damage, loss, injury, or liability caused by the intentional or willful and wanton misconduct of the receiver or any employee or for any bodily injury caused by the operation of a motor vehicle.

(c)   If any legal action is commenced against the receiver or any employee, whether against him personally or in his official capacity, alleging property damage, property loss, personal injury, or other civil liability caused by or resulting from any alleged act, error, or omission of the receiver or any employee arising out of or by reason of their duties or employment, the receiver and any employee shall be indemnified from the assets of the insurer for all expenses, attorneys' fees, judgments, settlements, decrees, or amounts due and owing or paid in satisfaction of or incurred in the defense of such legal action; unless it is determined upon a final adjudication on the merits that the alleged act, error, or omission of the receiver or employee giving rise to the claim did not arise out of or by reason of his duties or employment, or was caused by intentional or willful and wanton misconduct.

(d)   Attorneys' fees and all related expenses incurred in defending a legal action for which immunity or indemnity is available under this section shall be paid from the assets of the insurer, as they are incurred, before the final disposition of the action, upon receipt of any agreement by or on behalf of the receiver or employee to repay the attorneys' fees and expenses if it is ultimately determined upon a final adjudication on the merits that the receiver or employee is not entitled to immunity or indemnity under this section.

(e)   Any indemnification for expense payments, judgments, settlements, decrees, attorneys' fees, surety bond premiums, or other amounts paid or to be paid from the insurer's assets under this section shall be an administrative expense of the insurer.

(f)   In the event of any actual or threatened litigation against a receiver or any employee for which immunity or indemnity may be available under this section, a reasonable amount of funds, that in the judgment of the Commissioner may be needed to provide immunity or indemnity, shall be segregated and reserved from the assets of the insurer as security for the payment of indemnity until all applicable statutes of limitation have run, all actual or threatened actions against the receiver or any employee have been completely and finally resolved, and all obligations of the insurer and the Commissioner under this section have been satisfied.

(g) In lieu of segregation and reserving of funds, the Commissioner may, in his discretion, obtain a surety bond or make other arrangements that will enable the Commissioner to fully secure the payment of all obligations under this section.

(h) If any legal action against an employee for which indemnity may be available under this section is settled before final adjudication on the merits, the insurer must pay the settlement amount on behalf of the employee, or indemnify the employee for the settlement amount, unless the Commissioner determines:

(1) That the claim did not arise out of or by reason of the employee's duties or employment; or

(2) That the claims were caused by the intentional or willful and wanton misconduct of the employee.

(i) In any legal action in which the receiver is a defendant, that portion of any settlement relating to the alleged act, error, or omission of the receiver is subject to the approval of the court before which the delinquency proceeding is pending. The court shall not approve that portion of the settlement if it determines:

(1) That the claim did not arise out of or by reason of the receiver's duties or employment; or

(2) That the claim was caused by the intentional or willful and wanton misconduct of the receiver.

(j) Nothing in this section deprives the receiver or any employee of any immunity, indemnity, benefits of law, rights, or any defense otherwise available.

(k) Subsection (b) of this section applies to any suit based in whole or in part on any alleged act, error, or omission that occurs on or after October 1, 1993.

(l) No legal action shall lie against the receiver or any employee based in whole or in part on any alleged act, error, or omission that occurred before

October 1, 1993, unless suit is filed and valid service of process is obtained within 12 months after October 1, 1993.

(m)   Subsections (c), (h), and (i) of this section apply to any suit that is pending on or filed after October 1, 1993, without regard to when the alleged act, error, or omission took place. (1993, c. 452, s. 40.)

§ 58-30-75. Grounds for rehabilitation.

The Commissioner may petition the Court for an order authorizing him to rehabilitate a domestic insurer or an alien insurer domiciled in this State on any one or more of the following grounds:

(1)   The insurer is in such condition that the further transaction of business would be hazardous financially to its policyholders, creditors, or the public.

(2)   There is reasonable cause to believe that there has been embezzlement from the insurer, wrongful sequestration or diversion of the insurer's assets, forgery or fraud affecting the insurer, or other illegal conduct in, by, or with respect to the insurer that if established would endanger assets in an amount threatening the solvency of the insurer.

(3)   The insurer has failed to remove any person who in fact has executive authority in the insurer, whether an officer, manager, general agent, employee, or other person; if the person has been found after notice and hearing by the Commissioner to be dishonest or untrustworthy in a way affecting the insurer's business.

(4)   Control of the insurer, whether by stock ownership or otherwise, and whether direct or indirect, is in a person or persons found after notice and hearing to be untrustworthy.

(5)   Any person who in fact has executive authority in the insurer, whether an officer, manager, general agent, director or trustee, employee, or other person, has refused to be examined under oath by the Commissioner concerning its affairs, whether in this State or elsewhere; and after reasonable notice of the fact, the insurer has failed promptly and effectively to terminate the employment and status of the person and all his influence on management.

(6) After demand by the Commissioner the insurer has failed to promptly make available for examination any of its own property, books, accounts, documents, or other records; those of any subsidiary or related company within the control of the insurer; or those of any person having executive authority in the insurer insofar as they pertain to the insurer.

(7) Without first obtaining the written consent of the Commissioner, the insurer has (i) transferred, or attempted to transfer, in a manner contrary to Article 19 of this Chapter, substantially its entire property or business, or (ii) has entered into any transaction, the effect of which is to merge, consolidate, or reinsure substantially its entire property or business in or with the property or business of any other person.

(8) The insurer or its property has been or is the subject of an application for the appointment of a receiver, trustee, custodian, conservator, or sequestrator or similar fiduciary of the insurer or its property otherwise than as authorized under Articles 1 through 64 of this Chapter, and such appointment has been made or is imminent, and such appointment might oust the courts of this State of jurisdiction or might prejudice orderly delinquency proceedings under this Article.

(9) Within the previous four years the insurer has willfully violated its charter or articles of incorporation, its bylaws, Articles 1 through 67 of this Chapter, or any valid order of the Commissioner under G.S. 58-30-60.

(10) The insurer has failed to pay within 60 days after due any obligation to any state or any subdivision thereof or any judgment entered in any state, if the court in which such judgment was entered has jurisdiction over such subject matter; except that such nonpayment is not a ground until 60 days after any good faith effort by the insurer to contest the obligation has been terminated, whether it is before the Commissioner or in the courts, or the insurer has systematically attempted to compromise or renegotiate previously agreed settlements with its creditors on the ground that it is financially unable to pay its obligations in full.

(11) The insurer has failed to file its annual report or any other financial report required by statute within the time allowed by law and, after written demand by the Commissioner, has failed to immediately give an adequate explanation.

(12) The board of directors or the holders of a majority of the shares entitled to vote, or a majority of those individuals entitled to the control of those persons specified in G.S. 58-30-5, request or consent to rehabilitation under this Article. (1989, c. 452, s. 1; c. 770, s. 72.1; 1995, c. 193, s. 31; 2001-223, s. 19.)

§ 58-30-80. Rehabilitation orders.

(a) An order to rehabilitate the business of a domestic insurer or an alien insurer domiciled in this State, shall appoint the Commissioner and his successors in office as the rehabilitator, and shall direct the rehabilitator forthwith to take possession of the assets of the insurer and to administer them under the general supervision of the Court. The filing or recording of the order with the clerk of the Court or register of deeds of the county in which the principal business of the insurer is conducted, or the county in which its principal office or place of business is located, shall impart the same notice as a deed, bill of sale, or other evidence of title duly filed or recorded with that register of deeds would have imparted. The order to rehabilitate the insurer shall by operation of law vest title to all assets of the insurer in the rehabilitator.

(b) Any order issued under this section shall require accounting to the Court by the rehabilitator. Accountings shall be at such intervals as the Court specifies in its order.

(c) Entry of an order of rehabilitation shall not constitute an anticipatory breach of any contract of the insurer. (1989, c. 452, s. 1.)

§ 58-30-85. Powers and duties of the rehabilitator.

(a) The rehabilitator has the power:

(1) To appoint a special deputy to act for him under this Article, and to determine his reasonable compensation. The special deputy has all powers of the rehabilitator granted by this section. The special deputy serves at the pleasure of the rehabilitator.

(2) To employ employees and agents, legal counsel, actuaries, accountants, appraisers, consultants, and such other personnel as he may deem to be necessary to assist in the rehabilitation.

(3) To fix the reasonable compensation of employees and agents, legal counsel, actuaries, accountants, appraisers, and consultants, with the approval of the Court.

(4) To pay reasonable compensation to persons appointed; and to defray from the funds or assets of the insurer all expenses of taking possession of, conserving, conducting, rehabilitating, disposing of, or otherwise dealing with the business and property of the insurer.

(5) To hold hearings, to subpoena witnesses to compel their attendance, to administer oaths, to examine any person under oath, and to compel any person to subscribe to this testimony after it has been correctly reduced to writing; and in connection therewith to require the production of any books, papers, records, or other documents that he considers relevant to the inquiry.

(6) To collect all debts and moneys due and claims belonging to the insurer, wherever located, and for this purpose:

a. To institute timely action in other jurisdictions, in order to forestall garnishment and attachment proceedings against such debts;

b. To do such other acts that are necessary or expedient to collect, conserve, or protect its assets or property, including the power to sell, compound, compromise, or assign debts for purposes of collection upon such terms and conditions as he deems to be best; and

c. To pursue any creditor's remedies available to enforce his claims.

(7) To conduct public and private sales of the property of the insurer.

(8) To use assets of the estate of an insurer under a rehabilitation order to transfer policy obligations to a solvent assuming insurer, if the transfer can be arranged without prejudice to applicable priorities under G.S. 58-30-220.

(9) To acquire, hypothecate, encumber, lease, improve, sell, transfer, abandon, or otherwise dispose of or deal with, any property of the insurer at its market value or upon such terms and conditions that are fair and reasonable.

He also has the power to execute, acknowledge, and deliver any and all deeds, assignments, releases and other instruments necessary or proper to effectuate any sale of property or other transaction in connection with the rehabilitation.

(10) To borrow money on the security of the insurer's assets or without security and to execute and deliver all documents necessary to that transaction for the purpose of facilitating the rehabilitation.

(11) To enter into such contracts that are necessary to carry out the order to rehabilitate, and to affirm or disavow any contracts to which the insurer is a party.

(12) To continue to prosecute and to institute in the name of the insurer or in his own name any and all suits and other legal proceedings, in this State or elsewhere, and to abandon the prosecution of claims he deems unprofitable to pursue further.

(13) To prosecute any action that may exist in behalf of the creditors, members, policyholders, or shareholders of the insurer against any officer of the insurer or against any other person.

(14) To remove any or all records and property of the insurer to the offices of the Commissioner or to such other place as may be convenient for the purposes of efficient and orderly execution of the rehabilitation.

(15) To deposit in one or more banks in this State such sums as are required for meeting current administration expenses and dividend distributions.

(16) To invest all sums not currently needed, unless the Court orders otherwise.

(17) To file any necessary documents for recording in the office of any register of deeds in this State or elsewhere where property of the insurer is located.

(18) To assert all defenses available to the insurer as against third persons, including statutes of limitation, statutes of frauds, and the defense of usury. A waiver of any defense by the insurer after a petition in rehabilitation has been filed shall not bind the rehabilitator.

(19) To exercise and enforce all rights, remedies, and powers of any creditor, shareholder, policyholder, or member; including any power to avoid any transfer or lien that may be given by law and that is not included within G.S. 58-30-140 through 58-30-150.

(20) To intervene in any proceeding wherever instituted that might lead to the appointment of a receiver or trustee, and to act as the receiver or trustee whenever the appointment is offered.

(21) To enter into agreements with any receiver or insurance regulator of any other state relating to the rehabilitation, liquidation, conservation, or dissolution of an insurer doing business in both states.

(22) To exercise all powers now held or subsequently conferred upon receivers by laws of this State not inconsistent with the provisions of this Article.

(b) The enumeration in this section of the powers and authority of the rehabilitator shall not be construed as a limitation upon him, nor shall it exclude in any manner his right to do such other acts not specifically enumerated in this section or otherwise provided for, as may be necessary or appropriate for the accomplishment of or in aid of the purpose of rehabilitation.

(c) The rehabilitator may take such action as he considers necessary or appropriate to reform and revitalize the insurer. He shall have all the powers of the directors, officers, and managers, whose authority shall be suspended, except to the extent they may be redelegated by the rehabilitator. He shall have full power to direct, manage, hire, and discharge employees, subject to any contract rights they may have, and to deal with the property and business of the insurer.

(d) If it appears to the rehabilitator that there has been criminal or tortious conduct, or breach of any contractual or fiduciary obligation detrimental to the insurer by any officer, manager, agent, broker, employee or other person, he may pursue all available legal remedies on behalf of the insurer.

(e) If the rehabilitator determines that reorganization, consolidation, conversion, reinsurance, merger, runoff, or other transformation of the insurer is appropriate, he shall prepare a plan to effect such changes. Upon application of the rehabilitator for approval of the plan, and after such notice and hearings as the Court may prescribe, the Court may either approve or disapprove the plan proposed, or may modify it and approve it as modified. Any plan approved under this section shall be, in the opinion of the Court, fair and equitable to all parties concerned. If the plan is approved, the rehabilitator shall carry out the plan. In the case of a life insurer, the plan proposed may include the imposition of liens upon the policies of the insurer, if all rights of shareholders are first relinquished. A plan for a life insurer may also propose imposition of a moratorium upon loan and cash surrender rights under policies, for such period and to such an extent as may be necessary.

(f) The rehabilitator shall have the power under G.S. 58-30-140 and G.S. 58-30-145 to avoid fraudulent transfers. (1989, c. 452, s. 1; 2009-172, s. 2.)

§ 58-30-90. Actions by and against rehabilitator.

(a) When a rehabilitation order against an insurer is entered, every court in this State, before which any pending action or proceeding in which the insurer is a party or is obligated to defend a party, shall stay the action or proceeding for 120 days and such additional time that is necessary for the rehabilitator to obtain proper representation and prepare for further proceedings. The rehabilitator may take such action respecting pending litigation as he deems necessary in the interests of justice and for the protection of creditors, policyholders, and the public. The rehabilitator may immediately consider all litigation pending outside this State and may petition the courts having jurisdiction over that litigation for stays whenever necessary to protect the estate of the insurer.

(b) No statute of limitations or defense of laches shall run with respect to any action by or against an insurer between the filing of a petition for appointment of a rehabilitator for that insurer and the order granting or denying that petition.

(c) Any domestic or foreign guaranty association has standing to appear in any Court proceeding concerning the rehabilitation of an insurer if such association is or may become liable to act as a result of the rehabilitation. (1989, c. 452, s. 1.)

§ 58-30-95. Termination of rehabilitation.

(a) Whenever the rehabilitator believes further attempts to rehabilitate an insurer would substantially increase the risk of loss to creditors, policyholders or the public, or would be futile, the rehabilitator may petition the Court for an order of liquidation. A petition under this subsection shall have the same effect as a petition under G.S. 58-30-100. The Court may make such findings and issue such orders at any time upon its own motion. The Court shall permit the directors of the insurer to take such actions as are reasonably necessary to defend against the petition and may order payment from the estate of the insurer of such costs and other expenses of defense as justice may require. The court may allow the payment of costs and expenses incurred in defending against the petition for an order of liquidation only upon a specific finding that the defense was conducted, and the costs and expenses were incurred, in good faith. The directors shall have the burden of proving good faith. Evidence of good faith shall be the existence of a reasonable basis to conclude that the insurer is actually solvent or that there exists a viable means to accomplish rehabilitation without jeopardizing the remaining assets of the insurer and that continued operation of the insurer is in the best interest of the policyholders, stockholders, and creditors.

(b) The rehabilitator may at any time petition the Court for an order terminating rehabilitation of an insurer. The Court shall also permit the directors of the insurer to petition the Court for an order terminating rehabilitation of the insurer and may order payment from the estate of the insurer of such costs and other expenses of such petition as justice may require. The court may allow the payment of costs and expenses incurred in defending against the petition for an order terminating rehabilitation only upon a specific finding that the defense was conducted, and the costs and expenses were incurred, in good faith. The directors shall have the burden of proving good faith. Evidence of good faith shall be the existence of a reasonable basis to conclude that the insurer is actually solvent or that there exists a viable means to accomplish rehabilitation without jeopardizing the remaining assets of the insurer and that continued operation of the insurer is in the best interest of the policyholders, stockholders, and creditors. If the Court finds that rehabilitation has been accomplished and that grounds for rehabilitation under G.S. 58-30-75 no longer exist, it shall order that the insurer be restored to possession of its property and the control of the business. The Court may also make that finding and issue that order at any time upon its own motion. (1989, c. 452, s. 1; 1993, c. 452, s. 41.)

§ 58-30-100. Grounds for liquidation.

The Commissioner may petition the Court for an order directing him to liquidate a domestic insurer or an alien insurer domiciled in this State on the basis:

(1)   Of any ground for an order of rehabilitation as specified in G.S. 58-30-75, whether or not there has been a prior order directing the rehabilitation of the insurer;

(2)   That the insurer is insolvent; or

(3)   That the insurer is in such condition that the further transaction of business would be hazardous, financially or otherwise, to its policyholders, its creditors, or the public. (1989, c. 452, s. 1.)

§ 58-30-105. Liquidation orders.

(a)   An order to liquidate the business of a domestic insurer shall appoint the Commissioner and his successors in office liquidator and shall direct the liquidator forthwith to take possession of the assets of the insurer and to administer them under the general supervision of the Court. The liquidator is vested by operation of law with the title to all of the property, contracts, and rights of action, and all of the books and records of the insurer ordered liquidated, wherever located, as of the entry of the final order of liquidation. The filing or recording of the order with the clerk of the superior court and the register of deeds of the county in which its principal office or place of business is located; or, in the case of real estate, with the register of deeds of the county where the property is located, shall impart the same notice as a deed, bill of sale, or other evidence of title duly filed or recorded with that register of deeds would have imparted.

(b)   Upon issuance of the order, the rights and liabilities of any such insurer and of its creditors, policyholders, shareholders, members and all other persons interested in its estate shall become fixed as of the date of entry of the order of liquidation, except as provided in G.S. 58-30-110 and G.S. 58-30-195.

(c)   An order to liquidate the business of an alien insurer domiciled in this State shall be in the same terms and have the same legal effect as an order to liquidate a domestic insurer; except that the assets and the business in the United States shall be the only assets and business included therein.

(d) At the time of petitioning for an order of liquidation or at any time thereafter the Commissioner, after making appropriate findings of an insurer's insolvency, may petition the Court for a judicial declaration of such insolvency. After providing such notice and hearing as it deems to be proper, the Court may make the declaration.

(e) Any order issued under this section requires accounting to the Court by the liquidator. Accountings shall be at such intervals as the Court specifies in its order. (1989, c. 452, s. 1.)

§ 58-30-110. Continuance of coverage.

(a) All policies, other than life or health insurance or annuities, that are in effect at the time of the issuance of an order of liquidation shall continue in force only for the lesser of:

(1) A period of 30 days from the date of entry of the liquidation orders;

(2) The expiration of the policy coverage;

(3) The date when the insured has replaced the insurance coverage with equivalent insurance in another insurer or otherwise terminated the policy; or

(4) The liquidator has effected a transfer of the policy obligation pursuant to G.S. 58-30-120(a)(8).

(b) An order of liquidation under G.S. 58-30-105 terminates coverages at the time specified in subsection (a) of this section for the purposes of any other statute.

(c) Policies of life or health insurance or annuities shall continue in force for such period and under such terms as is provided for by any applicable domestic or foreign guaranty association.

(d) Policies of life or health insurance or annuities or any period of coverage of such policies that are not covered by a domestic or foreign guaranty association shall terminate under subsections (a) and (b) of this section. (1989, c. 452, s. 1.)

§ 58-30-115. Dissolution of insurer.

The Commissioner may petition for an order dissolving the corporate existence of a domestic insurer or the United States branch of an alien insurer domiciled in this State at the time he applies for a liquidation order. The Court shall order dissolution of the corporation upon petition by the Commissioner upon or after the granting of a liquidation order. If the dissolution has not previously been ordered, it shall be effected by operation of law upon the discharge of the liquidator if the insurer is under a liquidation order for some other reason. (1989, c. 452, s. 1.)

§ 58-30-120. Powers of liquidator.

(a) The liquidator has the power:

(1) To appoint a special deputy to act for him under this Article, and to determine his reasonable compensation. The special deputy has all powers of the liquidator granted by this section. The special deputy serves at the pleasure of the liquidator.

(2) To employ employees and agents, legal counsel, actuaries, accountants, appraisers, consultants, and such other personnel as he may deem to be necessary to assist in the liquidation.

(3) To fix the reasonable compensation of employees and agents, legal counsel, actuaries, accountants, appraisers, and consultants, with the approval of the Court.

(4) To pay reasonable compensation to persons appointed; and to defray from the funds or assets of the insurer all expenses of taking possession of, conserving, conducting, liquidating, disposing of, or otherwise dealing with the business and property of the insurer. In the event that the property of the insurer does not contain sufficient cash or liquid assets to defray the costs incurred, the Commissioner may advance the costs so incurred out of any appropriation for the maintenance of the Department. Any amounts so

advanced for expenses of administration shall be repaid to the Commissioner for the use of the Department out of the first available moneys of the insurer.

(5) To hold hearings, to subpoena witnesses to compel their attendance, to administer oaths, to examine any person under oath, and to compel any person to subscribe to this testimony after it has been correctly reduced to writing; and in connection therewith to require the production of any books, papers, records, or other documents that he considers relevant to the inquiry.

(6) To collect all debts and moneys due and claims belonging to the insurer, wherever located, and for this purpose:

a. To institute timely action in other jurisdictions, in order to forestall garnishment and attachment proceedings against such debts;

b. To do such other acts that are necessary or expedient to collect, conserve, or protect its assets or property, including the power to sell, compound, compromise, or assign debts for purposes of collection upon such terms and conditions as he deems to be best; and

c. To pursue any creditor's remedies available to enforce his claims.

(7) To conduct public and private sales of the property of the insurer.

(8) To use assets of the estate of an insurer under a liquidation order to transfer policy obligations to a solvent assuming insurer, if the transfer can be arranged without prejudice to applicable priorities under G.S. 58-30-220.

(9) To acquire, hypothecate, encumber, lease, improve, sell, transfer, abandon, or otherwise dispose of or deal with, any property of the insurer at its market value or upon such terms and conditions that are fair and reasonable. He also has the power to execute, acknowledge, and deliver any and all deeds, assignments, releases and other instruments necessary or proper to effectuate any sale of property or other transaction in connection with the liquidation.

(10) To borrow money on the security of the insurer's assets or without security and to execute and deliver all documents necessary to that transaction for the purpose of facilitating the liquidation.

(11) To enter into such contracts that are necessary to carry out the order to liquidate, and to affirm or disavow any contracts to which the insurer is a party.

(12) To continue to prosecute and to institute in the name of the insurer or in his own name any and all suits and other legal proceedings, in this State or elsewhere, and to abandon the prosecution of claims he deems unprofitable to pursue further. If the insurer is dissolved under G.S. 58-30-115, he shall have the power to apply to any court in this State or elsewhere for leave to substitute himself for the insurer as plaintiff.

(13) To prosecute any action that may exist in behalf of the creditors, members, policyholders, or shareholders of the insurer against any officer of the insurer or against any other person.

(14) To remove any or all records and property of the insurer to the offices of the Commissioner or to such other place as may be convenient for the purposes of efficient and orderly execution of the liquidation. Domestic and foreign guaranty associations shall have such reasonable access to the records of the insurer as is necessary for them to carry out their statutory obligations.

(15) To deposit in one or more banks in this State such sums as are required for meeting current administration expenses and dividend distributions.

(16) To invest all sums not currently needed, unless the Court orders otherwise.

(17) To file any necessary documents for recording in the office of any register of deeds in this State or elsewhere where property of the insurer is located.

(18) To assert all defenses available to the insurer as against third persons, including statutes of limitation, statutes of frauds, and the defense of usury. A waiver of any defense by the insurer after a petition in liquidation has been filed shall not bind the liquidator. Whenever a domestic or foreign guaranty association has an obligation to defend any suit, the liquidator shall give precedence to such obligation and may defend only in the absence of a defense by such guaranty associations.

(19) To exercise and enforce all rights, remedies, and powers of any creditor, shareholder, policyholder, or member; including any power to avoid any transfer or lien that may be given by law and that is not included within G.S. 58-30-140 through G.S. 58-30-150.

(20) To intervene in any proceeding wherever instituted that might lead to the appointment of a receiver or trustee, and to act as the receiver or trustee whenever the appointment is offered.

(21) To enter into agreements with any receiver or insurance regulator of any other state relating to the rehabilitation, liquidation, conservation, or dissolution of an insurer doing business in both states.

(22) To exercise all powers now held or subsequently conferred upon receivers by laws of this State not inconsistent with the provisions of this Article.

(b) The enumeration in this section of the powers and authority of the liquidator shall not be construed as a limitation upon him, nor shall it exclude in any manner his right to do such other acts not specifically enumerated in this section or otherwise provided for, as may be necessary or appropriate for the accomplishment of or in aid of the purpose of liquidation. (1989, c. 452, s. 1.)

§ 58-30-125. Notice to creditors and others.

(a) Unless the Court otherwise directs, the liquidator shall give or cause to be given notice of the liquidation order as soon as possible:

(1) By first-class mail and either by facsimile, electronic mail, or telephone to the insurance regulator of each jurisdiction in which the insurer is doing business;

(2) By first-class mail to any domestic or foreign guaranty association that is or may become obligated as a result of the liquidation;

(3) By first-class mail to all insurance agents of the insurer;

(4) By first-class mail to all persons known or reasonably expected to have claims against the insurer, including all policyholders, at their last known addresses indicated by the records of the insurer; and

(5) By publication in a newspaper of general circulation in the county in which the insurer has its principal place of business and in such other locations as the liquidator deems to be appropriate.

(b) Notice to potential claimants under subsection (a) of this section shall require claimants to file with the liquidator their claims, together with proper proofs thereof under G.S. 58-30-190, on or before a date the liquidator specifies in the notice. All claimants have a duty to keep the liquidator informed of any changes of address. The liquidator need not require the following to file claims under this section:

(1) Persons claiming cash surrender values or other investment values in life insurance and annuities.

(2) Persons claiming unearned premiums on property or casualty insurance.

(c) If notice is given in accordance with this section, the distribution of assets of the insurer under this Article shall be conclusive with respect to all claimants, whether or not they receive notice. (1989, c. 452, s. 1; 2006-105, s. 1.4.)

§ 58-30-127. Duties of agents.

(a) Every person who receives notice in the form prescribed in G.S. 58-30-125 that an insurer that person represents as an agent is the subject of a liquidation order shall, upon request of the liquidator and within 60 days after receipt of the request, provide to the liquidator the information in the agent's records related to any policy issued by the insurer through the agent; and if the agent is a general agent, the information in the general agent's records related to any policy issued by the insurer through a subagent under contract with the general agent, including the name and address of the subagent.

(b) For the purpose of this section, a policy is issued through an agent if the agent has a property interest in the expiration of the policy or if the agent has had in the agent's possession a copy of the declarations of the policy at any time during the life of the policy, except where the ownership of the expiration of the policy has been transferred to another person.

(c) Any agent failing to provide information to the liquidator as required by this section is to be subject to G.S. 58-2-70.

(d) The provisions of this section are in addition to any other duties in this Chapter that are placed on agents. (1991, c. 681, s. 45.)

§ 58-30-130. Actions by and against liquidator.

(a) Upon the issuance of an order appointing a liquidator of a domestic insurer or of an alien insurer domiciled in this State, no action at law or equity shall be brought against the insurer or liquidator, whether in this State or elsewhere, nor shall any such existing actions be maintained or further presented after issuance of such order. The Court shall give full faith and credit to injunctions against the liquidator or the insurer or the continuation of existing actions against the liquidator or the insurer, when such injunctions are included in an order to liquidate an insurer issued pursuant to corresponding provisions in other states. Whenever, in the liquidator's judgment, protection of the estate of the insurer necessitates intervention in an action against the insurer that is pending outside this State, he may intervene in the action. The liquidator may defend any action in which he intervenes under this section at the expense of the estate of the insurer.

(b) The liquidator may, upon or after an order for liquidation, within two years or such subsequent time period as applicable law may permit, institute an action or proceeding on behalf of the estate of the insurer upon any cause of action against which the period of limitation fixed by applicable law has not expired at the time of the filing of the petition upon which such order is entered. Where (i) by any agreement, a period of limitation is fixed for instituting a suit or proceeding upon any claim, or for filing any claim, proof of claim, proof of loss, demand, notice, or the like; or (ii) in any proceeding, judicial or otherwise, a period of limitation is fixed, either in the proceeding or by applicable law, for taking any action, filing any claim or pleading, or doing any act; and (iii) in any such case the period had not expired at the date of the filing of the petition; the liquidator may, for the benefit of the estate, take any such action or do any such act, required of or permitted to the insurer, within a period of 180 days subsequent to the entry of an order for liquidation, or within such further period as is shown to the satisfaction of the Court not to be unfairly prejudicial to the other party.

(c) Any domestic or foreign guaranty association has standing to appear in any Court proceeding concerning the liquidation of an insurer if such association is or may become liable to act as a result of the liquidation. (1989, c. 452, s. 1; 2009-570, s. 27.)

§ 58-30-135. Collection and list of assets.

(a) As soon as practicable after the liquidation order but not later than 120 days thereafter, the liquidator shall prepare in duplicate a list of the insurer's assets. The list shall be amended or supplemented from time to time as the liquidator determines. One copy shall be filed in the office of the clerk of the Court and one copy shall be retained for the liquidator's files. All amendments and supplements shall be similarly filed.

(b) The liquidator shall reduce the assets to a degree of liquidity that is consistent with the effective execution of the liquidation.

(c) A submittal to the Court for disbursement of assets in accordance with G.S. 58-30-180 fulfills the requirements of subsection (a) of this section. (1989, c. 452, s. 1.)

§ 58-30-140. Fraudulent transfers prior to petition.

(a) Every transfer made or suffered and every obligation incurred by an insurer within one year prior to the filing of a successful petition for rehabilitation or liquidation under this Article is fraudulent as to then existing and future creditors if made or incurred without fair consideration or if made or incurred with actual intent to hinder, delay, or defraud either existing or future creditors. A transfer made or an obligation incurred by an insurer ordered to be rehabilitated or liquidated under this Article, that is fraudulent under this section, may be avoided by the receiver, except as to a person who in good faith is a purchaser, lienor, or obligee, for a present fair equivalent value; and except that any purchaser, lienor, or obligee, who in good faith has given a consideration less than fair for such transfer, lien, or obligation, may retain the property, lien, or obligation as security for repayment. The Court may, on due notice, order any such transfer or obligation to be preserved for the benefit of the estate, and in that event, the receiver shall succeed to and may enforce the rights of the purchaser, lienor, or obligee.

(b) A transfer of property other than real property is made or suffered when it becomes so far perfected that no subsequent lien obtainable by legal or equitable proceedings on a simple contract could become superior to the rights of the transferee under G.S. 58-30-150(c). A transfer of real property is made or suffered when it becomes so far perfected that no subsequent bona fide purchaser from the insurer could obtain rights superior to the rights of the transferee. A transfer that creates an equitable lien is not perfected if there are available means by which a legal lien could be created. Any transfer that is not perfected prior to the filing of a petition for liquidation shall be deemed to be made immediately before the filing of the successful petition. The provisions of this subsection apply whether or not there are or were creditors who might have obtained any liens or persons who might have become bona fide purchasers.

(c) Any transaction of the insurer with a reinsurer is fraudulent and may be avoided by the receiver under subsection (a) of this section if:

(1) The transaction consists of the termination, adjustment, or settlement of a reinsurance contract in which the reinsurer is released from any part of its duty to pay the originally specified share of losses that had occurred prior to the time of the transaction, unless the reinsurer gives a present fair equivalent value for the release; and

(2) Any part of the transaction took place within one year prior to the date of filing of the petition through which the receivership was commenced.

(d) Every person receiving any property from the insurer or any benefit thereof as the result of a fraudulent transfer under subsection (a) of this section is personally liable therefor and is bound to account to the liquidator. (1989, c. 452, s. 1; 1991, c. 681, s. 46.)

§ 58-30-145. Fraudulent transfer after petition.

(a) After a petition for rehabilitation or liquidation has been filed, a transfer of any of the real property of the insurer made to a person acting in good faith shall be valid against the receiver if made for a present fair equivalent value; or, if not made for a present fair equivalent value, then to the extent of the present consideration actually paid therefor, for which amount the transferee shall have a lien on the property so transferred. The commencement of a proceeding in rehabilitation or liquidation shall be constructive notice upon the recording of a copy of the petition for or order of rehabilitation or liquidation with the register of deeds in the county in which any real property in question is located. The exercise by a court of the United States or any state to authorize or effect a judicial sale of real property of the insurer within any county in any state is not impaired by the pendency of such a proceeding unless the copy is recorded in the county prior to the consummation of the judicial sale.

(b) After a petition for rehabilitation or liquidation has been filed and before either the receiver takes possession of the property of the insurer or an order of rehabilitation or liquidation is granted:

(1) A transfer of any of the property of the insurer, other than real property, made to a person acting in good faith is valid against the receiver if made for a present fair equivalent value; or, if not made for a present fair equivalent value, then to the extent of the present consideration actually paid therefor, for which amount the transferee shall have a lien on the property so transferred.

(2) A person indebted to the insurer or holding property of the insurer may, if acting in good faith, pay the indebtedness or deliver the property, or any part thereof, to the insurer or upon his order, with the same effect as if the petition were not pending.

(3) A person having actual knowledge of the pending rehabilitation or liquidation shall be deemed not to act in good faith.

(4) A person asserting the validity of a transfer under this section has the burden of proof. Except as elsewhere provided in this section, no transfer by or on behalf of the insurer after the date of the petition for liquidation by any person other than the liquidator is valid as against the liquidator.

(c) Nothing in this Article impairs the validity of currency or the negotiability of any instrument. (1989, c. 452, s. 1.)

§ 58-30-150. Voidable preferences and liens.

(a) A preference is a transfer of any of the property of an insurer to or for the benefit of a creditor, for or on account of an antecedent debt, made or suffered by the insurer within one year before the filing of a successful petition for liquidation under this Article, the effect of which transfer may be to enable the creditor to obtain a greater percentage of this debt than another creditor of the same class would receive. If a liquidation order is entered while the insurer is already subject to a rehabilitation order, then such transfers shall be deemed to be preferences if made or suffered within one year before the filing of the successful petition for rehabilitation, or within two years before the filing of the successful petition for liquidation, whichever time is shorter. Any preference may be avoided by the liquidator if:

(1)   The insurer was insolvent at the time of the transfer;

(2)   The transfer was made within four months before the filing of the petition;

(3)   The creditor receiving it or to be benefited thereby or his agent acting with reference thereto had, at the time the transfer was made, reasonable cause to believe that the insurer was insolvent or was about to become insolvent; or

(4)   The creditor receiving it was an officer, or any employee, attorney, or other person who was in fact in a position of comparable influence in the insurer to an officer, whether or not he held such position, or any shareholder holding directly or indirectly more than five percent (5%) of any class of any equity security issued by the insurer, or any other person, firm, corporation, association, or aggregation of persons with whom the insurer did not deal at arm's length.

Where the preference is voidable, the liquidator may recover the property or, if it has been converted, its value from any person who has received or converted the property; except where a bona fide purchaser or lienor has given less than fair equivalent value, he shall have a lien upon the property to the extent of the consideration actually given by him. Where a preference by way of lien or security title is voidable, the Court may on due notice order the lien or title to be preserved for the benefit of the estate, in which event the lien or title shall pass to the liquidator.

(b)   A transfer of property other than real property shall be deemed to be made or suffered when it becomes so far perfected that no subsequent lien obtainable by legal or equitable proceedings on a simple contract could become superior to the rights of the transferee. A transfer of real property shall be deemed to be made or suffered when it becomes so far perfected that no subsequent bona fide purchaser from the insurer could obtain rights superior to the rights of the transferee. A transfer that creates an equitable lien shall not be deemed to be perfected if there are available means by which a legal lien could be created. A transfer not perfected prior to the filing of a petition for liquidation shall be deemed to be made immediately before the filing of the successful petition. The provisions of this subsection apply whether or not there are or were creditors who might have obtained liens or persons who might have become bona fide purchasers.

(c) A lien obtainable by legal or equitable proceedings upon a simple contract is one arising in the ordinary course of such proceedings upon the entry or docketing of a judgment or decree, or upon attachment, garnishment, execution, or like process, whether before, upon, or after judgment or decree and whether before or upon levy. It does not include liens that under applicable law are given a special priority over other liens that are prior in time. A lien obtainable by legal or equitable proceedings could become superior to the rights of a transferee, or a purchaser could obtain rights superior to the rights of a transferee within the meaning of subsection (b) of this section, if such consequences would follow only from the lien or purchase itself, or from the lien or purchase followed by any step wholly within the control of the respective lienholder or purchaser, with or without the aid of ministerial action by public officials. Such a lien could not, however, become superior and such a purchase could not create superior rights for the purpose of subsection (b) of this section through any acts subsequent to the obtaining of such a lien or subsequent to such a purchase that require the agreement or concurrence of any third party or that require any further judicial action or ruling.

(d) A transfer of property for or on account of a new and contemporaneous consideration that is deemed under subsection (b) of this section to be made or suffered after the transfer because of delay in perfecting it does not thereby become a transfer for or on account of any antecedent debt if any acts required by the applicable law to be performed in order to perfect the transfer as against liens or bona fide purchasers' rights are performed within 21 days or any period expressly allowed by the law, whichever is less. A transfer to secure a future loan, if such a loan is actually made, or a transfer that becomes security for a future loan, shall have the same effect as a transfer for or on account of a new and contemporaneous consideration.

(e) If any lien deemed to be voidable under subdivision (a)(2) of this section has been dissolved by the furnishing of a bond or other obligation, the surety on which has been indemnified directly or indirectly by the transfer of or the creation of a lien upon any property of an insurer before the filing of a petition under this Article that results in a liquidation order, the indemnifying transfer or lien shall also be deemed to be voidable.

(f) The property affected by any lien deemed to be voidable under subsections (a) and (e) of this section shall be discharged from such lien, and that property and any of the indemnifying property transferred to or for the benefit of a surety shall pass to the liquidator; except that the Court may on due notice order any such lien to be preserved for the benefit of the estate, and the Court may direct that such conveyance be executed as may be proper or adequate to evidence the title of the liquidator.

(g)   The Court shall have summary jurisdiction of any proceeding by the liquidator to hear and determine the rights of any parties under this section. Reasonable notice of any hearing in the proceeding shall be given to all parties in interest, including the obligee of a releasing bond or other like obligation. Where an order is entered for the recovery of indemnifying property in kind or for the avoidance of an indemnifying lien, the Court, upon application of any party in interest, shall in the same proceeding ascertain the value of the property or lien. If such value is less than the amount for which the property is indemnity or than the amount of the lien, the transferee or lienholder may elect to retain the property or lien upon payment of its value, as ascertained by the Court, to the liquidator, within such reasonable times as the Court shall fix.

(h)   The liability of the surety under a releasing bond or other like obligation shall be discharged to the extent of the value of the indemnifying property recovered or the indemnifying lien nullified and avoided by the liquidator; or where the property is retained under subsection (g) of this section to the extent of the amount paid to the liquidator.

(i)   If a creditor has been preferred and afterward in good faith gives the insurer further credit, without security of any kind, for property that becomes a part of the insurer's estate, the amount of the new credit remaining unpaid at the time of the petition may be set off against the preference that would otherwise be recoverable from him.

(j)   If an insurer, within four months before the filing of a successful petition for liquidation under this Article, or at any time in contemplation of a proceeding to liquidate it, directly or indirectly pays money or transfers property to an attorney at law for services rendered or to be rendered, such transactions may be examined by the Court on its own motion or on petition of the liquidator, and shall be held valid only to the extent of a reasonable amount to be determined by the Court. Any excess may be recovered by the liquidator for the benefit of the estate; provided that where the attorney is in a position of influence in the insurer or an affiliate thereof, payment of any money or the transfer of any property to the attorney at law for services rendered or to be rendered shall be governed by the provision of subdivision (a)(4) of this section.

(k) Every officer, manager, employee, shareholder, member, subscriber, attorney, or any other person acting on behalf of the insurer who knowingly participates in giving any preference, when he has reasonable cause to believe the insurer is or is about to become insolvent at the time of the preference, shall be personally liable to the liquidator for the amount of the preference. It is permissible to infer that there is a reasonable cause to so believe if the transfer was made within four months before the date of filing of the successful petition for liquidation. Every person receiving any property from the insurer or the benefit thereof as a preference voidable under subsection (a) of this section shall be personally liable therefor and shall be bound to account to the liquidator. Nothing in this subsection prejudices any other claim by the liquidator against any person. (1989, c. 452, s. 1.)

§ 58-30-155. Claims of holders of void or voidable rights.

(a) No claims of a creditor who has received or acquired a preference, lien, conveyance, transfer, assignment, or encumbrance voidable under this Article shall be allowed unless he surrenders the preference, lien, conveyance, transfer, assignment or encumbrance. If the avoidance is effected by a proceeding in which a final judgment has been entered, the claim shall not be allowed unless the money is paid or the property is delivered to the liquidator within 30 days from the date of the entering of the final judgment; except that the Court having jurisdiction over the liquidation may allow further time if there is an appeal or other continuation of the proceeding.

(b) A claim allowable under subsection (a) of this section by reason of the avoidance, whether voluntary or involuntary, of a preference, lien, conveyance, transfer, assignment, or encumbrance, may be filed as an excused late filing under G.S. 58-30-185 if filed within 30 days from the date of the avoidance, or within the further time allowed by the Court under subsection (a) of this section. (1989, c. 452, s. 1.)

§ 58-30-160. Setoffs.

(a) Mutual debts or mutual credits, whether arising out of one or more contracts between the insurer and another person in connection with any action or proceeding under this Article shall be set off and the balance only shall be allowed or paid, except as provided in subsections (b), (d), and (e) of this section and in G.S. 58-30-175.

(b) No setoff shall be allowed in favor of any person where:

(1) The obligation of the insurer to the person would not at the date of the filing of a petition for liquidation entitle the person to share as a claimant in the assets of the insurer;

(2) The obligation of the insurer to the person was purchased by or transferred to the person with a view to its being used as a setoff;

(3) The obligation of the person is to pay an assessment levied against the members or subscribers of the insurer, or is to pay a balance upon a subscription to the capital stock of the insurer, or is in any other way in the nature of a capital contribution;

(4) Repealed by Session Laws 1995 (Regular Session, 1996), c. 658, s. 1.

(5) The obligation of the insurer is owed to an affiliate of the person, or to any other entity or association other than the person;

(6) The obligation of the person is owed to an affiliate of the insurer, or to any other entity or association other than the insurer;

(7) The obligations between the person and the insurer arise out of transactions where either the person or the insurer has assumed risks and obligations from the other party and then has ceded back to that party substantially the same risks and obligations;

(8) The obligation of the person is to pay to the insurer sums held in a fiduciary capacity for the insurer; or

(9) The person alone or together with any other member of its insurance company holding system owns fifty percent (50%) or more of the voting stock of the insurer.

(c) A setoff shall be permitted to local agents against agents' balances otherwise payable to the domiciliary or ancillary receiver for the amount expended by the agents to replace insurance coverage of their insureds and the reasonable expenses incident thereto as a result of any domestic, foreign or alien insurer being placed in delinquency proceedings. Agents claiming a setoff shall within 60 days of replacing coverage provide a verified accounting of the replacement of the insurance to the domiciliary receiver, the ancillary receiver, if any, and the North Carolina Insurance Guaranty Association or similar organization in the state of residence of the policyholder. The verified accounting shall include the name of the agent, the name of the insured, the policy number, the replacement policy number, the cost of the replacement policy, the amount of unearned premium under each policy as to which setoff is claimed, any claimed expenses and a verification that the accounting has been provided to each of the persons and entities described herein. Unearned premiums set off as provided above in any amount shall be deemed paid in full by the insurer and no person shall have a claim for the unearned premiums against the North Carolina Insurance Guaranty Association or similar organization in the state of residence of the policyholder.

(d)   The receiver shall provide persons with accounting statements identifying debts which are currently due and payable. Where a person owes to the insurer currently due and payable balances, against which the person asserts setoff of mutual credits which may become due and payable from the insurer in the future, the person shall promptly pay to the receiver the currently due and payable amount; provided that, notwithstanding any other provision of this Article, the receiver shall promptly and fully refund, to the extent of the person's prior payments, any mutual credits that become due and payable to the person by the insurer.

(e)   Notwithstanding any other provision of this section, a setoff of sums due on obligations in the nature of those set forth in subdivision (b)(7) of this section shall be allowed for those sums accruing from business written where the contracts were entered into, renewed, or extended with the express written approval of the insurance regulator of the state of domicile of the now insolvent insurer, when in the judgment of the regulator it was necessary to provide reinsurance in order to prevent or mitigate a threatened impairment or insolvency of the insurer in connection with the exercise of the regulator's official responsibilities. (1989, c. 452, s. 1; 1991, c. 681, s. 47; 1995 (Reg. Sess., 1996), c. 658, s. 1.)

§ 58-30-165. Assessments.

(a) As soon as practicable but not more than two years from the date of an order of liquidation under G.S. 58-30-105 of an insurer issuing assessable policies, the liquidator shall make a report to the Court setting forth:

(1) The reasonable value of the assets of the insurer;

(2) The insurer's probable total liabilities;

(3) The probable aggregate amount of the assessment necessary to pay all claims of creditors and expenses in full, including expenses of administration and costs of collecting the assessment; and

(4) A recommendation as to whether an assessment should be made and in what amount.

(b) Upon the basis of the report provided in subsection (a) of this section, including any supplements and amendments thereto, the Court may levy one or more assessments against all members of the insurer who are subject to assessment. Subject to any applicable legal limits on assessability, the aggregate assessment shall be for the amount that the sum of the probable liabilities, the expenses of administration, and the estimated cost of collection of the assessment, exceeds the value of existing assets, with due regard given to assessments that cannot be collected economically.

(c) After a levy of assessment under subsection (b) of this section, the liquidator shall issue an order directing each member who has not paid the assessment pursuant to the order, to show cause why the liquidator should not pursue a judgment therefor.

(d) The liquidator shall give notice of the order to show cause by publication or by certified mail to each member liable thereunder mailed to his last known address as it appears on the insurer's records, at least 20 days before the return day of the order to show cause.

(e) If a member does not appear and serve duly verified objections upon the liquidator on or before the return day of the order to show cause under subsection (c) of this section, the Court shall make an order adjudging the member liable for the amount of the assessment against him pursuant to subsection (c) of this section, together with costs, and the liquidator shall have a judgment against the member therefor. If on or before such return day, the member appears and serves duly verified objections upon the liquidator, the

Commissioner may hear and determine the matter or may appoint a referee to hear it and make such order as the facts warrant. In the event that the Commissioner determines that such objections do not warrant relief from assessment, the member may request the Court to review the matter and vacate the order to show cause.

(f)   The liquidator may enforce any order or collect any judgment under subsection (e) of this section by any lawful means. (1989, c. 452, s. 1; 2009-172, s. 3.)

§ 58-30-170. Reinsurer's liability.

The amount recoverable by the liquidator from reinsurers shall not be reduced as a result of the delinquency proceedings, regardless of any provision in the reinsurance contract or other agreement. Payment made directly to an insured or other creditor does not diminish the reinsurer's obligation to the insurer's estate except;

(1)   Where the contract specifically provides for another payee of the reinsurance in the event of the insolvency of the ceding insurer or

(2)   Where the assuming insurer, with the consent of the direct insured or insureds, has assumed the policy obligations of the ceding insurer as direct obligations of the assuming insurer to the payees under policies and in substitution of the obligations of the ceding insurer to the payees. (1989, c. 452, s. 1.)

§ 58-30-175. Recovery of premiums owed.

(a)   An agent, broker, premium finance company, or any other person, other than the insured, responsible for the payment of a premium is obligated to pay an unpaid premium for the full policy term due the insurer at the time of the declaration of insolvency, whether earned or unearned, as shown on the records of the insurer. The liquidator also has the right to recover from such person any part of an unearned premium that represents commission of such person. Except as provided in G.S. 58-30-160, credits or setoffs or both are not allowed to an agent, broker, or premium finance company for any amounts advanced to the insurer by the agent, broker, or premium finance company on behalf of, but in the absence of a payment by, the insured.

(b) An insured is obligated to pay any unpaid premium due the insurer at the time of the declaration of insolvency, as shown on the records of the insurer. (1989, c. 452, s. 1.)

§ 58-30-180. Domiciliary liquidator's proposal to distribute assets.

(a) Within one year after a final determination of insolvency of an insurer by the Court, the liquidator shall make application to the Court for approval of a proposal to disburse assets out of marshalled assets, from time to time as such assets become available, to a domestic or foreign guaranty association having obligations because of such insolvency. If the liquidator determines that there are insufficient assets to disburse, the application required by this section shall be considered satisfied by a filing by the liquidator stating the reasons for this determination.

(b) Such proposal shall at least include provisions for:

(1) Reserving amounts for the payment of expenses of administration and the payment of claims of secured creditors, to the extent of the value of the security held, and claims falling within the priorities established in G.S. 58-30-220(1) and (4);

(2) Disbursement of the assets marshalled to date and subsequent disbursement of assets as they become available;

(3) Equitable allocation of disbursements to each of the domestic and foreign guaranty associations entitled thereto;

(4) The securing by the liquidator from each of the associations entitled to disbursements pursuant to this section of an agreement to return to the liquidator such assets, together with income earned on assets previously disbursed, as may be required to pay claims of secured creditors and claims falling within the priorities established in G.S. 58-30-220 in accordance with such priorities. No bond shall be required of any such association; and

(5) A full report to be made by each association to the liquidator accounting for all assets so disbursed to the association, all disbursements made therefrom, any interest earned by the association on such assets and any other matter as the Court directs.

(c) The liquidator's proposal shall provide for disbursements to the associations in amounts estimated at least equal to the claim payments made or to be made thereby for which such associations could assert a claim against the liquidator; and shall further provide that if the assets available for disbursement from time to time do not equal or exceed the amount of such claim payments made or to be made by the association then disbursements shall be in the amount of available assets.

(d) The liquidator's proposal shall, with respect to an insolvent insurer writing life or health insurance or annuities, provide for disbursements of assets to any domestic or foreign guaranty association covering life or health insurance or annuities or to any other entity reinsuring, assuming, or guaranteeing policies or contracts of insurance under the acts creating such associations.

(e) Notice of such application shall be given to the association in and to the insurance regulators of each of the states. Any such notice shall be deemed to have been given when deposited in United States certified mail, first class postage prepaid, at least 30 days prior to submission of such application to the Court. Action on the application may be taken by the Court provided the above required notice has been given and provided further that the liquidator's proposal complies with subdivisions (b)(1) and (b)(2) of this section. (1989, c. 452, s. 1; 1995, c. 517, s. 13; 2006-105, s. 1.5.)

§ 58-30-185. Filing of claims.

(a) Proof of all claims shall be filed with the liquidator in the form required by G.S. 58-30-190 on or before the last day for filing specified in the notice required under G.S. 58-30-125, except that proof of claims for cash surrender values or other investment values in life insurance and annuities need not be filed unless the liquidator expressly so requires.

(b) The liquidator may permit a claimant making a late filing to share in distributions, whether past or future, as if he were not late, to the extent that any such payment will not prejudice the orderly administration of the liquidation, under the following circumstances:

(1) The existence of the claim was not known to the claimant and that he filed his claim as promptly thereafter as reasonably possible after learning of it;

(2) A transfer to a creditor was avoided under G.S. 58-30-140 through 58-30-150, or was voluntarily surrendered under G.S. 58-30-155, and that the filing satisfies the conditions of G.S. 58-30-155; and

(3) The valuation under G.S. 58-30-215, of security held by a secured creditor shows a deficiency, that is filed within 30 days after the valuation.

(c) The liquidator shall permit late filing claims to share in distributions, whether past or future, as if they were not late, if such claims are claims of a guaranty association or foreign guaranty association for reimbursement of covered claims paid or expenses incurred, or both, subsequent to the last day for filing where such payments were made and expenses incurred as provided by law. Claims of domestic and foreign guaranty associations for reimbursement of covered claims paid or expenses incurred shall be deemed to be absolute.

(d) The liquidator may consider any claim filed late that is not covered by subsection (b) of this section, and permit it to receive distributions that are subsequently declared on any claims of the same or lower priority if the payment does not prejudice the orderly administration of the liquidation. The late-filing claimant shall receive, at each distribution, the same percentage of the amount allowed on his claim as is then being paid to claimants of any lower priority. This shall continue until his claim has been paid in full. (1989, c. 452, s. 1.)

§ 58-30-190. Proof of claim.

(a) Proof of claim shall consist of a statement signed by the claimant that includes all of the following that are applicable:

(1) The particulars of the claim, including the consideration given for it;

(2) The identity and amount of the security on the claim;

(3) The payments made on the debt, if any;

(4) That the sum claimed is justly owing and that there is no setoff, counterclaim, or defense to the claim;

(5) Any right of priority of payment or other specific right asserted by the claimant;

(6) A copy of the written instrument that is the foundation of the claim; and

(7) The name and address of the claimant and any attorney who represents him.

(b) No claim need be considered or allowed if it does not contain all the information in subsection (a) of this section that may be applicable. The liquidator may require that a prescribed form be used, and may require that other information and documents be included.

(c) At any time the liquidator may request the claimant to present information or evidence supplementary to that required under subsection (a) of this section; and may take testimony under oath, require production of affidavits or depositions, or otherwise obtain additional information or evidence.

(d) No judgment or order against an insured or the insurer entered after the date of filing of a successful petition for liquidation, and no judgment or order against an insured or the insurer entered at any time by default or by collusion, need be considered as evidence of liability or of amount of damages. No judgment or order against an insured or the insurer entered within four months before the filing of the petition need be considered as evidence of liability or of the amount of damages.

(e) All claims of a guaranty association or foreign guaranty association shall be in such form and contain such substantiation as may be agreed to by the association and the liquidator; and failing such agreement as ordered by the Court. (1989, c. 452, s. 1.)

§ 58-30-195. Special claims.

(a)   No contingent claim shall share in a distribution of the assets of an insurer that has been adjudicated to be insolvent by an order made pursuant to G.S. 58-30-105; except that such claims shall be considered, if properly presented, and may be allowed to share where:

(1)   Such claim becomes absolute against the insurer on or before the last day fixed for filing of proofs of claim against the assets of such insurer, or

(2)   There is a surplus and the liquidation is thereafter conducted upon the basis that such insurer is solvent.

(b)   Where an insurer has been so adjudicated to be insolvent, any person who has a cause of action against an insured of such insurer under a liability insurance policy issued by such insurer, has the right to file a claim in the liquidation proceedings, regardless of the fact that such claim may be contingent, and such claim may be allowed:

(1)   If it may be reasonably inferred from the proof presented upon such claim that such person would be able to obtain a judgment upon such cause of action against such insured; and

(2)   If such person furnishes suitable proof, unless the Court for good cause shown otherwise directs, that no further valid claims against such insurer arising out of his cause of action other than those already presented can be made; and

(3)   If the total liability of such insurer to all claimants arising out of the same act of its insured is no greater than its total liability would be were it not in liquidation.

No judgment against such an insured taken after the date of the entry of the liquidation order shall be considered in the liquidation proceedings as evidence of liability or of the amount of damages, and no judgment against an insured taken by default, inquest, or by collusion prior to the entry of the liquidation order shall be considered as conclusive evidence in the liquidation proceeding, either of the liability of such insured to such person upon such cause of action or of the amount of damages to which such person is therein entitled.

(c)   No claim of any secured claimant shall be allowed at a sum greater than the difference between the value of the claim without security and the value of the security itself as of the date of entry of the order of liquidation or such other date set by the Court for fixation of rights and liabilities as provided in G.S. 58-

30-105 unless the claimant surrenders his security to the Commissioner, in which event the claim shall be allowed in the full amount for which it is valued.

(d)   Claims that are due but for the passage of time, including any structured settlements or judgments involving periodic payments, shall be treated the same as absolute claims, except that such claims may be discounted at the legal rate of interest.

(e)   Claims made under employment contracts by directors, principal officers, or persons in fact performing similar functions or having similar powers, are limited to payment for services rendered prior to the issuance of any order of rehabilitation or liquidation under this Article. (1989, c. 452, s. 1.)

§ 58-30-200. Special provisions for third party claims.

(a)   Whenever any third party asserts a cause of action against an insured of an insurer in liquidation, the third party may file a claim with the liquidator.

(b)   Whether or not the third party files a claim, the insured may file a claim on his own behalf in the liquidation. If the insured fails to file a claim by the date for filing claims specified in the order of liquidation or within 60 days after mailing of the notice required by G.S. 58-30-125, whichever is later, he is an unexcused late filer.

(c)   The liquidator shall make his recommendations to the Court under G.S. 58-30-225 for the allowance of an insured's claim under subsection (b) of this section after consideration of the probable outcome of any pending action against the insured on which the claim is based, the probable damages recoverable in the action, and the probable costs and expenses of defense. After allowance by the Court, the liquidator shall withhold any dividends payable on the claim, pending the outcome of litigation and negotiation with the insured. Whenever it seems appropriate, he shall reconsider the claim on the basis of additional information and amend his recommendations to the Court. The insured shall be afforded the same notice and opportunity to be heard on all changes in the recommendation as in its initial determination. The Court may amend its allowance as it thinks appropriate. As claims against the insured are settled or barred, the insured shall be paid from the amount withheld the same percentage dividend as was paid on other claims of like property, based on the lesser of (i) the amount actually recovered from the insured by action or paid by agreement plus the reasonable costs and expense of defense, or (ii) the amount allowed on the claims by the Court. After all claims are settled or barred, any sum remaining from the amount withheld shall revert to the undistributed assets of the insurer. Delay in final payment under this subsection shall not be a reason for unreasonable delay of final distribution and discharge of the liquidator.

(d)   No claim may be presented under this section if it is or may be covered by any domestic or foreign guaranty association. (1989, c. 452, s. 1; 2003-221, s. 14.)

§ 58-30-205. Disputed claims.

(a)   When a claim is denied in whole or in part by the liquidator, written notice of the determination shall be given to the claimant or his attorney by first class mail at the address shown in the proof of claim. Within 60 days from the mailing of the notice, the claimant may file his objections with the liquidator. If no such filing is made, the claimant may not further object to the determination.

(b)   Whenever objections are filed with the liquidator and the liquidator does not alter his denial of the claim as a result of the objections, the liquidator shall ask the Court for a hearing as soon as practicable and give notice of the hearing by first class mail to the claimant or his attorney and to any other persons directly affected, not less than 10 nor more than 30 days before the date of the hearing. The matter may be heard by the Court or by a court-appointed referee who shall submit findings of fact along with his recommendation. (1989, c. 452, s. 1.)

§ 58-30-210. Claims of surety.

Whenever a creditor, whose claim against an insurer is secured in whole or in part by the undertaking of another person, fails to prove and file that claim, the other person may do so in the creditor's name and shall be subrogated to the rights of the creditor, whether the claim has been filed by the creditor or by the other person in the creditor's name, to the extent that he discharges the undertaking. In the absence of an agreement with the creditor to the contrary, the other person shall not be entitled to any distribution until the amount paid to the creditor on the undertaking plus the distributions paid on the claim from the insurer's estate to the creditor equals the amount of the entire claim of the creditor. Any excess received by the creditor shall be held by him in trust for such other person. As used in this section, "other person" does not mean a guaranty association or foreign guaranty association. (1989, c. 452, s. 1.)

§ 58-30-215. Secured creditor's claims.

(a) The value of any security held by a secured creditor shall be determined in one of the following ways, as the Court may direct:

(1) By converting the same into money according to the terms of the agreement pursuant to which the security was delivered to such creditors; or

(2) By agreement, arbitration, compromise or litigation between the creditor and the liquidator.

(b) The determination shall be under the supervision and control of the Court with due regard for the recommendation of the liquidator. The amount so determined shall be credited upon the secured claim, and any deficiency shall be treated as an unsecured claim. If the claimant surrenders his security to the liquidator, the entire claim shall be allowed as if unsecured. (1989, c. 452, s. 1; 1991, c. 720, s. 68.)

§ 58-30-220. Priority of distribution.

The priority of distribution of claims from the insurer's estate shall be in accordance with the order in which each class of claims is set forth in this section. Every claim in each class shall be paid in full or adequate funds shall be retained for payment before the members of the next class receive any payment. No subcategories shall be established within the categories in a class. The order of distribution of claims shall be:

(1) The receiver's expenses for the administration and conservation of assets of the insurer.

(2) Claims or portions of claims for benefits under policies and for losses incurred, including claims of third parties under liability policies; claims of HMO

enrollees and HMO enrollees' beneficiaries; claims for unearned premiums; claims for funds or consideration held under funding agreements, as defined in G.S. 58-7-16; claims under life insurance and annuity policies, whether for death proceeds, annuity proceeds, or investment values; and claims of domestic and foreign guaranty associations, including claims for the reasonable administrative expenses of domestic and foreign guaranty associations; but excluding claims of insurance pools, underwriting associations, or those arising out of reinsurance agreements, claims of other insurers for subrogation, and claims of insurers for payments and settlements under uninsured and underinsured motorist coverages.

(2a) For HMOs, claims of providers and participating providers, as defined in G.S. 58-67-5(h) and G.S. 58-67-5(1)[(l)], who are obligated by statute, agreement, or court order to hold enrollees harmless from liability for services provided and covered by an HMO.

(3) Claims of the federal or any state or local government or taxing authority, including claims for taxes.

(4) Compensation actually owing to employees other than officers of the insurer for services rendered within three months before the commencement of a delinquency proceeding against the insurer under this Article, but not exceeding one thousand dollars ($1,000) for each employee. In the discretion of the Commissioner, this compensation may be paid as soon as practicable after the proceeding has been commenced. This priority is in lieu of any other similar priority that may be authorized by law as to wages or compensation of those employees.

(5) Claims of general creditors, including claims of insurance pools, underwriting associations, or those arising out of reinsurance agreements; claims of other insurers for subrogation; and claims of insurers for payments and settlements under uninsured and underinsured motorist coverages. (1989, c. 452, s. 1; 1993 (Reg. Sess., 1994), c. 600, s. 2; 1995, c. 517, s. 14; 1998-211, s. 4.)

§ 58-30-225. Liquidator's recommendations to the Court.

(a) The liquidator shall review all claims duly filed in the liquidation and shall make such further investigation as necessary. He may compound, compromise, or in any other manner negotiate the amount for which claims will be recommended to the Court except where he is required by law to accept claims as settled by any person or organization, including any domestic or foreign guaranty association. Unresolved disputes shall be determined under G.S. 58-30-205. As soon as practicable, the liquidator shall present to the Court a report of the claims against the insurer with his recommendations. The report shall include the name and address of each claimant and the amount of any claim finally recommended. If the insurer has issued annuities or life insurance policies, the liquidator shall report the persons to whom, according to the records of the insurer, amounts are owed as cash surrender values or other investment values and the amounts owed.

(b) The Court may approve, disapprove, or modify the report on claims by the liquidator. Such reports that are not modified by the Court within a period of 60 days following submission by the liquidator shall be treated by the liquidator as allowed claims, subject thereafter to later modification or to rulings made by the Court pursuant to G.S. 58-30-205. No claim under a policy of insurance shall be allowed for an amount in excess of the applicable policy benefits. (1989, c. 452, s. 1.)

§ 58-30-230. Distribution of assets.

(a) Under the direction of the Court, the liquidator shall pay distributions in a manner that will assure the proper recognition of priorities and a reasonable balance between the expeditious completion of the liquidation and the protection of unliquidated and undetermined claims, including third party claims. Distribution of assets in kind may be made at valuations set by agreement between the liquidator and the creditor and approved by the Court.

(b) Interest on claims shall be paid only after all claims have been paid under subsection (a) of this section. This subsection does not apply to interest awarded as part of a judgment. (1989, c. 452, s. 1.)

§ 58-30-235. Unclaimed and withheld funds.

(a) All unclaimed funds subject to distribution remaining in the liquidator's hands when he is ready to apply to the Court for discharge, including the amount distributable to any creditor, shareholder, member, or other person who is unknown or cannot be found, shall be deposited with the State Treasurer, and shall be paid without interest except in accordance with G.S. 58-30-220 to the person entitled thereto or his legal representative upon proof satisfactory to the State Treasurer of his right thereto. Any amount on deposit not claimed within six years from the discharge of the liquidator shall be considered abandoned and shall be escheated without formal escheat proceedings.

(b)   All funds withheld under G.S. 58-30-195 and not distributed shall upon discharge of the liquidator be deposited with the State Treasurer and paid by him in accordance with G.S. 58-30-220. Any sums remaining that under G.S. 58-30-220 would revert to the undistributed assets of the insurer shall be transferred to the State Treasurer and become the property of the State under subsection (a) of this section, unless the Commissioner in his discretion petitions the Court to reopen the liquidation under G.S. 58-30-245. (1989, c. 452, s. 1.)

§ 58-30-240. Termination of proceedings.

(a)   When all assets justifying the expense of collection and distribution have been collected and distributed under this Article, the liquidator shall apply to the Court for discharge. The Court may grant the discharge and make any other orders, including an order to transfer any remaining funds that are uneconomic to distribute, as may be deemed appropriate.

(b)   Any other person may apply to the Court at any time for an order under subsection (a) of this section. If the application is denied, the applicant shall pay the costs and expenses of the liquidator in resisting the application, including reasonable attorney fees. (1989, c. 452, s. 1.)

§ 58-30-245. Reopening liquidation.

After the liquidation proceeding has been terminated and the liquidator discharged, the Commissioner or other interested party may at any time petition the Court to reopen the proceedings for good cause, including the discovery of additional assets. If the Court is satisfied that there is justification for reopening, it shall so order. (1989, c. 452, s. 1.)

§ 58-30-250. Disposition of records during and after termination of liquidation.

Whenever it appears to the Commissioner that the records of any insurer in process of liquidation or completely liquidated are no longer useful, he may recommend to the Court and the Court shall direct what records should be retained for future reference and what should be destroyed. (1989, c. 452, s. 1.)

§ 58-30-255. External audit of the receiver's books.

The Court may, as it deems to be desirable, cause audits to be made of the books of the Commissioner relating to any receivership established under this Article, and a report of each audit shall be filed with the Commissioner and with the Court. The books, records, and other documents of the receivership shall be made available to any auditor at any time without notice. The expense of each audit shall be considered a cost of administration of the receivership. (1989, c. 452, s. 1.)

§ 58-30-260. Conservation of property of foreign or alien insurers found in this State.

(a) If a domiciliary liquidator has not been appointed, the Commissioner may apply to the Court by verified petition for an order directing him to act as conservator to conserve the property of an alien insurer not domiciled in this State or a foreign insurer on any one or more of the following grounds:

(1) Any of the grounds in G.S. 58-30-75;

(2) That any of its property has been sequestered by official action in its domiciliary state, or in any other state;

(3) That enough of its property has been sequestered in an alien country to give reasonable cause to fear that the insurer is or may become insolvent;

(4) That its license to do business in this State has been revoked or that none was ever issued; and that there are residents of this State with outstanding claims or outstanding policies.

(b) When an order is sought under subsection (a) of this section, the Court shall cause the insurer to be given such notice and time to respond thereto as is reasonable under the circumstances.

(c) The Court may issue the order in whatever terms it shall deem appropriate. The filing or recording of the order with the clerk of court or the register of deeds of the county in which the principal business of the company is located, shall impart the same notice as a deed, bill of sale or other evidence of title duly filed or recorded with that register of deeds would have imparted.

(d) The conservator may at any time petition for and the Court may grant an order under G.S. 58-30-265 to liquidate assets of a foreign or alien insurer under conservation, or, if appropriate, for an order under G.S. 58-30-275, to be appointed ancillary receiver.

(e) The conservator may at any time petition the Court for an order terminating conservation of an insurer. If the Court finds that the conservation is no longer necessary, it shall order that the insurer be restored to possession of its property and the control of its business. The Court may also make such finding and issue such order at any time upon motion of any interested party, but if such motion is denied all costs shall be assessed against such party. (1989, c. 452, s. 1; 1999-132, s. 9.1.)

§ 58-30-265. Liquidation of property of foreign or alien insurers found in this State.

(a) If no domiciliary receiver has been appointed, the Commissioner may apply to the Court by verified petition for an order directing him to liquidate the assets found in this State of a foreign insurer or an alien insurer not domiciled in this State, on any of the following grounds:

(1) Any of the grounds in G.S. 58-30-75 or G.S. 58-30-100; or

(2) Any of the grounds specified in G.S. 58-30-260(a)(2) through (4).

(b) When an order is sought under subsection (a) of this section, the Court shall cause the insurer to be given such notice and time to respond thereto as is reasonable under the circumstances.

(c) If it appears to the Court that the best interests of creditors, policyholders, and the public require, the Court may issue an order to liquidate in whatever terms it deems to be appropriate. The filing or recording of the order with the clerk of the Court or the register of deeds of the county in which the principal business of the insurer is located or the county in which its principal office or place of business is located, shall impart the same notice as a deed, bill of sale, or other evidence of title duly filed or recorded with that register of deeds would have imparted.

(d) If a domiciliary liquidator is appointed in a reciprocal state while a liquidation is proceeding under this section, the liquidator under this section shall thereafter act as ancillary receiver under G.S. 58-30-275. If a domiciliary liquidator is appointed in a nonreciprocal state while a liquidation is proceeding under this section, the liquidator under this section, may petition the court for permission to act as ancillary receiver under G.S. 58-30-275.

(e) On the same grounds as are specified in subsection (a) of this section, the Commissioner may petition any appropriate federal district court to be appointed receiver to liquidate that portion of the insurer's assets and business over which that court will exercise jurisdiction, or any lesser part thereof that the Commissioner considers desirable for the protection of the policyholders and creditors in this State.

(f) The Court may order the Commissioner, when he has liquidated the assets of a foreign or alien insurer under this section, to pay claims of residents of this State against the insurer under such rules as to the liquidation of insurers under this Article as are otherwise compatible with the provisions of this section. (1989, c. 452, s. 1.)

§ 58-30-270. Domiciliary liquidators in other states.

(a) The domiciliary liquidator of an insurer domiciled in a reciprocal state is, except as to special deposits and security on secured claims under G.S. 58-30-275(c), vested by operation of law with the title to all of the assets, property, contracts and rights of action, agents' balances, and all of the books, accounts, and other records of the insurer located in this State. The date of vesting shall be the date of the filing of the petition, if that date is specified by the domiciliary law for the vesting of property in the domiciliary state. Otherwise, the date of vesting shall be the date of entry of the order directing possession to be taken. The domiciliary liquidator shall have the immediate right to recover the balances due from agents and to obtain possession of the books, accounts, and other records of the insurer located in this State. He also shall have the right to recover all other assets of the insurer located in this State, subject to G.S. 58-30-275.

(b)   If a domiciliary liquidator is appointed for an insurer not domiciled in a reciprocal state, the Commissioner shall be vested by operation of law with the title to all of the property, contracts, and rights of action, and all of the books, accounts and other records of the insurer located in this State, at the same time that the domiciliary liquidator is vested with title in the domicile. The Commissioner may petition for a conservation or liquidation order under G.S. 58-30-260 and G.S. 58-30-265, or for an ancillary receivership under G.S. 58-30-275, or after approval by the Court may transfer title to the domiciliary liquidator, as the interests of justice and the equitable distribution of the assets require.

(c)   Claimants residing in this State may file claims with the liquidator or ancillary receiver, if any, in this State or with the domiciliary liquidator, if the domiciliary law permits. The claims must be filed on or before the last date fixed for the filing of claims in the domiciliary liquidation proceedings. (1989, c. 452, s. 1.)

§ 58-30-275. Ancillary formal proceedings.

(a)   If a domiciliary liquidator has been appointed for an insurer not domiciled in this State, the Commissioner may file a petition with the Court requesting appointment as ancillary receiver in this State:

(1)   If he finds that there are sufficient assets of the insurer located in this State to justify the appointment of an ancillary receiver;

(2)   If the protection of creditors or policyholders in this State so requires.

(b) The Court may issue an order appointing an ancillary receiver in whatever terms it deems to be appropriate, including provisions for payment of the reasonable and necessary expenses of the proceedings. The filing or recording of the order with a register of deeds in this State imparts the same notice as a deed, bill of sale, or other evidence of title duly filed or recorded with that register of deeds.

(c) When a domiciliary liquidator has been appointed in a reciprocal state, then the ancillary receiver appointed in this State, may, whenever necessary, aid and assist the domiciliary liquidator in recovering assets of the insurer located in this State. The ancillary receiver shall, as soon as practicable, liquidate from their respective securities those special deposit claims and secured claims which are proved and allowed in the ancillary proceedings in this State, and shall pay the necessary expenses of the proceedings. He shall promptly transfer all remaining assets, books, accounts, and records to the domiciliary liquidator. Subject to this section, the ancillary receiver and his deputies shall have the same powers and be subject to the same duties with respect to the administration of assets as a liquidator of an insurer domiciled in this State.

(d) When a domiciliary liquidator has been appointed in this State, ancillary receivers appointed in reciprocal states shall have, as to assets and books, accounts, and other records in their respective states, corresponding rights, duties and powers to those provided in subsection (c) of this section for ancillary receivers appointed in this State. (1989, c. 452, s. 1; 1993 (Reg. Sess., 1994), c. 678, s. 17.)

§ 58-30-280. Ancillary summary proceedings.

The Commissioner in his sole discretion may institute proceedings under G.S. 58-30-60 through 58-30-70 at the request of the insurance regulator of the domiciliary state of any foreign or alien insurer having property located in this State. (1989, c. 452, s. 1.)

§ 58-30-285. Claims of nonresidents against insurers domiciled in this State.

(a) In a liquidation proceeding begun in this State against an insurer domiciled in this State, claimants residing in foreign countries or in states not reciprocal states must file claims in this State, and claimants residing in reciprocal states may file claims either with the ancillary receivers, if any, in their respective states, or with the domiciliary liquidator. Claims must be filed on or before the last date fixed for the filing of claims in the domiciliary liquidation proceeding.

(b) Claims belonging to claimants residing in reciprocal states may be proved either in the liquidation proceeding in this State as provided in this Article, or in ancillary proceedings, if any, in the reciprocal states. If notice of the claims and opportunity to appear and be heard is afforded the domiciliary liquidator of this State as provided in G.S. 58-30-290(b) with respect to ancillary proceedings, the final allowance of claims by the courts in ancillary proceedings in reciprocal states shall be conclusive as to amount and as to priority against special deposits or other security located in such ancillary states, but shall not be conclusive with respect to priorities against general assets under G.S. 58-30-220. (1989, c. 452, s. 1.)

§ 58-30-290. Claims of residents against insurers domiciled in reciprocal states.

(a) In a liquidation proceeding in a reciprocal state against an insurer domiciled in that state, claimants against the insurer who reside within this State may file claims either with the ancillary receiver, if any, in this State, or with the domiciliary liquidator. Claims must be filed on or before the last dates fixed for the filing of claims in the domiciliary proceeding.

(b) Claims belonging to claimants residing in this State may be proved either in the domiciliary state under the law of that state, or in ancillary proceedings, if any, in this State. If a claimant elects to prove his claim in this State, he shall file his claim with the liquidator in the manner provided in G.S. 58-30-185 and G.S. 58-30-190. The ancillary receiver shall make his recommendation to the Court as under G.S. 58-30-225. He shall also arrange a date for hearing if necessary under G.S. 58-30-205 and shall give notice to the liquidator in the domiciliary state, either by certified mail or by personal service at least 40 days prior to the date set for hearing. If the domicilary liquidator, within 30 days after the giving of such notice, gives notice in writing to the ancillary receiver and to the claimant, either by certified mail or by personal service, of his intention to contest the claim, he shall be entitled to appear or to be represented in any proceedings in this State involving the adjudication of the claim.

(c)   The final allowance of the claim by the courts of this State shall be accepted as conclusive as to amount and as to priority against special deposits or other security located in this State. (1989, c. 452, s. 1.)

§ 58-30-295. Attachment, garnishment and levy of execution.

During the pendency in this or any other state of a liquidation proceeding, whether called by that name or not, no action or proceeding in the nature of an attachment, garnishment, or levy of execution shall be commenced or maintained in this State against the delinquent insurer or its assets. (1989, c. 452, s. 1.)

§ 58-30-300. Interstate priorities.

(a)   In a liquidation proceeding in this State involving one or more reciprocal states, the order of distribution of the domiciliary state shall control as to all claims of residents of this and reciprocal states. All claims of residents of reciprocal states shall be given equal priority of payment from general assets regardless of where such assets are located.

(b)   The owners of special deposit claims against an insurer for which a liquidator is appointed in this or any other state shall be given priority against the special deposits in accordance with the statutes governing the creation and maintenance of the deposits. If there is a deficiency in any deposit, so that the claims secured by it are not fully discharged from it, the claimants may share in the general assets, but the sharing shall be deferred until general creditors, and also claimants against other special deposits who have received smaller percentages from their respective special deposits, have been paid percentages of their claims equal to the percentage paid from the special deposit.

(c)   The owner of a secured claim against an insurer for which a liquidator has been appointed in this or any other state may surrender the owner's security and file the claim as a general creditor, or the claim may be discharged by resort to the security in accordance with G.S. 58-30-215 in which case the deficiency, if any, shall be treated as a claim against the general assets of the insurer on the same basis as claims of unsecured creditors. (1989, c. 452, s. 1; 1995, c. 193, s. 32.)

§ 58-30-305. Subordination of claims for noncooperation.

If an ancillary receiver in another state or foreign country, whether called by that name or not, fails to transfer to the domiciliary liquidator in this State any assets within his control other than special deposits, diminished only by the expenses of the ancillary receivership, if any, the claims filed in the ancillary receivership, other than special deposit claims or secured claims shall be placed in the class of claims under G.S. 58-30-220(5). (1989, c. 452, s. 1.)

§ 58-30-310. Exemption from filing fees.

As used in this section, "Commissioner" includes the Commissioner's deputies, employees, or attorneys of record. The Commissioner is not required to pay any fee to any public officer in this State for filing, recording, issuing a transcript or certificate, or authenticating any paper or instrument pertaining to the exercise by the Commissioner of any of the powers or duties conferred upon him under this Article. This section applies whether or not the paper or instrument is connected with the commencement of an action or proceeding by or against the Commissioner or with the subsequent conduct of an action or proceeding. (1989 (Reg. Sess., 1990), c. 1069, s. 15.)

§ 58-31-26. Medical liability insurance for certain physicians and dentists.

(a) The Secretary of the Department of Health and Human Services and the Secretary of the Department of Public Safety may provide medical liability insurance not to exceed one million dollars ($1,000,000) per incident on behalf of employees of these Departments who are licensed to practice medicine or dentistry; on behalf of all licensed physicians who are faculty members of The University of North Carolina who perform work on a contractual basis for the Division of Mental Health, Developmental Disabilities, and Substance Abuse Services for incidents that occur in Division programs; and on behalf of physicians in all residency training programs from The University of North Carolina who are in training at institutions operated by the Department of Health and Human Services. This coverage may include commercial insurance or self-insurance and shall cover these individuals for their acts or omissions only while they are engaged in providing medical and dental services pursuant to their State employment or training.

(b) The coverage provided pursuant to this section shall not cover any individual for any act or omission that the individual knows or reasonably should know constitutes a violation of the applicable criminal laws of any state or the United States, or that arises out of any sexual, fraudulent, criminal, or malicious act or out of any act amounting to willful or wanton negligence.

(c) The coverage provided pursuant to this section shall not require any additional appropriations and, except as provided in subsection (a) of this section, shall not apply to any individual providing contractual service to the Department of Health and Human Services or the Department of Public Safety. (2013-360, s. 12A.7.)

Article 31.

Insuring State Property, Officials and Employees.

§ 58-31-1. State Property Fire Insurance Fund created.

Upon the expiration of all existing policies of fire insurance upon state-owned buildings, fixtures, furniture, and equipment, including all such property the title to which may be in any State department, institution, or agency, the State of North Carolina shall not reinsure any of such properties.

There is hereby created a "State Property Fire Insurance Fund," which shall be as a special fund in the State treasury, for the purpose of providing a reserve against loss from fire at State departments and institutions. The State Treasurer shall be the custodian of the "State Property Fire Insurance Fund" and shall invest its assets in accordance with the provisions of G.S. 147-69.2 and 147-69.3. The unexpended appropriations of State departments and institutions for fire insurance premiums for the fiscal year 1944-1945 and the appropriations for fire insurance premiums made for the biennium 1945-1947 or that may thereafter be made for this purpose shall be transferred to the "State Property Fire Insurance Fund." (1945, c. 1027, s. 1; 1963, c. 462; 1975, c. 519, s. 1; 1979, c. 467, s. 4.)

§ 58-31-5. Appropriations; fund to pay administrative expenses.

Upon the expiration of the existing fire insurance policies on said properties and in making appropriations for any biennium after the next biennium, the Commissioner shall file with the Department of Administration his estimate of the appropriations which will be necessary in order to set up and maintain an adequate reserve to provide a fund sufficient to protect the State, its departments, institutions, and agencies from loss or damage to any of said properties up to fifty per centum (50%) of the value thereof. Appropriations made for the creating of such fire insurance reserves against property of the Department of Agriculture and Consumer Services, or the Department of Transportation or any special operating fund shall be charged against the funds of such departments.

The State Property Fire Insurance Fund is authorized and empowered to pay all the administrative expenses occasioned by the administration of Article 31 of Chapter 58 of the General Statutes. (1945, c. 1027, s. 2; 1957, c. 65, s. 11; c. 269, s. 1; 1959, c. 182, s. 1; 1973, c. 507, s. 5; 1977, c. 464, s. 34; 1991, c. 720, s. 4; 1997-261, s. 109.)

§ 58-31-10. Payment of losses on basis of actual cost of restoration or replacement; rules; insurance and reinsurance; sprinkler leakage insurance.

(a)   In the case of total or partial loss of any property of any State agency or institution, the Commissioner shall determine the amount of loss and certify that amount to the agency or institution concerned and to the Director of the Budget and Council of State. The Director of the Budget and Council of State may authorize transfers from the Fund to the agency or institution that suffered the loss in amounts that are necessary to pay for the actual cost of restoration or replacement of the property. In the event there is not a sufficient amount in the Fund to pay for the actual cost of restoration or replacement, the Director of the

Budget and the Council of State may supplement the Fund by transferring amounts from the Contingency and Emergency Fund.

(b) The Commissioner, with the approval of the Council of State, is authorized to adopt rules necessary to carry out the purpose of this Article, which rules shall be binding on all State agencies and institutions. The Commissioner, with the approval of the Director of the Budget and the Council of State, is authorized to purchase from qualified insurers insurance or reinsurance necessary to protect the Fund against loss on any one building and its contents in excess of fifty thousand dollars ($50,000), and the premiums for this coverage shall be paid from the Fund.

(c) Upon the request of any State agency or institution, sprinkler leakage insurance shall be provided on designated property of the agency or institution that is insured by the Fund. Premiums for this coverage shall be paid by the requesting agency or institution in accordance with rates fixed by the Commissioner. Losses covered by this insurance may be paid out of the Fund in the same manner as other losses. The Commissioner, with the approval of the Director of the Budget and the Council of State, is authorized to purchase from qualified insurers insurance or reinsurance necessary to protect the Fund against loss with respect to sprinkler leakage insurance coverage. (1945, c. 1027, s. 3; 1951, c. 802; 1959, c. 182, s. 2; 1983, c. 913, s. 7; 1985, c. 786.)

§ 58-31-12. Policy forms.

The Commissioner, with the approval of the Council of State, may adopt insurance forms for coverages provided by the State Property Fire Insurance Fund under this Article. (1993, c. 409, s. 13.)

§ 58-31-13. Hazardous conditions in State-owned buildings.

If the Commissioner determines that an undue hazard to life, safety, or property exists because of a condition or the use of a building owned by the State, the Commissioner shall advise the proper agency how to limit or prohibit use of the building until the hazard is abated. (1993, c. 409, s. 13.)

§ 58-31-15. Extended coverage insurance.

Upon request of any State department, agency or institution, extended coverage insurance, and other property insurance, may be provided on designated state-owned property of such department, agency or institution which is insured by the State Property Fire Insurance Fund. Premiums for such insurance coverage shall be paid by each requesting department, agency or institution in accordance with rates fixed by the Commissioner. Losses covered by such insurance may be paid for out of the State Property Fire Insurance Fund in the same manner as fire losses. The Commissioner, with the approval of the Governor and Council of State, is authorized and empowered to purchase from insurers admitted to do business in North Carolina such insurance or reinsurance as may be necessary to protect the State Property Fire Insurance Fund against loss with respect to such insurance coverage. The words "extended coverage insurance," as used in this section, mean insurance against loss or damage caused by windstorm, hail, explosion, riot, riot attending a strike, civil commotion, aircraft, vehicles or smoke. (1957, c. 67; 1975, c. 519, s. 2; 1991, c. 720, s. 4.)

§ 58-31-20. Use and occupancy and business interruption insurance.

Upon request of any State department, agency or institution, use and occupancy and business interruption insurance shall be provided on state-owned property of such department, agency or institution which is insured by the State Property Fire Insurance Fund. Premiums for such insurance coverage shall be paid by each requesting department, agency or institution in accordance with rates fixed by the Commissioner. Losses covered by such insurance may be paid for out of the State Property Fire Insurance Fund in the same manner as fire losses. The Commissioner, with the approval of the Governor and Council of State, is authorized and empowered to purchase from insurers admitted to do business in North Carolina such insurance or reinsurance as may be necessary to protect the State Property Fire Insurance Fund against loss with respect to such insurance coverage. (1957, c. 67; 1991, c. 720, s. 4.)

§ 58-31-25. Professional liability insurance for officials and employees of the State.

The Commissioner may acquire professional liability insurance covering the officers and employees of any State department, institution or agency upon the request of such State department, institution or agency. Premiums for such insurance coverage shall be paid by the requesting department, institution or agency at rates fixed by the Commissioner from funds made available to it for the purpose. The Commissioner, in placing a contract for such insurance is authorized to place such insurance through the Public Officers and Employees' Liability Insurance Commission, and shall exercise all efforts to place such insurance through the said commission prior to attempting to procure such insurance through any other source.

The Commissioner, pursuant to this section, may acquire professional liability insurance covering the officers and employees of a department, institution or agency of State government only if the coverage to be provided by such policy is coverage of claims in excess of the protection provided by Articles 31 and 31A of Chapter 143 of the General Statutes.

The purchase, by any State department, institution or agency of professional liability insurance covering the law-enforcement officers, officers or employees of such department, institution or agency shall not be construed as a waiver of any defense of sovereign immunity by such department, institution or agency. The purchase of such insurance shall not be deemed a waiver by any employee of the defense of sovereign immunity to the extent that such defense may be available to him.

The payment, by any State department, institution or agency of funds as premiums for professional liability insurance through the plan provided herein, covering the law-enforcement officers or officials or employees of such department, institution or agency is hereby declared to be for a public purpose. (1979, c. 206, s. 1; 1987, c. 864, s. 53; 1991, c. 720, s. 4.)

§ 58-31-30: Expired at the end of the 1993-94 fiscal year by its own terms.

§ 58-31-35. Information furnished Commissioner by officers in charge.

It is the duty of the different officers or boards having in their custody any property belonging to the State to inform the Commissioner, giving him in detail a full description of same, and to keep him informed of any changes in such property or its location or surroundings. (1901, c. 710, ss. 1, 2; 1903, c. 771, s. 2; Rev., s. 4828; C.S., s. 6452.)

§ 58-31-40. Commissioner to inspect State property.

(a) The Commissioner shall, as often as is required in the fire code adopted by the North Carolina Building Code Council or more often if the Commissioner considers it necessary, visit, inspect, and thoroughly examine every State property to analyze and determine its protection from fire, including the property's occupants or contents. The Commissioner shall notify in writing the agency or official in charge of the property of any defect noted by the Commissioner or any improvement considered by the Commissioner to be necessary, and a copy of that notice shall be forwarded by the Commissioner to the Department of Administration.

(b) No agency or person authorized or directed by law to select a plan or erect a building comprising 20,000 square feet or more for the use of any county, city, or school district shall receive and approve of the plan until it is submitted to and approved by the Commissioner as to the safety of the proposed building from fire, including the property's occupants or contents.

(c) Repealed by Session Laws 2009-474, s. 1, effective October 1, 2009. (1901, c. 710, ss. 1, 2; 1903, c. 771, s. 3; Rev., s. 4829; 1909, c. 880; 1919, c. 186, s. 3; C.S., s. 6453; 2000-122, s. 10; 2001-487, s. 19; 2001-496, s. 11.1; 2007-303, s. 1; 2009-474, s. 1; 2012-161, s. 2.)

§ 58-31-45. Report required of Commissioner.

The Commissioner must submit to the Governor a full report of his official action under this Article, with such recommendations as commend themselves to the Commissioner. (1901, c. 710, ss. 1, 2; 1903, c. 771, s. 4; Rev., s. 4830; C.S., s. 6454; 1945, c. 386; 1991, c. 720, s. 4; 2013-199, s. 7.)

§ 58-31-50. Liability insurance required for state-owned vehicles.

Every department, agency or institution of the State shall acquire motor vehicle liability insurance on all state-owned motor vehicles under its control. (1959, c. 1248; 1983, c. 717, s. 10.)

§ 58-31-52. State motor vehicle safety program.

(a)   Findings, Policy, and Purpose. - Motor vehicle accidents exact a terrible toll of human tragedy and suffering as well as national resources within the United States. The same is true, on a smaller scale, within North Carolina State government. Every year State employees or members of the general public are killed or injured, and a significant portion of the State's financial resources is expended as a direct result of accidents involving State-owned vehicles. Accordingly, it is North Carolina policy that the State-owned motor vehicle fleet and vehicles used on behalf of the State be operated and maintained in such a manner as to minimize deaths, injuries, and costs. The purpose of this section is to direct the Commissioner of Insurance to develop a program to provide policy, requirements, procedures, technical information, and standards for administering a State vehicle safety program which will apply to all State personnel involved in the administration and operation of vehicles on behalf of the State.

(b)   The Commissioner shall develop and adopt a State motor vehicle safety program to assure that State-owned motor vehicles are operated and maintained in a safe manner.

(c)   In developing the program, the Commissioner shall include the following:

(1)   Basic criteria concerning qualifications, screening, and education of drivers.

(2)   Required and prohibited driving practices.

(3)   Safety maintenance requirements.

(4)   Accident reporting and review procedures.

(d) The requirements and procedures established under the program apply to all agencies and persons operating vehicles on behalf of the State, unless specifically exempted by the Commissioner. Agencies may adopt more stringent requirements and procedures than those adopted by the Commissioner under this section. The administration of the program in each agency is the responsibility of each agency head or that person's designee.

(e) The provisions of Chapter 150B of the General Statutes do not apply to the program developed and adopted under this section. (1995, c. 517, s. 15.)

§ 58-31-55. Insurance and official fidelity bonds for State agencies to be placed by Department; exception; costs of placement.

Except as provided in G.S. 58-32-15, all insurance and all official fidelity and surety bonds authorized for State departments, institutions, and agencies shall be effected and placed by the Department, and the cost of such placement shall be paid by the State department, institution, or agency involved upon bills rendered to and approved by the Commissioner. (1975, c. 875, s. 11; 1981, c. 1109, s. 4; 1993, c. 504, s. 21.)

§ 58-31-60. Competitive selection of payroll deduction insurance products paid for by State employees.

(a) Employee Insurance Committee. - The head of each State government employee payroll unit offering payroll deduction insurance products to employees shall appoint an Employee Insurance Committee for the following purposes:

(1) To review insurance products currently offered through payroll deduction to the State employees in the Employee Insurance Committee's payroll unit to determine if those products meet the needs and desires of employees in the Employee Insurance Committee's payroll unit.

(2) To select the types of insurance products that reflect the needs and desires of employees in the Employee Insurance Committee's payroll unit.

(3) To competitively select the best insurance products of the types determined by the Employee Insurance Committee to reflect the needs and desires of the employees of that payroll unit.

As used in this section, "insurance product" includes a prepaid legal services plan registered under G.S. 84-23.1.

(b) Appointment of Employee Insurance Committee Members. - The members of the Employee Insurance Committee shall be appointed by the head of the payroll unit. The Committee shall consist of not less than five or more than nine individuals a majority of whom have been employed in the payroll unit for at least one year. The committee members shall, except where necessary initially to establish the rotation herein prescribed, serve three-year terms with approximately one-third of the terms expiring annually. Committee membership make-up shall fairly represent the work force in the payroll unit and be selected without regard to any political or other affiliations. It shall be the duty of the payroll unit head to assure that the Employee Insurance Committee is completely autonomous in its selection of insurance products and insurance companies and that no member of the Employee Insurance Committee has any conflict of interest in serving on the Committee. A committee on employee benefits elected or appointed by the faculty representative body of a constituent institution of The University of North Carolina shall be deemed constituted and functioning as an employee insurance committee in accordance with this section. Any decision rendered by the Employee Insurance Committee where the autonomy of the Committee or a conflict of interest is questioned shall be subject to appeal pursuant to the Administrative Procedure Act, or in the case of departments, boards and commissions which are specifically exempt from the Administrative Procedure Act, pursuant to the appeals procedure prescribed for such department, board or commission.

(c) Payroll Deduction Slots. - Each payroll unit shall be entitled to not less than four payroll deduction slots to be used for payment of insurance premiums for products selected by the Employee Insurance Committee and offered to the employees of the payroll unit. The Employee Insurance Committee shall select only one company per payroll deduction slot. The Company selected by the Employee Insurance Committee shall be permitted to sell through payroll deduction only the products specifically approved by the Employee Insurance Committee. The assignment by the Employee Insurance Committee of a payroll deduction slot shall be for a period of not less than two years unless the insurance company shall be in violation of the terms of the written agreement specified in this subsection. The insurance company awarded a payroll deduction slot shall, pursuant to a written agreement setting out the rights and duties of the insurance company, be afforded an adequate opportunity to solicit employees of the payroll unit by making such employees aware that a representative of the company will be available at a specified time and at a location convenient to the employees.

Notwithstanding any other provision of the General Statutes, once an employee has selected an insurance product for payroll deduction, that product may not be removed from payroll deduction for that employee without his or her specific written consent.

When an employee retires from State employment and payroll deduction under this section is no longer available, the insurance company may not terminate life insurance products purchased under the payroll deduction plan without the retiree's specific written consent solely because the premium is no longer deducted from payroll.

(c1)   Procedure for Selection of Insurance Product Proposals. - All insurance product proposals shall be sealed. The Committee shall open all proposals in public and record them in the minutes of the Committee, at which time the proposals become public records open to public inspection.

After the public opening, the Committee shall review the proposals, examining the cost and quality of the products, the reputation and capabilities of the insurance companies submitting the proposals, and other appropriate criteria. The Committee shall determine which proposal, if any, would meet the needs and desires of the employees of that Committee's payroll unit and shall award a payroll deduction slot to the company submitting the proposal that meets those needs and desires. The Committee may reject any or all proposals.

A company may seek to modify or withdraw a proposal only after the public opening and only on the basis that the proposal contains an unintentional clerical error as opposed to an error in judgment. A company seeking to modify or withdraw a proposal shall submit to the Committee a written request, with facts and evidence in support of its position, prior to the award of the payroll deduction slot, but not later than two days after the public opening of the proposals. The Committee shall promptly review the request, examine the nature of the error, and determine whether to permit or deny the request.

(d)   Criminal Penalty. - It shall be a Class 3 misdemeanor for any State employee, who has supervisory authority over any member of the Employee

Insurance Committee, to attempt to influence the autonomy of any Employee Insurance Committee either in the appointment of members to such Committee or in the operation of such Committee; or for anyone to open a sealed insurance product proposal or disclose or exhibit the contents of a sealed insurance product proposal, prior to the public opening of the proposal. The Commissioner of Insurance shall have the authority to investigate complaints alleging acts subject to the criminal penalty and shall report his findings to the Attorney General of North Carolina. (1985, c. 213, s. 1; 1985 (Reg. Sess., 1986), c. 1013, s. 15; 1987, c. 752, s. 12; c. 864, s. 92; 1989, c. 299; 1991, c. 644, s. 3.1; 1993, c. 539, s. 456; 1994, Ex. Sess., c. 24, s. 14(c); 1995, c. 193, s. 33; 1998-187, s. 1.)

§ 58-31-65. Owner-controlled or wrap-up insurance authorized.

(a) To the extent it is determined necessary and in the best interest of this State, the Department may obtain design and construction insurance or provide for self-insurance against property damage caused by this State, its departments, agencies, boards, and commissions and all officers and employees of this State in connection with the construction of public works projects. Workers' compensation and general liability insurance may be purchased to cover both general contractors and subcontractors doing work on a specific contracted work site. In connection with the construction of public works projects, the Department may also use an owner-controlled or wrap-up insurance program if all of the following conditions are met:

(1) The total cost of the project or group of projects is over fifty million dollars ($50,000,000).

(2) The program maintains completed operations coverage for a term during which coverage is reasonably commercially available as determined by the Commissioner, but in no event for fewer than three years.

(3) Bid specifications clearly specify for all bidders the insurance coverage provided under the program and the minimum safety requirements that shall be met.

(4) The program does not prohibit a contractor or subcontractor from purchasing any additional insurance coverage that a contractor believes is necessary for protection from any liability arising out of the contract. The cost of

the additional insurance shall not be passed through to this State on a contract bid.

(5) The program does not include surety insurance.

(6) The State may purchase an owner-controlled or wrap-up policy that has a deductible or self-insured retention as long as the deductible or self-insured retention does not exceed one million dollars ($1,000,000).

(b) For the purposes of subsection (a) of this section:

(1) "Owner-controlled or wrap-up insurance" means a series of insurance policies issued to cover this State and all of the construction managers, contractors, subcontractors, architects, and engineers on a specified contracted work site or work sites for purposes of general liability, property damage, and workers' compensation. A State agency or the State may be a secondary insured under owner-controlled or wrap-up insurance.

(2) "Specific contracted work site" means construction being performed at one site or a series of contiguous sites separated only by a street, roadway, waterway, or railroad right-of-way, or along a continuous system for the provision of water and power. (2001-167, s. 1.)

§ 58-31-66. Public construction contract surety bonds.

(a) Neither the State nor any county, city, or other political subdivision of the State, or any officer, employee, or other person acting on behalf of any such entity shall, with respect to any public building or construction contract, require any contractor, bidder, or proposer to procure a bid bond, payment bond, or performance bond from a particular surety, agent, producer, or broker.

(b) (1) Repealed by Session Laws 2004-203, s. 74(b), effective October 1, 2004.

(2) Repealed by Session Laws 2006-264, s. 7, effective August 27, 2006.

(c) Repealed by Session Laws 2004-203, s. 74(b), effective October 1, 2004. (2003-212, s. 27; 2004-203, s. 74(b); 2006-264, s. 7.)

Article 30.

Insurers Supervision, Rehabilitation, and Liquidation.

§ 58-30-1. Construction and purpose.

(a)   This Article does not limit powers granted to the Commissioner by any other provision of law. To the extent practicable, the Commissioner may supplement the provisions of this Article with those of Part 2 of Article 38 of Chapter 1 of the General Statutes.

(b)   This Article shall be liberally construed to effect the purpose stated in subsection (c) of this section.

(c)   The purpose of this Article is to protect the interests of policyholders, claimants, creditors, and the public generally with minimum interference with the normal prerogatives of the owners and managers of insurers, through:

(1)   Early detection of any potentially dangerous condition in an insurer, and prompt application of appropriate corrective measures;

(2)   Improved methods for rehabilitating insurers, involving the cooperation and management expertise of the insurance industry;

(3)   Enhanced efficiency and economy of liquidation, through clarification of the law, to minimize legal uncertainty and litigation;

(4)   Equitable apportionment of any unavoidable loss;

(5)   Lessening the problems of interstate rehabilitation and liquidation by facilitating cooperation between states in the liquidation process, and by extending the scope of personal jurisdiction over debtors of the insurer outside this State; and

(6)   Regulation of the insurance business by the impact of the law relating to delinquency procedures and substantive rules on the entire insurance business. (1989, c. 452, s. 1.)

§ 58-30-5. Persons covered.

The proceedings authorized by this Article may be applied to:

(1)   All insurers that are doing, or have done, an insurance business in this State, and against whom claims arising from that business may exist now or in the future.

(2)   All insurers that purport to do an insurance business in this State.

(3)   All insurers that have insureds resident in this State.

(4)   All persons organized or in the process of organizing with the intent to do an insurance business in this State.

(5)   All persons subject to Articles 64, 65 and 66, or 67 of this Chapter; except to the extent there is a conflict between the provisions of this Article and the provisions of those Articles, in which case those Articles will govern.

(6)   Self-insured group workers' compensation funds subject to Article 47 of this Chapter. (1989, c. 452, s. 1; 1995, c. 471, s. 3; 1995 (Reg. Sess., 1996), c. 582, s. 1; 1999-132, s. 7.2.)

§ 58-30-10. Definitions.

For the purposes of this Article only:

(1)   "Alien country" means any other jurisdiction not in any state.

(2)   "Ancillary state" means any state other than a domiciliary state.

(3)   "Court" means the Superior Court of Wake County.

(4)   "Creditor" means a person having any claim, whether matured or unmatured, liquidated or unliquidated, secured or unsecured, absolute, fixed, or contingent.

(5) "Delinquency proceeding" means any proceeding instituted against an insurer for the purpose of supervising, rehabilitating, conserving, or liquidating such insurer.

(6) "Doing business" includes any of the following acts by insurers, whether effected by mail or otherwise:

a. The issuance or delivery of contracts of insurance to persons resident in this State;

b. The solicitation of applications for such contracts, or other negotiations preliminary to the execution of such contracts;

c. The collection of premiums, membership fees, assessments, or other consideration for such contracts;

d. The transaction of matters subsequent to execution of such contracts and arising out of them;

e. Operating as an insurer under a license issued by the Department; or

f. The purchase of contracts of insurance issued to persons in this State by an assumption agreement.

(7) "Domestic guaranty association" means the Postassessment Insurance Guaranty Association in Article 48 of this Chapter, as amended; the North Carolina Self-Insurance Security Association in Article 4 of Chapter 97 of the General Statutes; the Life and Accident and Health Insurance Guaranty Association in Article 62 of this Chapter, as amended; or any other similar entity hereafter created by the General Assembly for the payment of claims of insolvent insurers.

(8) "Domiciliary state" means the state in which an insurer is incorporated or organized; or, in the case of an alien insurer, its state of entry.

(9) "Fair consideration" is given for property or obligation when:

a. In exchange for such property or obligation, as a fair equivalent therefor, and in good faith, property is conveyed or services are rendered or an obligation is incurred or an antecedent debt is satisfied; or

b. Such property or obligation is received in good faith to secure a present advance or antecedent debt in amount not disproportionately small as compared to the value of the property or obligation obtained.

(10) "Foreign guaranty association" means a guaranty association now in existence in or hereafter created by the legislature of any other state.

(11) "Formal delinquency proceeding" means any liquidation or rehabilitation proceeding.

(12) "General assets" means all real, personal, or other property that is not specifically mortgaged, pledged, hypothecated, deposited, or otherwise encumbered for the security or benefit of specified persons or classes of persons. As to specifically encumbered property, "general assets" includes all such property or its proceeds in excess of the amount necessary to discharge the sum or sums secured thereby. Assets that are held in trust and on deposit for the security or benefit of all policyholders in more than one state or all policyholders and creditors in more than one state shall be treated as "general assets". No person shall have a claim against general assets unless that claim is in an amount in excess of fifty dollars ($50.00).

(13) "Insolvency" or "insolvent" means that an insurer is unable to pay its obligations when they are due, or that its admitted assets do not exceed its liabilities plus the greater of (i) any capital and surplus required by law for its organization; or (ii) the total par or stated value of its authorized and issued capital stock. For the purposes of this subdivision, "liabilities" includes reserves required by statute, by Department rules, or by specific requirements imposed by the Commissioner upon a subject company at the time of admission or subsequent thereto, except those reserves that are an allocation of surplus as specified in G.S. 58-65-95.

(14) "Insurer" means any entity that is or should be licensed under Articles 7, 16, 26, 47, 49, 64, 65, or 67 of this Chapter.

(15) "Preferred claim" means any claim with respect to which the provisions of this Article accord priority of payment from the general assets of the insurer.

(16) "Receiver" includes a liquidator, rehabilitator, or conservator, as the context requires.

(17) "Reciprocal state" means any state other than this State in which in substance and effect the provisions of G.S. 58-30-105(a), 58-30-270, 58-30-275, and 58-30-285 through 58-30-295 are in force, and in which provisions are in force requiring that the insurance regulator of that state be the receiver of a delinquent insurer; and in which provisions exist for the avoidance of fraudulent conveyances and preferential transfers.

(18) "Secured claim" means any claim secured by mortgage, trust deed, pledge, deposit as security, escrow, or otherwise; and includes any claim that has become a lien upon specific assets by reason of judicial process. "Secured claim" does not include a special deposit claim or a claim against general assets.

(19) "Special deposit claim" means any claim in excess of fifty dollars ($50.00) secured by a deposit made pursuant to statute for the security or benefit of a limited class or classes of persons, but does not include any claim secured by general assets.

(20) "Transfer" includes the sale and every other and different mode, whether direct or indirect, of disposing of or of parting with property, an interest therein, or the possession thereof; or of voluntarily fixing a lien upon property or an interest therein, whether absolutely or conditionally, by or without judicial proceedings. The retention of a security title to property delivered to a debtor is a transfer suffered by the debtor. (1989, c. 452, s. 1; 1995, c. 471, ss. 4, 5; 1995 (Reg. Sess., 1996), c. 582, s. 2; c. 742, s. 24; 1999-132, ss. 2.1, 7.3, 9.1; 1999-294, s. 11(a), (b); 2000-140, s. 13; 2001-223, ss. 24.2, 24.3; 2001-487, s. 103(a); 2005-400, s. 18; 2007-127, s. 9.)

§ 58-30-12. Duty to report insurer impairment; violations; penalties.

(a) As used in this section:

(1) "Chief executive officer", as used in subsection (b) of this section, means the person, irrespective of title, designated by the board of directors or trustees of an insurer as the person charged with administering and implementing an insurer's policies and procedures.

(2) "Impaired", as used in subsections (b) and (c) of this section, means a financial condition in which the assets of an insurer are less than the sum of the

insurer's minimum required capital, minimum required surplus, and all liabilities as determined in accordance with the requirements for the preparation and filing of a financial statement under G.S. 58-2-165 and under other provisions of this Chapter.

(3) "Insolvent", as used in subsection (c) of this section, has the same meaning as set forth in G.S. 58-30-10(13).

(b) Whenever an insurer is impaired, its chief executive officer shall, as soon as is reasonably possible, notify the Commissioner in writing of the impairment and shall at the same time notify in writing all of the members of the board of directors or trustees of the insurer, if the chief executive officer knows or has reason to know of the impairment. An officer, director, or trustee of an insurer shall notify the chief executive officer of the impairment of the insurer if the officer, director, or trustee knows or has reason to know that the insurer is impaired. Any person who knowingly violates this subsection shall, upon conviction, be guilty of a Class 1 misdemeanor.

(c) Any person who willfully:

(1) Conceals any property belonging to an insurer; or

(2) Transfers or conceals in contemplation of a delinquency proceeding the person's own property or property belonging to an insurer; or

(3) Conceals, destroys, mutilates, alters, or makes a false entry in any document that affects or relates to the property of an insurer or withholds any such document from a receiver, trustee, or other officer of a court entitled to its possession; or

(4) Gives, obtains, or receives a thing of value for acting or forbearing to act in any court proceedings;

and any such act results in or contributes to an insurer becoming impaired or insolvent; shall be guilty of a Class H felony. (1991, c. 681, s. 40; 1993, c. 539, s. 455; 1994, Ex. Sess., c. 24, s. 14(c).)

§ 58-30-15. Jurisdiction and venue.

(a) No delinquency proceeding shall be commenced by anyone other than the Commissioner and no other court has jurisdiction to entertain, hear, or determine any proceeding commenced by any other person.

(b) Except as provided in this Article, no court of this State has jurisdiction to entertain, hear, or determine any complaint praying for the dissolution, liquidation, rehabilitation, sequestration, conservation, or receivership of any insurer; or praying for an injunction or restraining order or other relief preliminary to, incidental to, or relating to such proceedings.

(c) In addition to other grounds for jurisdiction provided by the laws of this State, the Court has jurisdiction over a person served pursuant to Chapter 1A of the General Statutes or other applicable provisions of law in an action brought by the receiver of a domestic insurer or an alien insurer domiciled in this State:

(1) If the person served is obligated to the insurer in any way as an incident to any agency or brokerage arrangement that may exist or has existed between the insurer and the agent or broker, in any action on or incident to the obligation; or

(2) If the person served is a reinsurer who has at any time entered into a contract of reinsurance with an insurer against which a rehabilitation or liquidation order is in effect when the action is commenced, or is an agent or broker of or for the reinsurer, in any action on or incident to the reinsurance contract; or

(3) If the person served is or has been an officer, manager, trustee, organizer, promoter, or person in a position of comparable authority or influence, in an insurer against which a rehabilitation or liquidation order is in effect when the action is commenced, in any action resulting from such a relationship with the insurer; or

(4) If the person served is or was, when the delinquency proceeding was begun against the insurer, holding assets in which the receiver claims an interest on behalf of the insurer, in any action concerning the assets; or

(5) If the person served is obligated to the insurer in any way whatsoever, in any action on or incident to the obligation.

(d) All actions authorized in this Article shall be brought in the Superior Court of Wake County.

(e) The provisions of Chapter 150B of the General Statutes do not apply to this Article. (1989, c. 452, s. 1; 1991, c. 681, s. 41.)

§ 58-30-20. Injunctions and orders.

(a) Any receiver appointed in a proceeding under this Article may at any time apply for, and any court of general jurisdiction may grant, such restraining orders, preliminary and permanent injunctions, and other orders as may be deemed to be necessary and proper to prevent:

(1) The transaction of further business;

(2) The transfer of property;

(3) Interference with the receiver or with a proceeding under this Article;

(4) Waste of the insurer's assets;

(5) Dissipation and transfer of bank accounts;

(6) The institution or further prosecution of any actions or proceedings;

(7) The obtaining of preferences, judgments, attachments, garnishments, or liens against the insurer, its assets or its policyholders;

(8) The levying of execution against the insurer, its assets, or its policyholders;

(9) The making of any sale or deed for nonpayment of taxes or assessments that would lessen the value of the assets of the insurer;

(10) The withholding from the receiver of books, accounts, documents, or other records relating to the business of the insurer; or

(11) Any other threatened or contemplated action that might lessen the value of the insurer's assets or prejudice the rights of policyholders, creditors, or shareholders, or the administration of any proceeding under this Article.

(b) The receiver may apply to any court outside of this State for the relief described in subsection (a) of this section. (1989, c. 452, s. 1.)

§ 58-30-22. Powers of Commissioner and receiver to examine or audit books or records.

(a) As used in this section, "person" includes an agent of the insurer; a broker, ceding or assuming reinsurer, or reinsurance intermediary that has done business with the insurer; or any affiliate of the insurer.

(b) In addition to other powers granted under this Chapter, the Commissioner in any supervision proceeding under this Article and a receiver in any delinquency proceeding under this Article has the power to examine or audit the books or records of any person insofar as those books or records relate to the business activities of the insurer that is under supervision or subject to a delinquency proceeding.

(c) Repealed by Session Laws 1995, c. 360, s. 2(a). (1991, c. 681, s. 42; 1995, c. 360, s. 2(a).)

§ 58-30-25. Cooperation of officers, owners and employees.

(a) Any officer, manager, director, trustee, owner, employee, or agent of any insurer, and any other person with authority over or in charge of any segment of the insurer's affairs, shall cooperate with the Commissioner in any proceeding under this Article or any investigation preliminary to the proceeding. As used in this section, "person" includes any person who exercises direct or indirect control over activities of an insurer through any holding company or other affiliate of the insurer. "Cooperate" includes replying promptly in writing to any inquiry from the Commissioner requesting such a reply and making available to the Commissioner any books, accounts, documents, or other records or information or property of or pertaining to the insurer and in his possession, custody, or control.

(b) No person shall obstruct or interfere with the Commissioner in the conduct of any delinquency proceeding or any investigation preliminary or incidental thereto.

(c) This section does not abridge otherwise existing legal rights, including the right to resist a petition for any delinquency proceeding or other order.

(d) Any person described in subsection (a) of this section who fails to cooperate with the Commissioner, or any person who obstructs or interferes with the Commissioner in the conduct of any delinquency proceeding or any investigation preliminary or incidental thereto, or any person who knowingly and willfully violates any order the Commissioner issued validly under this Article is subject to the civil penalty and restitution provisions of G.S. 58-2-70 and is subject further to the revocation or suspension of any licenses issued by the Commissioner. (1989, c. 452, s. 1.)

§ 58-30-30. Bonds.

In any proceeding under this Article, the Commissioner and his deputies shall be responsible on their official bonds for the faithful performance of their duties. (1989, c. 452, s. 1.)

§ 58-30-35. Executory contracts and unexpired leases.

(a) Except as provided in subsections (b), (c), and (d) of this section, the receiver, subject to the Court's approval, may assume or reject any executory contract or unexpired lease of the insurer.

(b) (1) If there has been a default in an executory contract or unexpired lease of the insurer, the receiver may not assume such contract or lease unless, at the time of assumption of such contract or lease, the receiver:

a. Cures, or provides adequate assurance that the receiver will promptly cure, such default;

b. Compensates, or provides adequate assurance that the receiver will promptly compensate, a party, other than the insurer to such contract or lease, for any actual pecuniary loss to such party resulting from such default; and

c. Provides adequate assurance of future performance under such contract or lease.

(2) Subdivision (1) of this subsection does not apply to a default that is a breach of a provision relating to;

a. The insolvency or financial condition of the insurer at any time before the closing of the case;

b. The commencement of a proceeding under this Article; or

c. The appointment of or taking possession by a receiver in a proceeding under this Article or a custodian before such commencement.

(3) Notwithstanding any other provision of this section, if there has been a default in an unexpired lease of the insurer, other than a default of a kind specified in subdivision (2) of this subsection, the receiver may not require a lessor to provide services or supplies incidental to such lease before assumption of such lease unless the lessor is compensated under the terms of such lease for any services and supplies provided under such lease before assumption of such lease.

(c) The receiver may not assume or assign an executory contract or unexpired lease of the insurer, whether or not such contract or lease prohibits or restricts assignment of rights or delegation of duties, if:

(1) a. Applicable law excuses a party, other than the insurer, to such contract or lease from accepting performance from or rendering performance to the receiver or an assignee of such contract or lease, whether or not such contract or lease prohibits or restricts assignment of rights or delegation of duties; and

b. Such party does not consent to such assumption or assignment; or

(2) Such contract is a contract to make a loan, or extend other debt financing or financial accommodations, to or for the benefit of the insurer, or to issue a security of the insurer.

(d) (1) In a proceeding under G.S. 58-30-105, if the receiver does not assume or reject an executory contract or unexpired lease of the insurer within 60 days after the order for liquidation, or within such additional time as the

Court, for cause, within such 60-day period, fixes, then such contract or lease is deemed to be rejected.

(2) In a proceeding under G.S. 58-30-80 the receiver may assume or reject an executory contract or unexpired lease of the insurer at any time before the order for a plan of rehabilitation, but the Court, on request of any party to such contract or lease, may order the receiver to determine within a specified period of time whether to assume or reject such contract or lease.

(e) (1) Notwithstanding a provision in an executory contract or unexpired lease, or in applicable law, an executory contract or unexpired lease of the insurer may not be terminated or modified, and any right or obligation under such contract or lease may not be terminated or modified, at any time after the commencement of the proceeding solely because of a provision in such contract or lease that is conditioned on:

a. The insolvency or financial condition of the insurer at any time before the closing of the proceeding;

b. The commencement of a proceeding under this Article; or

c. The appointment of or taking possession by a receiver in a proceeding under this Article or a custodian before such commencement.

(2) Subdivision (1) of this subsection does not apply to an executory contract or unexpired lease of the insurer, whether or not such contract or lease prohibits or restricts assignment of rights or delegation of duties, if:

a. Applicable law excused a party, other than the insurer, to such contract or lease from accepting performance from or rendering performance to the receiver or to an assignee of such contract or lease, whether or not such contract or lease prohibits or restricts assignment of rights or delegation of duties and such party does not consent to such assumption or assignment; or

b. Such contract is a contract to make a loan, or extend other debt financing or financial accommodations, to or for the benefit of the insurer, or to issue a security of the insurer.

(f) (1) Except as provided in subsection (c) of this section, notwithstanding a provision in an executory contract or unexpired lease of the insurer, or in applicable law, that prohibits, restricts, or conditions the assignment of such contract or lease, the receiver may assign such contract or lease under subdivision (2) of this subsection.

(2)   The receiver may assign an executory contract or unexpired lease of the insurer only if:

a.   The receiver assumes such contract or lease in accordance with the provisions of this section; and

b.   Adequate assurance of future performance by the assignee of such contract or lease is provided, whether or not there has been a default in such contract or lease.

(3)   Notwithstanding a provision in an executory contract or unexpired lease of the insurer, or in applicable law that terminates or modifies, or permits a party other than the insurer to terminate or modify, such contract or lease or a right or obligation under such contract or lease on account of an assignment of such contract or lease, such contract, lease, right, or obligation may not be terminated or modified under such provision because of the assumption or assignment of such contract or lease by the receiver.

(g)   Except as provided in subdivisions (h)(2) and (i)(2) of this section, the rejection of an executory contract or unexpired lease of the insurer constitutes a breach of such contract or lease:

(1)   If such contract or lease has not been assumed under this section or under a plan of rehabilitation under G.S. 58-30-80, immediately before the date of the filing of the petition; or

(2)   If such contract or lease has been assumed under this section or under a plan of rehabilitation under G.S. 58-30-80:

a.   If before such rejection the proceeding has not been converted to a proceeding under G.S. 58-30-105 at the time of such rejection; or

b.   If before such rejection the case has been converted to a proceeding under G.S. 58-30-105: (i) immediately before the date of such conversion, if such contract or lease was assumed before such conversion; or (ii) at the time of such rejection, if such contract or lease was assumed after such conversion.

(h) (1) If the receiver rejects an unexpired lease of real property of the insurer under which the insurer is the lessor, the lessee under such lease may treat the lease as terminated by such rejection, or, in the alternative, may remain in possession for the balance of the term of such lease and any renewal or extension of such term that is enforceable by such lessee under applicable provision of law outside of this Article.

(2) If such lessee remains in possession, such lessee may offset against the rent reserved under such lease for the balance of the term after the date of the rejection of such lease, and any such renewal or extension, any damages occurring after such date caused by the nonperformance of any obligation of the insurer after such date, but such lessee does not have any rights against the estate on account of any damages arising after such date from such rejection, other than such offset.

(i) (1) If the receiver rejects an executory contract of the insurer for the sale of real property under which the purchaser is in possession, such purchaser may treat such contract as terminated, or, in the alternative, may remain in possession of such real property.

(2) If such purchaser remains in possession:

a. Such purchaser shall continue to make all payments due under such contract but may offset against such payments any damages occurring after the date of the rejection of such contract caused by the nonperformance of any obligation of the insurer after such date, but such purchaser does not have any rights against the estate on account of any damages arising after such date from such rejection, other than such offset; and

b. The receiver shall deliver title to such purchaser in accordance with the provisions of such contract, but is relieved of all other obligations to perform under such contract.

(j) A purchaser that treats an executory contract as terminated under subsection (i) of this section, or a party whose executory contract to purchase real property from the insurer is rejected and under which such party is not in possession, has a lien on the interest of the insurer in such property for the recovery of any portion of the purchase price that such purchaser or party has paid.

(k) Assignment by the receiver to a person of a contract or lease assumed under this section relieves the receiver and the estate from any liability for any breach of such contract or lease occurring after such assignment. (1989, c. 452, s. 1.)

§ 58-30-40. Turnover of property by a custodian.

(a) As used in this section "custodian" means:

(1) A receiver or trustee of any of the property of the insurer, appointed in a case or proceeding not under this Article;

(2) An assignee under a general assignment for the benefit of the insurer's creditors; or

(3) A trustee, receiver, or agent under applicable law, or under a contract, that is appointed or authorized to take charge of property of the insurer for the purpose of enforcing a lien against such property, or for the purpose of general administration of such property for the benefit of the insurer's creditors.

(b) A custodian with knowledge of the commencement of a proceeding under this Article may not make any disbursement from, or take any action in the administration of property of the insurer, proceeds of such property, or property of the estate, in the possession, custody, or control of such custodian, except such action as is necessary to preserve such property.

(c) A custodian shall:

(1) Deliver to the receiver any property of the insurer transferred to such custodian, or proceeds of such property, that is in such custodian's possession, custody, or control on the date that such custodian acquires knowledge of the commencement of the proceeding; and

(2) File an accounting of any property of the insurer, or proceeds of such property, that, at any time, came into the possession, custody, or control of such custodian.

(d) The Court, after notice and a hearing, shall:

(1) Protect all entities to which a custodian has become obligated with respect to such property;

(2) Provide for the payment of reasonable compensation for services rendered and costs and expenses incurred by such custodian; and

(3) Surcharge such custodian, other than an assignee for the benefit of the insurer's creditors that was appointed or took possession more than 120 days before the date of the filing of the petition, for any improper excessive disbursement, other than a disbursement that has been made in accordance with applicable law or approved, after notice and a hearing, by a court of competent jurisdiction before the commencement of the proceeding under this Article.

(e) The Court may, after notice and a hearing, excuse compliance with subsection (a), (b), or (c) of this section, if the interests of policyholders, creditors, and any equity security holders would be better served by permitting a custodian to continue in possession, custody, or control of such property. (1989, c. 452, s. 1.)

§ 58-30-45. Utility service.

(a) Except as provided in subsection (b) of this section, a utility may not alter, refuse, or discontinue service to, or discriminate against, the receiver or the insurer solely on the basis that a debt owed by the insurer to such utility for service rendered before an order of rehabilitation or liquidation was not paid when due.

(b) Such utility may alter, refuse, or discontinue service if neither the receiver nor the insurer, within 20 days after the date of an order of rehabilitation or liquidation, furnishes adequate assurance of payment, in the form of a deposit or other security, for services after such date. On request of a party in interest and after notice and a hearing, the Court may order reasonable modification of the amount of the deposit or other security necessary to provide adequate assurance of payment. (1989, c. 452, s. 1.)

§ 58-30-50. Continuation of delinquency proceedings.

Every proceeding that was commenced under the laws in effect before June 26, 1989, is deemed to have been commenced under this Article for the purpose of conducting the proceeding; except that in the discretion of the Commissioner the proceeding may be continued, in whole or in part, as it would have been continued had this Article not been enacted. (1989, c. 452, s. 1.)

§ 58-30-55. Condition on release from delinquency proceedings.

No insurer that is subject to any delinquency proceedings, whether formal or informal, administrative or judicial, shall:

(1) Be released from such proceeding, unless such proceeding is converted into a judicial rehabilitation or liquidation proceeding;

(2) Be permitted to solicit or accept new business or request or accept the restoration of any suspended or revoked license;

(3) Be returned to the control of its shareholders or private management; or

(4) Have any of its assets returned to the control of its shareholders or private management;

until all payments of or on account of the insurer's contractual obligations by all guaranty associations, along with all expenses thereof and interest on all such payments and expenses, have been repaid to the guaranty associations or a plan of repayment by the insurer shall have been approved by the guaranty associations. (1989, c. 452, s. 1; 1999-132, s. 9.1; 2000-140, s. 14.)

§ 58-30-60. Commissioner's summary orders and supervision proceedings.

(a) Whenever the Commissioner has reasonable cause to believe, and determines after a hearing held under subsection (e) of this section, that any domestic insurer has committed or is engaged in, or is about to commit or engage in, any act, practice, or transaction that would subject it to delinquency proceedings under this Article, he may make and serve upon the insurer and any other persons involved, such orders as are reasonably necessary to correct, eliminate, or remedy such conduct, condition, or ground.

(b) The Commissioner may consider any or all of the following standards to determine whether the continued operation of any licensed insurer is hazardous to its policyholders, creditors, or the general public:

(1) Adverse findings reported in financial condition and market conduct examination reports, audit reports, and actuarial opinions, reports, or summaries;

(2) The NAIC Insurance Regulatory Information System and its other financial analysis solvency tools and reports;

(3) Repealed by Session Laws 2013-199, s. 6, effective July 1, 2013.

(4) Whether the insurer has made adequate provision, according to presently accepted actuarial standards of practice, for the anticipated cash flows required by the contractual obligations and related expenses of the insurer, when considered in light of the assets held by the insurer with respect to such reserves and related actuarial items, including, but not limited to, the investment earnings on such assets, and the considerations anticipated to be received and retained under such policies and contracts;

(5) The ability of an assuming reinsurer to perform and whether the insurer's reinsurance program provides sufficient protection for the insurer's remaining surplus, after taking into account the insurer's cash flow and the classes of business written as well as the financial condition of the assuming reinsurer;

(6) Whether an insurer's operating loss in the last 12-month period or any shorter period of time, including, but not limited to, net capital gain or loss, changes in nonadmitted assets, and cash dividends paid to shareholders, is greater than fifty percent (50%) of the insurer's remaining policyholders' surplus in excess of the minimum required;

(6a) Whether the insurer's operating loss in the last 12-month period or any shorter period of time, excluding net capital gains, is greater than twenty percent (20%) of the insurer's remaining policyholders' surplus in excess of the minimum required;

(7) Whether a reinsurer, obligor, or any entity within the insurer's insurance holding company system is insolvent, threatened with insolvency, or delinquent in payment of its monetary or any other obligation and which in the opinion of the Commissioner may affect the solvency of the insurer;

(8) Contingent liabilities, pledges, or guaranties that either individually or collectively involve a total amount that in the Commissioner's opinion may affect an insurer's solvency;

(9) Whether any controlling person of an insurer is delinquent in the transmitting to or payment of net premiums to the insurer;

(10) The age and collectibility of receivables;

(11) Whether the management of an insurer, including officers, directors, or any other person who directly or indirectly controls the operation of the insurer, fails to possess and demonstrate the competence, fitness, or reputation considered by the Commissioner to be necessary to serve the insurer in that position;

(12) Whether the management of an insurer has failed to respond to the Commissioner's inquiries about the condition of the insurer or has furnished false and misleading information in response to an inquiry by the Commissioner;

(12a) Whether the insurer has failed to meet financial and holding company filing requirements in the absence of a reason satisfactory to the Commissioner;

(13) Whether the management of an insurer has filed any false or misleading sworn financial statement, has released a false or misleading financial statement to a lending institution or to the general public, or has made a false or misleading entry or omitted an entry of material amount in the insurer's books;

(14) Whether the insurer has grown so rapidly and to such an extent that it lacks adequate financial and administrative capacity to meet its obligations in a timely manner;

(15) Whether the insurer has experienced or will experience in the foreseeable future cash flow or liquidity problems;

(16)   Whether management has established reserves that do not comply with minimum standards established by State insurance laws, regulations, statutory accounting standards, sound actuarial principles, and standards of practice;

(17)   Whether management persistently engages in material under reserving that results in adverse development;

(18)   Whether transactions among affiliates, subsidiaries, or controlling persons for which the insurer receives assets or capital gains, or both, do not provide sufficient value, liquidity, or diversity to assure the insurer's ability to meet its outstanding obligations as they mature; or

(19)   Any other finding determined by the Commissioner to be hazardous to the insurer's policyholders, creditors, or general public.

To determine an insurer's financial condition under this Article, the Commissioner may: disregard any credit or amount receivable resulting from transactions with a reinsurer that is insolvent, impaired, or otherwise subject to a delinquency proceeding; make appropriate adjustments to asset values attributable to investments in or transactions with parents, subsidiaries, or affiliates of an insurer; refuse to recognize the stated value of accounts receivable if the insurer's ability to collect receivables is highly speculative in view of the age of the account or the financial condition of the debtor; or increase the insurer's liability in an amount equal to any contingent liability, pledge, or guarantee not otherwise included if there is a substantial risk that the insurer will be called upon to meet the obligation undertaken within the next 12-month period.

If upon examination or at any other time the Commissioner has reasonable cause to believe that any domestic insurer is in such condition as to render the continuance of its business hazardous to the public or to holders of its policies or certificates of insurance, or if the domestic insurer gives its consent, then the Commissioner shall upon the Commissioner's determination:

(1)   Issue an order notifying the insurer of that determination; and

(2)   Furnish to the insurer a written list of the Commissioner's requirements to abate that determination that may include any of the following:

a.   A reduction in the total amount of present and potential liability for policy benefits by reinsurance.

b. A reduction, suspension, or limitation of the volume of insurance being accepted or renewed.

c. A reduction in general insurance and commission expenses by specified methods.

d. An increase in the insurer's capital and surplus.

e. A suspension or limitation in the insurer's declaration and payment of dividends to its stockholders or policyholders.

f. The filing of reports in a form acceptable to the Commissioner concerning the market value of its assets.

g. A limitation or withdrawal from certain investments or the discontinuance of certain investment practices to the extent the Commissioner considers necessary.

h. Documentation of the adequacy of premium rates in relation to the risks insured.

i. The filing, in addition to regular annual financial statements, of interim financial reports on the form adopted by the NAIC or on such format prescribed by the Commissioner.

j. The correction of corporate governance practice deficiencies.

k. The adoption and utilization of governance practices acceptable to the Commissioner.

l. The provision of a business plan to the Commissioner in order to continue to transact business in the State.

Notwithstanding any other provision of law limiting the frequency or amount of premium rate adjustments, the Commissioner may adjust rates for any nonlife insurance product written by the insurer that the Commissioner considers necessary to improve the financial condition of the insurer.

(c) If the Commissioner makes a determination to supervise an insurer subject to an order under subsections (a) or (b) of this section, he shall notify the insurer that it is under the supervision of the Commissioner. During the period of supervision, the Commissioner may appoint a supervisor to supervise such insurer. The order appointing a supervisor shall direct the supervisor to enforce orders issued under subsections (a) and (b) of this section and may also require that the insurer may not do any of the following things during the period of supervision, without the prior approval of the Commissioner or his supervisor:

(1)   Dispose of, convey, or encumber any of its assets or its business in force;

(2)   Withdraw from any of its bank accounts;

(3)   Lend any of its funds;

(4)   Invest any of its funds;

(5)   Transfer any of its property;

(6)   Incur any debt, obligation, or liability;

(7)   Merge or consolidate with another company; or

(8)   Enter into any new reinsurance contract or treaty.

(d)   Any insurer subject to an order under this section shall comply with the lawful requirements of the Commissioner and, if placed under supervision, shall comply with the requirements of the Commissioner within such period of time established by the Commissioner. The Commissioner may in his discretion extend the time for compliance beyond such period of time for cause. In the event of such insurer's failure to comply within such period of time, the Commissioner may institute proceedings under this Article to have a rehabilitator or liquidator appointed, or extend the period of supervision.

(e)   The notice of hearing under subsection (a) of this section and any order issued pursuant to that subsection shall be served upon the insurer pursuant to the applicable rules of civil procedure. The notice of hearing shall state the time and place of hearing, and the conduct, condition, or ground upon which the Commissioner would base his order. Unless mutually agreed upon between the Commissioner and the insurer, the hearing shall occur not less than 10 days nor more than 30 days after notice is served and shall be either in Wake County or in some other place designated by the Commissioner. The Commissioner shall hold all hearings under subsection (a) of this section privately unless the insurer requests a public hearing, in which case the hearing shall be public.

(f)   Any insurer subject to an order under subsection (b) of this section may request an administrative hearing before the Commissioner or his designee to review that order. Such hearing shall be held as provided in subsection (e) of this section, but the request for a hearing shall not stay the effect of the order. If the Commissioner issues an order under subsection (b) of this section, the insurer may, at any time, waive the hearing and apply for immediate judicial relief by means of any remedy afforded by law without first exhausting its administrative remedies. Subsequent to an administrative hearing, any party to the proceedings whose interests are substantially affected is entitled to judicial review of any order issued by the Commissioner.

(g)   During the period of supervision the insurer may request the Commissioner to review any action taken or proposed to be taken by the supervisor, specifying wherein the action complained of is believed not to be in the best interest of the insurer.

(h)   If any person violates any supervision order issued under this section that as to him is then still in effect, he shall be liable to pay a civil penalty imposed by the Court not to exceed ten thousand dollars ($10,000). The clear proceeds of civil penalties imposed pursuant to this subsection shall be remitted to the Civil Penalty and Forfeiture Fund in accordance with G.S. 115C-457.2.

(i)   The Commissioner may apply for, and any court of general jurisdiction may grant, such restraining orders, preliminary and permanent injunctions, and other orders as may be deemed to be necessary and proper to enforce a supervision order.

(j)   In the event that any person subject to the provisions of this Article, including any person described in G.S. 58-30-25(a), knowingly and willfully violates any valid order of the Commissioner issued under the provisions of this section and, as a result of such violation, the net worth of the insurer is reduced or the insurer suffers loss that it would not otherwise have suffered, said person shall become personally liable to the insurer for the amount of any such reduction or loss. The Commissioner or supervisor is authorized to bring an action on behalf of the insurer in the Court to recover the amount of the reduction or loss together with any costs. (1989, c. 452, s. 1; 1989 (Reg. Sess., 1990), c. 1021, s. 6; 1991, c. 681, s. 43; 1998-215, s. 86; 2013-199, s. 6.)

§ 58-30-62. Administrative supervision of insurers.

(a)   As used in this section, an insurer has "exceeded its powers" when it: has refused to permit examination of its books, papers, accounts, records or affairs by the Commissioner; has in violation of G.S. 58-7-50 removed from this State books, papers, accounts or records necessary for an examination of the insurer; has failed to comply promptly with applicable financial reporting statutes or rules and related Department requests; continues to transact the business of insurance after its license has been revoked or suspended by the Commissioner; by contract or otherwise, has unlawfully, or has in violation of an order of the Commissioner, or has without first having obtained any legally required written approval of the Commissioner, totally reinsured its entire outstanding business or merged or consolidated substantially its entire property or business with another insurer; has engaged in any transaction in which it is not authorized to engage under the laws of this State; has not complied with G.S. 58-7-73; or has refused to comply with a lawful order of the Commissioner. As used in this section, "Commissioner" includes an authorized representative or designee of the Commissioner.

(b)   This section applies to all domestic insurers and any other insurer doing business in this State whose state of domicile has asked the Commissioner to apply the provisions of this section to that insurer.

(c)   An insurer may be subject to administrative supervision by the Commissioner if upon examination or at any other time it appears to the Commissioner that the insurer: has exceeded its powers; has failed to comply with applicable provisions of this Chapter; is conducting its business in a manner that is hazardous to the public or to its insureds; or consents to administrative supervision.

(d)   If the Commissioner determines that the conditions set forth in subsection (c) of this section exist, the Commissioner shall: notify the insurer of that determination; furnish to the insurer a written list of the requirements to abate those conditions; and notify the insurer that it is under the supervision of the Commissioner and that the Commissioner is applying and effectuating the provisions of this section.

(e) If placed under administrative supervision, the insurer shall have 60 days, or a different period of time determined by the Commissioner, to comply with the requirements of the Commissioner under this section. If the Commissioner determines after notice and hearing that the conditions giving rise to the supervision still exist at the end of the supervision period specified in this subsection, the Commissioner may extend the period; or if the Commissioner determines that none of the conditions giving rise to the supervision exist, the Commissioner shall release the insurer from supervision.

(f) Notwithstanding any other provision of law and except as set forth in this section, all proceedings, hearings, notices, correspondence, reports, records, and other information in the possession of the Commissioner or the Department relating to the supervision of any insurer are confidential. The Department shall have access to such proceedings, hearings, notices, correspondence, reports, records, or other information as permitted by the Commissioner. The Commissioner may open the proceedings or hearings, or disclose the notices, correspondence, reports, records, or information to a department, agency or instrumentality of this or another state of the United States if the Commissioner determines that the disclosure is necessary or proper for the enforcement of the laws of this or another state of the United States. The Commissioner may open the proceedings or hearings or make public the notices, correspondence, reports, records, or other information if the Commissioner considers that it is in the best interest of the insurer, its insureds or creditors, or the general public. This section does not apply to hearings, notices, correspondence, reports, records, or other information obtained upon the appointment of a receiver for the insurer by a court of competent jurisdiction.

(g) During the period of supervision, the Commissioner shall serve as the administrative supervisor. The Commissioner may provide that the insurer shall not do any of the following during the period of supervision, without the Commissioner's prior approval: dispose of, convey, or encumber any of its assets or its business in force; withdraw from any of its bank accounts; lend or invest any of its funds; transfer any of its property; incur any debt, obligation, or liability; merge or consolidate with another company; establish new premiums or renew any policies; enter into any new reinsurance contract or treaty; terminate, surrender, forfeit, convert, or lapse any insurance coverage, except for nonpayment of premiums due; release, pay, or refund premium deposits, accrued cash, or loan values, unearned premiums, or other reserves on any insurance coverage; make any material change in management; increase salaries or benefits of officers or directors or make preferential payment of bonuses, dividends, or other payments considered preferential; or make any other change in its operations that the Commissioner considers to be material.

(h)   During the period of supervision the insurer may contest an action taken or proposed to be taken by the Commissioner, specifying why the action being complained of would not result in improving the insurer's condition.

(i)   This section does not limit powers granted to the Commissioner by any other provision of law. This section does not preclude the Commissioner from initiating judicial proceedings to place an insurer in a delinquency proceeding under this Article, regardless of whether the Commissioner has previously initiated administrative supervision proceedings under this section or under G.S. 58-30-60 against the insurer. The determination as to actions under this section is in the Commissioner's discretion.

(j)   Notwithstanding any other provision of law, the Commissioner may meet with a supervisor appointed under this section and with the attorney or other representative of the supervisor, without the presence of any other person, at the time of any proceeding or during the pendency of any proceeding held under the authority of this section, to carry out the Commissioner's duties under this section or for the supervisor to carry out the supervisor's duties under this section.

(k)   There is no liability by, and no cause of action of any nature arises against, the Commissioner for any acts or omissions by the Commissioner in the performance of the Commissioner's powers and duties under this section. (1991, c. 681, s. 44; 2002-187, s. 2.10; 2003-212, s. 26(i).)

§ 58-30-65. Court's seizure order.

(a)   The Commissioner may file in the Court a petition alleging, with respect to a domestic insurer:

(1)   That there exist grounds that justify a judicial order for a formal delinquency proceeding against an insurer under this Article;

(2)   That the interests of policyholders, creditors, or the public will be endangered by delay; and

(3) The contents of an order deemed by the Commissioner to be necessary.

(b) Upon a filing under subsection (a) of this section, the Court may issue forthwith, ex parte, the requested order, that directs the Commissioner to take possession and control of all or a part of the property, books, accounts, documents, and other records of an insurer, and of the premises occupied by it for transaction of its business, and that, until further order of the Court, enjoins the insurer and its officers, managers, agents, and employees from disposing of its property and from transacting its business except with the written consent of the Commissioner.

(c) The Court shall specify in the order what its duration shall be, which shall be such time as the Court considers necessary for the Commissioner to ascertain the condition of the insurer. On motion of either party or on its own motion, the Court may from time to time hold such hearings as it considers desirable after such notice as it considers appropriate; and may extend, shorten, or modify the terms of the seizure order. The Court shall vacate the seizure order if the Commissioner fails to commence a formal proceeding under this Article after having a reasonable opportunity to do so. An order of the Court pursuant to a formal proceeding under this Article shall ipso facto vacate the seizure order.

(d) Entry of a seizure order under this section does not constitute an anticipatory breach of any contract of the insurer.

(e) An insurer subject to an ex parte order under this section may petition the Court at any time after the issuance of such order for a hearing and review of the order. The Court shall hold such a hearing and review not more than 15 days after the request. A hearing under this subsection may be held privately in chambers, and it shall be so held if the insurer proceeded against so requests.

(f) If, at any time after the issuance of such an order, it appears to the Court that any person whose interest is or will be substantially affected by the order did not appear at the hearing and has not been served, the Court may order that notice be given. An order that notice be given does not stay the effect of any order previously issued by the Court. (1989, c. 452, s. 1.)

§ 58-30-70. Confidentiality of hearings.

In all proceedings and judicial reviews thereof under G.S. 58-30-60 and G.S. 58-30-65, all records of the insurer, other documents, and all Department files and Court records and papers, insofar as they pertain to or are a part of the record of the proceedings, shall be and remain confidential except as is necessary to obtain compliance therewith, unless the Court, after hearing arguments from the parties in chambers, orders otherwise; or unless the insurer requests that the matter be made public. Until such Court order, all papers filed with the clerk of the Court shall be held by him in a confidential file. (1989, c. 452, s. 1.)

§ 58-30-71. Immunity and indemnification of the receiver and employees.

(a) For the purposes of this section, the persons entitled to protection under this section are:

(1) All receivers responsible for the conduct of a delinquency proceeding under this Article, including present and former receivers; and

(2) Their employees meaning all present and former special deputies and assistant special deputies appointed by the Commissioner, staff assigned to the delinquency proceeding employed by the Attorney General's Office, and all persons whom the Commissioner, special deputies, or assistant special deputies have employed to assist in a delinquency proceeding under this Article. Attorneys, accountants, auditors, and other professional persons or firms, who are retained by the receiver as independent contractors and their employees are not employees of the receiver for purposes of this section.

(b) The receiver and his employees have official immunity and are immune from suit and liability, both personally and in their official capacities, for any claim for damage to or loss of property or personal injury or other civil liability caused by or resulting from any alleged act, error, or omission of the receiver or any employee arising out of or by reason of their duties or employment; provided that nothing in this section holds the receiver or any employee immune from suit or liability for any damage, loss, injury, or liability caused by the intentional or willful and wanton misconduct of the receiver or any employee or for any bodily injury caused by the operation of a motor vehicle.

(c) If any legal action is commenced against the receiver or any employee, whether against him personally or in his official capacity, alleging property damage, property loss, personal injury, or other civil liability caused by or resulting from any alleged act, error, or omission of the receiver or any employee arising out of or by reason of their duties or employment, the receiver and any employee shall be indemnified from the assets of the insurer for all expenses, attorneys' fees, judgments, settlements, decrees, or amounts due and owing or paid in satisfaction of or incurred in the defense of such legal action; unless it is determined upon a final adjudication on the merits that the alleged act, error, or omission of the receiver or employee giving rise to the claim did not arise out of or by reason of his duties or employment, or was caused by intentional or willful and wanton misconduct.

(d)   Attorneys' fees and all related expenses incurred in defending a legal action for which immunity or indemnity is available under this section shall be paid from the assets of the insurer, as they are incurred, before the final disposition of the action, upon receipt of any agreement by or on behalf of the receiver or employee to repay the attorneys' fees and expenses if it is ultimately determined upon a final adjudication on the merits that the receiver or employee is not entitled to immunity or indemnity under this section.

(e)   Any indemnification for expense payments, judgments, settlements, decrees, attorneys' fees, surety bond premiums, or other amounts paid or to be paid from the insurer's assets under this section shall be an administrative expense of the insurer.

(f)   In the event of any actual or threatened litigation against a receiver or any employee for which immunity or indemnity may be available under this section, a reasonable amount of funds, that in the judgment of the Commissioner may be needed to provide immunity or indemnity, shall be segregated and reserved from the assets of the insurer as security for the payment of indemnity until all applicable statutes of limitation have run, all actual or threatened actions against the receiver or any employee have been completely and finally resolved, and all obligations of the insurer and the Commissioner under this section have been satisfied.

(g)   In lieu of segregation and reserving of funds, the Commissioner may, in his discretion, obtain a surety bond or make other arrangements that will enable the Commissioner to fully secure the payment of all obligations under this section.

(h)   If any legal action against an employee for which indemnity may be available under this section is settled before final adjudication on the merits, the insurer must pay the settlement amount on behalf of the employee, or indemnify the employee for the settlement amount, unless the Commissioner determines:

(1) That the claim did not arise out of or by reason of the employee's duties or employment; or

(2) That the claims were caused by the intentional or willful and wanton misconduct of the employee.

(i) In any legal action in which the receiver is a defendant, that portion of any settlement relating to the alleged act, error, or omission of the receiver is subject to the approval of the court before which the delinquency proceeding is pending. The court shall not approve that portion of the settlement if it determines:

(1) That the claim did not arise out of or by reason of the receiver's duties or employment; or

(2) That the claim was caused by the intentional or willful and wanton misconduct of the receiver.

(j) Nothing in this section deprives the receiver or any employee of any immunity, indemnity, benefits of law, rights, or any defense otherwise available.

(k) Subsection (b) of this section applies to any suit based in whole or in part on any alleged act, error, or omission that occurs on or after October 1, 1993.

(l) No legal action shall lie against the receiver or any employee based in whole or in part on any alleged act, error, or omission that occurred before October 1, 1993, unless suit is filed and valid service of process is obtained within 12 months after October 1, 1993.

(m) Subsections (c), (h), and (i) of this section apply to any suit that is pending on or filed after October 1, 1993, without regard to when the alleged act, error, or omission took place. (1993, c. 452, s. 40.)

§ 58-30-75. Grounds for rehabilitation.

The Commissioner may petition the Court for an order authorizing him to rehabilitate a domestic insurer or an alien insurer domiciled in this State on any one or more of the following grounds:

(1)   The insurer is in such condition that the further transaction of business would be hazardous financially to its policyholders, creditors, or the public.

(2)   There is reasonable cause to believe that there has been embezzlement from the insurer, wrongful sequestration or diversion of the insurer's assets, forgery or fraud affecting the insurer, or other illegal conduct in, by, or with respect to the insurer that if established would endanger assets in an amount threatening the solvency of the insurer.

(3)   The insurer has failed to remove any person who in fact has executive authority in the insurer, whether an officer, manager, general agent, employee, or other person; if the person has been found after notice and hearing by the Commissioner to be dishonest or untrustworthy in a way affecting the insurer's business.

(4)   Control of the insurer, whether by stock ownership or otherwise, and whether direct or indirect, is in a person or persons found after notice and hearing to be untrustworthy.

(5)   Any person who in fact has executive authority in the insurer, whether an officer, manager, general agent, director or trustee, employee, or other person, has refused to be examined under oath by the Commissioner concerning its affairs, whether in this State or elsewhere; and after reasonable notice of the fact, the insurer has failed promptly and effectively to terminate the employment and status of the person and all his influence on management.

(6)   After demand by the Commissioner the insurer has failed to promptly make available for examination any of its own property, books, accounts, documents, or other records; those of any subsidiary or related company within the control of the insurer; or those of any person having executive authority in the insurer insofar as they pertain to the insurer.

(7)   Without first obtaining the written consent of the Commissioner, the insurer has (i) transferred, or attempted to transfer, in a manner contrary to Article 19 of this Chapter, substantially its entire property or business, or (ii) has entered into any transaction, the effect of which is to merge, consolidate, or

reinsure substantially its entire property or business in or with the property or business of any other person.

(8) The insurer or its property has been or is the subject of an application for the appointment of a receiver, trustee, custodian, conservator, or sequestrator or similar fiduciary of the insurer or its property otherwise than as authorized under Articles 1 through 64 of this Chapter, and such appointment has been made or is imminent, and such appointment might oust the courts of this State of jurisdiction or might prejudice orderly delinquency proceedings under this Article.

(9) Within the previous four years the insurer has willfully violated its charter or articles of incorporation, its bylaws, Articles 1 through 67 of this Chapter, or any valid order of the Commissioner under G.S. 58-30-60.

(10) The insurer has failed to pay within 60 days after due any obligation to any state or any subdivision thereof or any judgment entered in any state, if the court in which such judgment was entered has jurisdiction over such subject matter; except that such nonpayment is not a ground until 60 days after any good faith effort by the insurer to contest the obligation has been terminated, whether it is before the Commissioner or in the courts, or the insurer has systematically attempted to compromise or renegotiate previously agreed settlements with its creditors on the ground that it is financially unable to pay its obligations in full.

(11) The insurer has failed to file its annual report or any other financial report required by statute within the time allowed by law and, after written demand by the Commissioner, has failed to immediately give an adequate explanation.

(12) The board of directors or the holders of a majority of the shares entitled to vote, or a majority of those individuals entitled to the control of those persons specified in G.S. 58-30-5, request or consent to rehabilitation under this Article. (1989, c. 452, s. 1; c. 770, s. 72.1; 1995, c. 193, s. 31; 2001-223, s. 19.)

§ 58-30-80. Rehabilitation orders.

(a) An order to rehabilitate the business of a domestic insurer or an alien insurer domiciled in this State, shall appoint the Commissioner and his successors in office as the rehabilitator, and shall direct the rehabilitator forthwith to take possession of the assets of the insurer and to administer them under the general supervision of the Court. The filing or recording of the order with the clerk of the Court or register of deeds of the county in which the principal business of the insurer is conducted, or the county in which its principal office or place of business is located, shall impart the same notice as a deed, bill of sale, or other evidence of title duly filed or recorded with that register of deeds would have imparted. The order to rehabilitate the insurer shall by operation of law vest title to all assets of the insurer in the rehabilitator.

(b)   Any order issued under this section shall require accounting to the Court by the rehabilitator. Accountings shall be at such intervals as the Court specifies in its order.

(c)   Entry of an order of rehabilitation shall not constitute an anticipatory breach of any contract of the insurer. (1989, c. 452, s. 1.)

§ 58-30-85. Powers and duties of the rehabilitator.

(a)   The rehabilitator has the power:

(1)   To appoint a special deputy to act for him under this Article, and to determine his reasonable compensation. The special deputy has all powers of the rehabilitator granted by this section. The special deputy serves at the pleasure of the rehabilitator.

(2)   To employ employees and agents, legal counsel, actuaries, accountants, appraisers, consultants, and such other personnel as he may deem to be necessary to assist in the rehabilitation.

(3)   To fix the reasonable compensation of employees and agents, legal counsel, actuaries, accountants, appraisers, and consultants, with the approval of the Court.

(4)   To pay reasonable compensation to persons appointed; and to defray from the funds or assets of the insurer all expenses of taking possession of, conserving, conducting, rehabilitating, disposing of, or otherwise dealing with the business and property of the insurer.

(5)   To hold hearings, to subpoena witnesses to compel their attendance, to administer oaths, to examine any person under oath, and to compel any person

to subscribe to this testimony after it has been correctly reduced to writing; and in connection therewith to require the production of any books, papers, records, or other documents that he considers relevant to the inquiry.

(6) To collect all debts and moneys due and claims belonging to the insurer, wherever located, and for this purpose:

a. To institute timely action in other jurisdictions, in order to forestall garnishment and attachment proceedings against such debts;

b. To do such other acts that are necessary or expedient to collect, conserve, or protect its assets or property, including the power to sell, compound, compromise, or assign debts for purposes of collection upon such terms and conditions as he deems to be best; and

c. To pursue any creditor's remedies available to enforce his claims.

(7) To conduct public and private sales of the property of the insurer.

(8) To use assets of the estate of an insurer under a rehabilitation order to transfer policy obligations to a solvent assuming insurer, if the transfer can be arranged without prejudice to applicable priorities under G.S. 58-30-220.

(9) To acquire, hypothecate, encumber, lease, improve, sell, transfer, abandon, or otherwise dispose of or deal with, any property of the insurer at its market value or upon such terms and conditions that are fair and reasonable. He also has the power to execute, acknowledge, and deliver any and all deeds, assignments, releases and other instruments necessary or proper to effectuate any sale of property or other transaction in connection with the rehabilitation.

(10) To borrow money on the security of the insurer's assets or without security and to execute and deliver all documents necessary to that transaction for the purpose of facilitating the rehabilitation.

(11) To enter into such contracts that are necessary to carry out the order to rehabilitate, and to affirm or disavow any contracts to which the insurer is a party.

(12) To continue to prosecute and to institute in the name of the insurer or in his own name any and all suits and other legal proceedings, in this State or

elsewhere, and to abandon the prosecution of claims he deems unprofitable to pursue further.

(13) To prosecute any action that may exist in behalf of the creditors, members, policyholders, or shareholders of the insurer against any officer of the insurer or against any other person.

(14) To remove any or all records and property of the insurer to the offices of the Commissioner or to such other place as may be convenient for the purposes of efficient and orderly execution of the rehabilitation.

(15) To deposit in one or more banks in this State such sums as are required for meeting current administration expenses and dividend distributions.

(16) To invest all sums not currently needed, unless the Court orders otherwise.

(17) To file any necessary documents for recording in the office of any register of deeds in this State or elsewhere where property of the insurer is located.

(18) To assert all defenses available to the insurer as against third persons, including statutes of limitation, statutes of frauds, and the defense of usury. A waiver of any defense by the insurer after a petition in rehabilitation has been filed shall not bind the rehabilitator.

(19) To exercise and enforce all rights, remedies, and powers of any creditor, shareholder, policyholder, or member; including any power to avoid any transfer or lien that may be given by law and that is not included within G.S. 58-30-140 through 58-30-150.

(20) To intervene in any proceeding wherever instituted that might lead to the appointment of a receiver or trustee, and to act as the receiver or trustee whenever the appointment is offered.

(21) To enter into agreements with any receiver or insurance regulator of any other state relating to the rehabilitation, liquidation, conservation, or dissolution of an insurer doing business in both states.

(22) To exercise all powers now held or subsequently conferred upon receivers by laws of this State not inconsistent with the provisions of this Article.

(b) The enumeration in this section of the powers and authority of the rehabilitator shall not be construed as a limitation upon him, nor shall it exclude in any manner his right to do such other acts not specifically enumerated in this section or otherwise provided for, as may be necessary or appropriate for the accomplishment of or in aid of the purpose of rehabilitation.

(c) The rehabilitator may take such action as he considers necessary or appropriate to reform and revitalize the insurer. He shall have all the powers of the directors, officers, and managers, whose authority shall be suspended, except to the extent they may be redelegated by the rehabilitator. He shall have full power to direct, manage, hire, and discharge employees, subject to any contract rights they may have, and to deal with the property and business of the insurer.

(d) If it appears to the rehabilitator that there has been criminal or tortious conduct, or breach of any contractual or fiduciary obligation detrimental to the insurer by any officer, manager, agent, broker, employee or other person, he may pursue all available legal remedies on behalf of the insurer.

(e) If the rehabilitator determines that reorganization, consolidation, conversion, reinsurance, merger, runoff, or other transformation of the insurer is appropriate, he shall prepare a plan to effect such changes. Upon application of the rehabilitator for approval of the plan, and after such notice and hearings as the Court may prescribe, the Court may either approve or disapprove the plan proposed, or may modify it and approve it as modified. Any plan approved under this section shall be, in the opinion of the Court, fair and equitable to all parties concerned. If the plan is approved, the rehabilitator shall carry out the plan. In the case of a life insurer, the plan proposed may include the imposition of liens upon the policies of the insurer, if all rights of shareholders are first relinquished. A plan for a life insurer may also propose imposition of a moratorium upon loan and cash surrender rights under policies, for such period and to such an extent as may be necessary.

(f) The rehabilitator shall have the power under G.S. 58-30-140 and G.S. 58-30-145 to avoid fraudulent transfers. (1989, c. 452, s. 1; 2009-172, s. 2.)

§ 58-30-90. Actions by and against rehabilitator.

(a) When a rehabilitation order against an insurer is entered, every court in this State, before which any pending action or proceeding in which the insurer is a party or is obligated to defend a party, shall stay the action or proceeding for 120 days and such additional time that is necessary for the rehabilitator to obtain proper representation and prepare for further proceedings. The rehabilitator may take such action respecting pending litigation as he deems necessary in the interests of justice and for the protection of creditors, policyholders, and the public. The rehabilitator may immediately consider all litigation pending outside this State and may petition the courts having jurisdiction over that litigation for stays whenever necessary to protect the estate of the insurer.

(b) No statute of limitations or defense of laches shall run with respect to any action by or against an insurer between the filing of a petition for appointment of a rehabilitator for that insurer and the order granting or denying that petition.

(c) Any domestic or foreign guaranty association has standing to appear in any Court proceeding concerning the rehabilitation of an insurer if such association is or may become liable to act as a result of the rehabilitation. (1989, c. 452, s. 1.)

§ 58-30-95. Termination of rehabilitation.

(a) Whenever the rehabilitator believes further attempts to rehabilitate an insurer would substantially increase the risk of loss to creditors, policyholders or the public, or would be futile, the rehabilitator may petition the Court for an order of liquidation. A petition under this subsection shall have the same effect as a petition under G.S. 58-30-100. The Court may make such findings and issue such orders at any time upon its own motion. The Court shall permit the directors of the insurer to take such actions as are reasonably necessary to defend against the petition and may order payment from the estate of the insurer of such costs and other expenses of defense as justice may require. The court may allow the payment of costs and expenses incurred in defending against the petition for an order of liquidation only upon a specific finding that the defense was conducted, and the costs and expenses were incurred, in good faith. The directors shall have the burden of proving good faith. Evidence of good faith shall be the existence of a reasonable basis to conclude that the insurer is actually solvent or that there exists a viable means to accomplish rehabilitation without jeopardizing the remaining assets of the insurer and that continued operation of the insurer is in the best interest of the policyholders, stockholders, and creditors.

(b) The rehabilitator may at any time petition the Court for an order terminating rehabilitation of an insurer. The Court shall also permit the directors of the insurer to petition the Court for an order terminating rehabilitation of the insurer and may order payment from the estate of the insurer of such costs and other expenses of such petition as justice may require. The court may allow the payment of costs and expenses incurred in defending against the petition for an order terminating rehabilitation only upon a specific finding that the defense was conducted, and the costs and expenses were incurred, in good faith. The directors shall have the burden of proving good faith. Evidence of good faith shall be the existence of a reasonable basis to conclude that the insurer is actually solvent or that there exists a viable means to accomplish rehabilitation without jeopardizing the remaining assets of the insurer and that continued operation of the insurer is in the best interest of the policyholders, stockholders, and creditors. If the Court finds that rehabilitation has been accomplished and that grounds for rehabilitation under G.S. 58-30-75 no longer exist, it shall order that the insurer be restored to possession of its property and the control of the business. The Court may also make that finding and issue that order at any time upon its own motion. (1989, c. 452, s. 1; 1993, c. 452, s. 41.)

§ 58-30-100. Grounds for liquidation.

The Commissioner may petition the Court for an order directing him to liquidate a domestic insurer or an alien insurer domiciled in this State on the basis:

(1) Of any ground for an order of rehabilitation as specified in G.S. 58-30-75, whether or not there has been a prior order directing the rehabilitation of the insurer;

(2) That the insurer is insolvent; or

(3) That the insurer is in such condition that the further transaction of business would be hazardous, financially or otherwise, to its policyholders, its creditors, or the public. (1989, c. 452, s. 1.)

§ 58-30-105. Liquidation orders.

(a) An order to liquidate the business of a domestic insurer shall appoint the Commissioner and his successors in office liquidator and shall direct the liquidator forthwith to take possession of the assets of the insurer and to administer them under the general supervision of the Court. The liquidator is vested by operation of law with the title to all of the property, contracts, and rights of action, and all of the books and records of the insurer ordered liquidated, wherever located, as of the entry of the final order of liquidation. The filing or recording of the order with the clerk of the superior court and the register of deeds of the county in which its principal office or place of business is located; or, in the case of real estate, with the register of deeds of the county where the property is located, shall impart the same notice as a deed, bill of sale, or other evidence of title duly filed or recorded with that register of deeds would have imparted.

(b) Upon issuance of the order, the rights and liabilities of any such insurer and of its creditors, policyholders, shareholders, members and all other persons interested in its estate shall become fixed as of the date of entry of the order of liquidation, except as provided in G.S. 58-30-110 and G.S. 58-30-195.

(c) An order to liquidate the business of an alien insurer domiciled in this State shall be in the same terms and have the same legal effect as an order to liquidate a domestic insurer; except that the assets and the business in the United States shall be the only assets and business included therein.

(d) At the time of petitioning for an order of liquidation or at any time thereafter the Commissioner, after making appropriate findings of an insurer's insolvency, may petition the Court for a judicial declaration of such insolvency. After providing such notice and hearing as it deems to be proper, the Court may make the declaration.

(e) Any order issued under this section requires accounting to the Court by the liquidator. Accountings shall be at such intervals as the Court specifies in its order. (1989, c. 452, s. 1.)

§ 58-30-110. Continuance of coverage.

(a) All policies, other than life or health insurance or annuities, that are in effect at the time of the issuance of an order of liquidation shall continue in force only for the lesser of:

(1) A period of 30 days from the date of entry of the liquidation orders;

(2) The expiration of the policy coverage;

(3) The date when the insured has replaced the insurance coverage with equivalent insurance in another insurer or otherwise terminated the policy; or

(4) The liquidator has effected a transfer of the policy obligation pursuant to G.S. 58-30-120(a)(8).

(b) An order of liquidation under G.S. 58-30-105 terminates coverages at the time specified in subsection (a) of this section for the purposes of any other statute.

(c) Policies of life or health insurance or annuities shall continue in force for such period and under such terms as is provided for by any applicable domestic or foreign guaranty association.

(d) Policies of life or health insurance or annuities or any period of coverage of such policies that are not covered by a domestic or foreign guaranty association shall terminate under subsections (a) and (b) of this section. (1989, c. 452, s. 1.)

§ 58-30-115. Dissolution of insurer.

The Commissioner may petition for an order dissolving the corporate existence of a domestic insurer or the United States branch of an alien insurer domiciled in this State at the time he applies for a liquidation order. The Court shall order dissolution of the corporation upon petition by the Commissioner upon or after the granting of a liquidation order. If the dissolution has not previously been ordered, it shall be effected by operation of law upon the discharge of the liquidator if the insurer is under a liquidation order for some other reason. (1989, c. 452, s. 1.)

§ 58-30-120. Powers of liquidator.

(a) The liquidator has the power:

(1) To appoint a special deputy to act for him under this Article, and to determine his reasonable compensation. The special deputy has all powers of the liquidator granted by this section. The special deputy serves at the pleasure of the liquidator.

(2) To employ employees and agents, legal counsel, actuaries, accountants, appraisers, consultants, and such other personnel as he may deem to be necessary to assist in the liquidation.

(3) To fix the reasonable compensation of employees and agents, legal counsel, actuaries, accountants, appraisers, and consultants, with the approval of the Court.

(4) To pay reasonable compensation to persons appointed; and to defray from the funds or assets of the insurer all expenses of taking possession of, conserving, conducting, liquidating, disposing of, or otherwise dealing with the business and property of the insurer. In the event that the property of the insurer does not contain sufficient cash or liquid assets to defray the costs incurred, the Commissioner may advance the costs so incurred out of any appropriation for the maintenance of the Department. Any amounts so advanced for expenses of administration shall be repaid to the Commissioner for the use of the Department out of the first available moneys of the insurer.

(5) To hold hearings, to subpoena witnesses to compel their attendance, to administer oaths, to examine any person under oath, and to compel any person to subscribe to this testimony after it has been correctly reduced to writing; and in connection therewith to require the production of any books, papers, records, or other documents that he considers relevant to the inquiry.

(6) To collect all debts and moneys due and claims belonging to the insurer, wherever located, and for this purpose:

a. To institute timely action in other jurisdictions, in order to forestall garnishment and attachment proceedings against such debts;

b. To do such other acts that are necessary or expedient to collect, conserve, or protect its assets or property, including the power to sell, compound, compromise, or assign debts for purposes of collection upon such terms and conditions as he deems to be best; and

c. To pursue any creditor's remedies available to enforce his claims.

(7) To conduct public and private sales of the property of the insurer.

(8) To use assets of the estate of an insurer under a liquidation order to transfer policy obligations to a solvent assuming insurer, if the transfer can be arranged without prejudice to applicable priorities under G.S. 58-30-220.

(9) To acquire, hypothecate, encumber, lease, improve, sell, transfer, abandon, or otherwise dispose of or deal with, any property of the insurer at its market value or upon such terms and conditions that are fair and reasonable. He also has the power to execute, acknowledge, and deliver any and all deeds, assignments, releases and other instruments necessary or proper to effectuate any sale of property or other transaction in connection with the liquidation.

(10) To borrow money on the security of the insurer's assets or without security and to execute and deliver all documents necessary to that transaction for the purpose of facilitating the liquidation.

(11) To enter into such contracts that are necessary to carry out the order to liquidate, and to affirm or disavow any contracts to which the insurer is a party.

(12) To continue to prosecute and to institute in the name of the insurer or in his own name any and all suits and other legal proceedings, in this State or elsewhere, and to abandon the prosecution of claims he deems unprofitable to pursue further. If the insurer is dissolved under G.S. 58-30-115, he shall have the power to apply to any court in this State or elsewhere for leave to substitute himself for the insurer as plaintiff.

(13) To prosecute any action that may exist in behalf of the creditors, members, policyholders, or shareholders of the insurer against any officer of the insurer or against any other person.

(14) To remove any or all records and property of the insurer to the offices of the Commissioner or to such other place as may be convenient for the purposes of efficient and orderly execution of the liquidation. Domestic and foreign

guaranty associations shall have such reasonable access to the records of the insurer as is necessary for them to carry out their statutory obligations.

(15)   To deposit in one or more banks in this State such sums as are required for meeting current administration expenses and dividend distributions.

(16)   To invest all sums not currently needed, unless the Court orders otherwise.

(17)   To file any necessary documents for recording in the office of any register of deeds in this State or elsewhere where property of the insurer is located.

(18)   To assert all defenses available to the insurer as against third persons, including statutes of limitation, statutes of frauds, and the defense of usury. A waiver of any defense by the insurer after a petition in liquidation has been filed shall not bind the liquidator. Whenever a domestic or foreign guaranty association has an obligation to defend any suit, the liquidator shall give precedence to such obligation and may defend only in the absence of a defense by such guaranty associations.

(19)   To exercise and enforce all rights, remedies, and powers of any creditor, shareholder, policyholder, or member; including any power to avoid any transfer or lien that may be given by law and that is not included within G.S. 58-30-140 through G.S. 58-30-150.

(20)   To intervene in any proceeding wherever instituted that might lead to the appointment of a receiver or trustee, and to act as the receiver or trustee whenever the appointment is offered.

(21)   To enter into agreements with any receiver or insurance regulator of any other state relating to the rehabilitation, liquidation, conservation, or dissolution of an insurer doing business in both states.

(22)   To exercise all powers now held or subsequently conferred upon receivers by laws of this State not inconsistent with the provisions of this Article.

(b)   The enumeration in this section of the powers and authority of the liquidator shall not be construed as a limitation upon him, nor shall it exclude in any manner his right to do such other acts not specifically enumerated in this section or otherwise provided for, as may be necessary or appropriate for the accomplishment of or in aid of the purpose of liquidation. (1989, c. 452, s. 1.)

§ 58-30-125. Notice to creditors and others.

(a) Unless the Court otherwise directs, the liquidator shall give or cause to be given notice of the liquidation order as soon as possible:

(1) By first-class mail and either by facsimile, electronic mail, or telephone to the insurance regulator of each jurisdiction in which the insurer is doing business;

(2) By first-class mail to any domestic or foreign guaranty association that is or may become obligated as a result of the liquidation;

(3) By first-class mail to all insurance agents of the insurer;

(4) By first-class mail to all persons known or reasonably expected to have claims against the insurer, including all policyholders, at their last known addresses indicated by the records of the insurer; and

(5) By publication in a newspaper of general circulation in the county in which the insurer has its principal place of business and in such other locations as the liquidator deems to be appropriate.

(b) Notice to potential claimants under subsection (a) of this section shall require claimants to file with the liquidator their claims, together with proper proofs thereof under G.S. 58-30-190, on or before a date the liquidator specifies in the notice. All claimants have a duty to keep the liquidator informed of any changes of address. The liquidator need not require the following to file claims under this section:

(1) Persons claiming cash surrender values or other investment values in life insurance and annuities.

(2) Persons claiming unearned premiums on property or casualty insurance.

(c) If notice is given in accordance with this section, the distribution of assets of the insurer under this Article shall be conclusive with respect to all claimants, whether or not they receive notice. (1989, c. 452, s. 1; 2006-105, s. 1.4.)

§ 58-30-127. Duties of agents.

(a) Every person who receives notice in the form prescribed in G.S. 58-30-125 that an insurer that person represents as an agent is the subject of a liquidation order shall, upon request of the liquidator and within 60 days after receipt of the request, provide to the liquidator the information in the agent's records related to any policy issued by the insurer through the agent; and if the agent is a general agent, the information in the general agent's records related to any policy issued by the insurer through a subagent under contract with the general agent, including the name and address of the subagent.

(b) For the purpose of this section, a policy is issued through an agent if the agent has a property interest in the expiration of the policy or if the agent has had in the agent's possession a copy of the declarations of the policy at any time during the life of the policy, except where the ownership of the expiration of the policy has been transferred to another person.

(c) Any agent failing to provide information to the liquidator as required by this section is to be subject to G.S. 58-2-70.

(d) The provisions of this section are in addition to any other duties in this Chapter that are placed on agents. (1991, c. 681, s. 45.)

§ 58-30-130. Actions by and against liquidator.

(a) Upon the issuance of an order appointing a liquidator of a domestic insurer or of an alien insurer domiciled in this State, no action at law or equity shall be brought against the insurer or liquidator, whether in this State or elsewhere, nor shall any such existing actions be maintained or further presented after issuance of such order. The Court shall give full faith and credit to injunctions against the liquidator or the insurer or the continuation of existing actions against the liquidator or the insurer, when such injunctions are included in an order to liquidate an insurer issued pursuant to corresponding provisions in other states. Whenever, in the liquidator's judgment, protection of the estate of the insurer necessitates intervention in an action against the insurer that is pending outside this State, he may intervene in the action. The liquidator may defend any action in which he intervenes under this section at the expense of the estate of the insurer.

(b) The liquidator may, upon or after an order for liquidation, within two years or such subsequent time period as applicable law may permit, institute an action or proceeding on behalf of the estate of the insurer upon any cause of action against which the period of limitation fixed by applicable law has not expired at the time of the filing of the petition upon which such order is entered. Where (i) by any agreement, a period of limitation is fixed for instituting a suit or proceeding upon any claim, or for filing any claim, proof of claim, proof of loss, demand, notice, or the like; or (ii) in any proceeding, judicial or otherwise, a period of limitation is fixed, either in the proceeding or by applicable law, for taking any action, filing any claim or pleading, or doing any act; and (iii) in any such case the period had not expired at the date of the filing of the petition; the liquidator may, for the benefit of the estate, take any such action or do any such act, required of or permitted to the insurer, within a period of 180 days subsequent to the entry of an order for liquidation, or within such further period as is shown to the satisfaction of the Court not to be unfairly prejudicial to the other party.

(c) Any domestic or foreign guaranty association has standing to appear in any Court proceeding concerning the liquidation of an insurer if such association is or may become liable to act as a result of the liquidation. (1989, c. 452, s. 1; 2009-570, s. 27.)

§ 58-30-135. Collection and list of assets.

(a) As soon as practicable after the liquidation order but not later than 120 days thereafter, the liquidator shall prepare in duplicate a list of the insurer's assets. The list shall be amended or supplemented from time to time as the liquidator determines. One copy shall be filed in the office of the clerk of the Court and one copy shall be retained for the liquidator's files. All amendments and supplements shall be similarly filed.

(b) The liquidator shall reduce the assets to a degree of liquidity that is consistent with the effective execution of the liquidation.

(c) A submittal to the Court for disbursement of assets in accordance with G.S. 58-30-180 fulfills the requirements of subsection (a) of this section. (1989, c. 452, s. 1.)

§ 58-30-140. Fraudulent transfers prior to petition.

(a) Every transfer made or suffered and every obligation incurred by an insurer within one year prior to the filing of a successful petition for rehabilitation or liquidation under this Article is fraudulent as to then existing and future creditors if made or incurred without fair consideration or if made or incurred with actual intent to hinder, delay, or defraud either existing or future creditors. A transfer made or an obligation incurred by an insurer ordered to be rehabilitated or liquidated under this Article, that is fraudulent under this section, may be avoided by the receiver, except as to a person who in good faith is a purchaser, lienor, or obligee, for a present fair equivalent value; and except that any purchaser, lienor, or obligee, who in good faith has given a consideration less than fair for such transfer, lien, or obligation, may retain the property, lien, or obligation as security for repayment. The Court may, on due notice, order any such transfer or obligation to be preserved for the benefit of the estate, and in that event, the receiver shall succeed to and may enforce the rights of the purchaser, lienor, or obligee.

(b) A transfer of property other than real property is made or suffered when it becomes so far perfected that no subsequent lien obtainable by legal or equitable proceedings on a simple contract could become superior to the rights of the transferee under G.S. 58-30-150(c). A transfer of real property is made or suffered when it becomes so far perfected that no subsequent bona fide purchaser from the insurer could obtain rights superior to the rights of the transferee. A transfer that creates an equitable lien is not perfected if there are available means by which a legal lien could be created. Any transfer that is not perfected prior to the filing of a petition for liquidation shall be deemed to be made immediately before the filing of the successful petition. The provisions of this subsection apply whether or not there are or were creditors who might have obtained any liens or persons who might have become bona fide purchasers.

(c)   Any transaction of the insurer with a reinsurer is fraudulent and may be avoided by the receiver under subsection (a) of this section if:

(1)   The transaction consists of the termination, adjustment, or settlement of a reinsurance contract in which the reinsurer is released from any part of its duty to pay the originally specified share of losses that had occurred prior to the time of the transaction, unless the reinsurer gives a present fair equivalent value for the release; and

(2)   Any part of the transaction took place within one year prior to the date of filing of the petition through which the receivership was commenced.

(d)   Every person receiving any property from the insurer or any benefit thereof as the result of a fraudulent transfer under subsection (a) of this section is personally liable therefor and is bound to account to the liquidator. (1989, c. 452, s. 1; 1991, c. 681, s. 46.)

§ 58-30-145. Fraudulent transfer after petition.

(a)   After a petition for rehabilitation or liquidation has been filed, a transfer of any of the real property of the insurer made to a person acting in good faith shall be valid against the receiver if made for a present fair equivalent value; or, if not made for a present fair equivalent value, then to the extent of the present consideration actually paid therefor, for which amount the transferee shall have a lien on the property so transferred. The commencement of a proceeding in rehabilitation or liquidation shall be constructive notice upon the recording of a copy of the petition for or order of rehabilitation or liquidation with the register of deeds in the county in which any real property in question is located. The exercise by a court of the United States or any state to authorize or effect a judicial sale of real property of the insurer within any county in any state is not impaired by the pendency of such a proceeding unless the copy is recorded in the county prior to the consummation of the judicial sale.

(b)   After a petition for rehabilitation or liquidation has been filed and before either the receiver takes possession of the property of the insurer or an order of rehabilitation or liquidation is granted:

(1)   A transfer of any of the property of the insurer, other than real property, made to a person acting in good faith is valid against the receiver if made for a

present fair equivalent value; or, if not made for a present fair equivalent value, then to the extent of the present consideration actually paid therefor, for which amount the transferee shall have a lien on the property so transferred.

(2) A person indebted to the insurer or holding property of the insurer may, if acting in good faith, pay the indebtedness or deliver the property, or any part thereof, to the insurer or upon his order, with the same effect as if the petition were not pending.

(3) A person having actual knowledge of the pending rehabilitation or liquidation shall be deemed not to act in good faith.

(4) A person asserting the validity of a transfer under this section has the burden of proof. Except as elsewhere provided in this section, no transfer by or on behalf of the insurer after the date of the petition for liquidation by any person other than the liquidator is valid as against the liquidator.

(c) Nothing in this Article impairs the validity of currency or the negotiability of any instrument. (1989, c. 452, s. 1.)

§ 58-30-150. Voidable preferences and liens.

(a) A preference is a transfer of any of the property of an insurer to or for the benefit of a creditor, for or on account of an antecedent debt, made or suffered by the insurer within one year before the filing of a successful petition for liquidation under this Article, the effect of which transfer may be to enable the creditor to obtain a greater percentage of this debt than another creditor of the same class would receive. If a liquidation order is entered while the insurer is already subject to a rehabilitation order, then such transfers shall be deemed to be preferences if made or suffered within one year before the filing of the successful petition for rehabilitation, or within two years before the filing of the successful petition for liquidation, whichever time is shorter. Any preference may be avoided by the liquidator if:

(1) The insurer was insolvent at the time of the transfer;

(2) The transfer was made within four months before the filing of the petition;

(3) The creditor receiving it or to be benefited thereby or his agent acting with reference thereto had, at the time the transfer was made, reasonable cause to believe that the insurer was insolvent or was about to become insolvent; or

(4) The creditor receiving it was an officer, or any employee, attorney, or other person who was in fact in a position of comparable influence in the insurer to an officer, whether or not he held such position, or any shareholder holding directly or indirectly more than five percent (5%) of any class of any equity security issued by the insurer, or any other person, firm, corporation, association, or aggregation of persons with whom the insurer did not deal at arm's length.

Where the preference is voidable, the liquidator may recover the property or, if it has been converted, its value from any person who has received or converted the property; except where a bona fide purchaser or lienor has given less than fair equivalent value, he shall have a lien upon the property to the extent of the consideration actually given by him. Where a preference by way of lien or security title is voidable, the Court may on due notice order the lien or title to be preserved for the benefit of the estate, in which event the lien or title shall pass to the liquidator.

(b) A transfer of property other than real property shall be deemed to be made or suffered when it becomes so far perfected that no subsequent lien obtainable by legal or equitable proceedings on a simple contract could become superior to the rights of the transferee. A transfer of real property shall be deemed to be made or suffered when it becomes so far perfected that no subsequent bona fide purchaser from the insurer could obtain rights superior to the rights of the transferee. A transfer that creates an equitable lien shall not be deemed to be perfected if there are available means by which a legal lien could be created. A transfer not perfected prior to the filing of a petition for liquidation shall be deemed to be made immediately before the filing of the successful petition. The provisions of this subsection apply whether or not there are or were creditors who might have obtained liens or persons who might have become bona fide purchasers.

(c) A lien obtainable by legal or equitable proceedings upon a simple contract is one arising in the ordinary course of such proceedings upon the entry or docketing of a judgment or decree, or upon attachment, garnishment, execution, or like process, whether before, upon, or after judgment or decree and whether before or upon levy. It does not include liens that under applicable law are given a special priority over other liens that are prior in time. A lien obtainable by legal or equitable proceedings could become superior to the rights of a transferee, or a purchaser could obtain rights superior to the rights of a transferee within the meaning of subsection (b) of this section, if such consequences would follow only from the lien or purchase itself, or from the lien or purchase followed by any step wholly within the control of the respective lienholder or purchaser, with or without the aid of ministerial action by public officials. Such a lien could not, however, become superior and such a purchase could not create superior rights for the purpose of subsection (b) of this section through any acts subsequent to the obtaining of such a lien or subsequent to such a purchase that require the agreement or concurrence of any third party or that require any further judicial action or ruling.

(d) A transfer of property for or on account of a new and contemporaneous consideration that is deemed under subsection (b) of this section to be made or suffered after the transfer because of delay in perfecting it does not thereby become a transfer for or on account of any antecedent debt if any acts required by the applicable law to be performed in order to perfect the transfer as against liens or bona fide purchasers' rights are performed within 21 days or any period expressly allowed by the law, whichever is less. A transfer to secure a future loan, if such a loan is actually made, or a transfer that becomes security for a future loan, shall have the same effect as a transfer for or on account of a new and contemporaneous consideration.

(e) If any lien deemed to be voidable under subdivision (a)(2) of this section has been dissolved by the furnishing of a bond or other obligation, the surety on which has been indemnified directly or indirectly by the transfer of or the creation of a lien upon any property of an insurer before the filing of a petition under this Article that results in a liquidation order, the indemnifying transfer or lien shall also be deemed to be voidable.

(f) The property affected by any lien deemed to be voidable under subsections (a) and (e) of this section shall be discharged from such lien, and that property and any of the indemnifying property transferred to or for the benefit of a surety shall pass to the liquidator; except that the Court may on due notice order any such lien to be preserved for the benefit of the estate, and the Court may direct that such conveyance be executed as may be proper or adequate to evidence the title of the liquidator.

(g) The Court shall have summary jurisdiction of any proceeding by the liquidator to hear and determine the rights of any parties under this section. Reasonable notice of any hearing in the proceeding shall be given to all parties in interest, including the obligee of a releasing bond or other like obligation. Where an order is entered for the recovery of indemnifying property in kind or for the avoidance of an indemnifying lien, the Court, upon application of any party in interest, shall in the same proceeding ascertain the value of the property or lien. If such value is less than the amount for which the property is indemnity or than the amount of the lien, the transferee or lienholder may elect to retain the property or lien upon payment of its value, as ascertained by the Court, to the liquidator, within such reasonable times as the Court shall fix.

(h)   The liability of the surety under a releasing bond or other like obligation shall be discharged to the extent of the value of the indemnifying property recovered or the indemnifying lien nullified and avoided by the liquidator; or where the property is retained under subsection (g) of this section to the extent of the amount paid to the liquidator.

(i)   If a creditor has been preferred and afterward in good faith gives the insurer further credit, without security of any kind, for property that becomes a part of the insurer's estate, the amount of the new credit remaining unpaid at the time of the petition may be set off against the preference that would otherwise be recoverable from him.

(j)   If an insurer, within four months before the filing of a successful petition for liquidation under this Article, or at any time in contemplation of a proceeding to liquidate it, directly or indirectly pays money or transfers property to an attorney at law for services rendered or to be rendered, such transactions may be examined by the Court on its own motion or on petition of the liquidator, and shall be held valid only to the extent of a reasonable amount to be determined by the Court. Any excess may be recovered by the liquidator for the benefit of the estate; provided that where the attorney is in a position of influence in the insurer or an affiliate thereof, payment of any money or the transfer of any property to the attorney at law for services rendered or to be rendered shall be governed by the provision of subdivision (a)(4) of this section.

(k)   Every officer, manager, employee, shareholder, member, subscriber, attorney, or any other person acting on behalf of the insurer who knowingly participates in giving any preference, when he has reasonable cause to believe the insurer is or is about to become insolvent at the time of the preference, shall be personally liable to the liquidator for the amount of the preference. It is permissible to infer that there is a reasonable cause to so believe if the transfer was made within four months before the date of filing of the successful petition for liquidation. Every person receiving any property from the insurer or the benefit thereof as a preference voidable under subsection (a) of this section shall be personally liable therefor and shall be bound to account to the liquidator. Nothing in this subsection prejudices any other claim by the liquidator against any person. (1989, c. 452, s. 1.)

§ 58-30-155. Claims of holders of void or voidable rights.

(a) No claims of a creditor who has received or acquired a preference, lien, conveyance, transfer, assignment, or encumbrance voidable under this Article shall be allowed unless he surrenders the preference, lien, conveyance, transfer, assignment or encumbrance. If the avoidance is effected by a proceeding in which a final judgment has been entered, the claim shall not be allowed unless the money is paid or the property is delivered to the liquidator within 30 days from the date of the entering of the final judgment; except that the Court having jurisdiction over the liquidation may allow further time if there is an appeal or other continuation of the proceeding.

(b) A claim allowable under subsection (a) of this section by reason of the avoidance, whether voluntary or involuntary, of a preference, lien, conveyance, transfer, assignment, or encumbrance, may be filed as an excused late filing under G.S. 58-30-185 if filed within 30 days from the date of the avoidance, or within the further time allowed by the Court under subsection (a) of this section. (1989, c. 452, s. 1.)

§ 58-30-160. Setoffs.

(a) Mutual debts or mutual credits, whether arising out of one or more contracts between the insurer and another person in connection with any action or proceeding under this Article shall be set off and the balance only shall be allowed or paid, except as provided in subsections (b), (d), and (e) of this section and in G.S. 58-30-175.

(b) No setoff shall be allowed in favor of any person where:

(1) The obligation of the insurer to the person would not at the date of the filing of a petition for liquidation entitle the person to share as a claimant in the assets of the insurer;

(2) The obligation of the insurer to the person was purchased by or transferred to the person with a view to its being used as a setoff;

(3) The obligation of the person is to pay an assessment levied against the members or subscribers of the insurer, or is to pay a balance upon a subscription to the capital stock of the insurer, or is in any other way in the nature of a capital contribution;

(4) Repealed by Session Laws 1995 (Regular Session, 1996), c. 658, s. 1.

(5) The obligation of the insurer is owed to an affiliate of the person, or to any other entity or association other than the person;

(6) The obligation of the person is owed to an affiliate of the insurer, or to any other entity or association other than the insurer;

(7) The obligations between the person and the insurer arise out of transactions where either the person or the insurer has assumed risks and obligations from the other party and then has ceded back to that party substantially the same risks and obligations;

(8) The obligation of the person is to pay to the insurer sums held in a fiduciary capacity for the insurer; or

(9) The person alone or together with any other member of its insurance company holding system owns fifty percent (50%) or more of the voting stock of the insurer.

(c) A setoff shall be permitted to local agents against agents' balances otherwise payable to the domiciliary or ancillary receiver for the amount expended by the agents to replace insurance coverage of their insureds and the reasonable expenses incident thereto as a result of any domestic, foreign or alien insurer being placed in delinquency proceedings. Agents claiming a setoff shall within 60 days of replacing coverage provide a verified accounting of the replacement of the insurance to the domiciliary receiver, the ancillary receiver, if any, and the North Carolina Insurance Guaranty Association or similar organization in the state of residence of the policyholder. The verified accounting shall include the name of the agent, the name of the insured, the policy number, the replacement policy number, the cost of the replacement policy, the amount of unearned premium under each policy as to which setoff is claimed, any claimed expenses and a verification that the accounting has been provided to each of the persons and entities described herein. Unearned premiums set off as provided above in any amount shall be deemed paid in full by the insurer and no person shall have a claim for the unearned premiums against the North Carolina Insurance Guaranty Association or similar organization in the state of residence of the policyholder.

(d) The receiver shall provide persons with accounting statements identifying debts which are currently due and payable. Where a person owes to the insurer currently due and payable balances, against which the person asserts setoff of mutual credits which may become due and payable from the insurer in the future, the person shall promptly pay to the receiver the currently due and payable amount; provided that, notwithstanding any other provision of this Article, the receiver shall promptly and fully refund, to the extent of the person's prior payments, any mutual credits that become due and payable to the person by the insurer.

(e) Notwithstanding any other provision of this section, a setoff of sums due on obligations in the nature of those set forth in subdivision (b)(7) of this section shall be allowed for those sums accruing from business written where the contracts were entered into, renewed, or extended with the express written approval of the insurance regulator of the state of domicile of the now insolvent insurer, when in the judgment of the regulator it was necessary to provide reinsurance in order to prevent or mitigate a threatened impairment or insolvency of the insurer in connection with the exercise of the regulator's official responsibilities. (1989, c. 452, s. 1; 1991, c. 681, s. 47; 1995 (Reg. Sess., 1996), c. 658, s. 1.)

§ 58-30-165. Assessments.

(a) As soon as practicable but not more than two years from the date of an order of liquidation under G.S. 58-30-105 of an insurer issuing assessable policies, the liquidator shall make a report to the Court setting forth:

(1) The reasonable value of the assets of the insurer;

(2) The insurer's probable total liabilities;

(3) The probable aggregate amount of the assessment necessary to pay all claims of creditors and expenses in full, including expenses of administration and costs of collecting the assessment; and

(4) A recommendation as to whether an assessment should be made and in what amount.

(b) Upon the basis of the report provided in subsection (a) of this section, including any supplements and amendments thereto, the Court may levy one or more assessments against all members of the insurer who are subject to assessment. Subject to any applicable legal limits on assessability, the aggregate assessment shall be for the amount that the sum of the probable liabilities, the expenses of administration, and the estimated cost of collection of the assessment, exceeds the value of existing assets, with due regard given to assessments that cannot be collected economically.

(c) After a levy of assessment under subsection (b) of this section, the liquidator shall issue an order directing each member who has not paid the assessment pursuant to the order, to show cause why the liquidator should not pursue a judgment therefor.

(d) The liquidator shall give notice of the order to show cause by publication or by certified mail to each member liable thereunder mailed to his last known address as it appears on the insurer's records, at least 20 days before the return day of the order to show cause.

(e) If a member does not appear and serve duly verified objections upon the liquidator on or before the return day of the order to show cause under subsection (c) of this section, the Court shall make an order adjudging the member liable for the amount of the assessment against him pursuant to subsection (c) of this section, together with costs, and the liquidator shall have a judgment against the member therefor. If on or before such return day, the member appears and serves duly verified objections upon the liquidator, the Commissioner may hear and determine the matter or may appoint a referee to hear it and make such order as the facts warrant. In the event that the Commissioner determines that such objections do not warrant relief from assessment, the member may request the Court to review the matter and vacate the order to show cause.

(f) The liquidator may enforce any order or collect any judgment under subsection (e) of this section by any lawful means. (1989, c. 452, s. 1; 2009-172, s. 3.)

§ 58-30-170. Reinsurer's liability.

The amount recoverable by the liquidator from reinsurers shall not be reduced as a result of the delinquency proceedings, regardless of any provision in the reinsurance contract or other agreement. Payment made directly to an insured or other creditor does not diminish the reinsurer's obligation to the insurer's estate except;

(1) Where the contract specifically provides for another payee of the reinsurance in the event of the insolvency of the ceding insurer or

(2) Where the assuming insurer, with the consent of the direct insured or insureds, has assumed the policy obligations of the ceding insurer as direct obligations of the assuming insurer to the payees under policies and in substitution of the obligations of the ceding insurer to the payees. (1989, c. 452, s. 1.)

§ 58-30-175. Recovery of premiums owed.

(a) An agent, broker, premium finance company, or any other person, other than the insured, responsible for the payment of a premium is obligated to pay an unpaid premium for the full policy term due the insurer at the time of the declaration of insolvency, whether earned or unearned, as shown on the records of the insurer. The liquidator also has the right to recover from such person any part of an unearned premium that represents commission of such person. Except as provided in G.S. 58-30-160, credits or setoffs or both are not allowed to an agent, broker, or premium finance company for any amounts advanced to the insurer by the agent, broker, or premium finance company on behalf of, but in the absence of a payment by, the insured.

(b) An insured is obligated to pay any unpaid premium due the insurer at the time of the declaration of insolvency, as shown on the records of the insurer. (1989, c. 452, s. 1.)

§ 58-30-180. Domiciliary liquidator's proposal to distribute assets.

(a)   Within one year after a final determination of insolvency of an insurer by the Court, the liquidator shall make application to the Court for approval of a proposal to disburse assets out of marshalled assets, from time to time as such assets become available, to a domestic or foreign guaranty association having obligations because of such insolvency. If the liquidator determines that there are insufficient assets to disburse, the application required by this section shall be considered satisfied by a filing by the liquidator stating the reasons for this determination.

(b)   Such proposal shall at least include provisions for:

(1)   Reserving amounts for the payment of expenses of administration and the payment of claims of secured creditors, to the extent of the value of the security held, and claims falling within the priorities established in G.S. 58-30-220(1) and (4);

(2)   Disbursement of the assets marshalled to date and subsequent disbursement of assets as they become available;

(3)   Equitable allocation of disbursements to each of the domestic and foreign guaranty associations entitled thereto;

(4)   The securing by the liquidator from each of the associations entitled to disbursements pursuant to this section of an agreement to return to the liquidator such assets, together with income earned on assets previously disbursed, as may be required to pay claims of secured creditors and claims falling within the priorities established in G.S. 58-30-220 in accordance with such priorities. No bond shall be required of any such association; and

(5)   A full report to be made by each association to the liquidator accounting for all assets so disbursed to the association, all disbursements made therefrom, any interest earned by the association on such assets and any other matter as the Court directs.

(c)   The liquidator's proposal shall provide for disbursements to the associations in amounts estimated at least equal to the claim payments made or to be made thereby for which such associations could assert a claim against the liquidator; and shall further provide that if the assets available for disbursement from time to time do not equal or exceed the amount of such claim payments made or to be made by the association then disbursements shall be in the amount of available assets.

(d) The liquidator's proposal shall, with respect to an insolvent insurer writing life or health insurance or annuities, provide for disbursements of assets to any domestic or foreign guaranty association covering life or health insurance or annuities or to any other entity reinsuring, assuming, or guaranteeing policies or contracts of insurance under the acts creating such associations.

(e) Notice of such application shall be given to the association in and to the insurance regulators of each of the states. Any such notice shall be deemed to have been given when deposited in United States certified mail, first class postage prepaid, at least 30 days prior to submission of such application to the Court. Action on the application may be taken by the Court provided the above required notice has been given and provided further that the liquidator's proposal complies with subdivisions (b)(1) and (b)(2) of this section. (1989, c. 452, s. 1; 1995, c. 517, s. 13; 2006-105, s. 1.5.)

§ 58-30-185. Filing of claims.

(a) Proof of all claims shall be filed with the liquidator in the form required by G.S. 58-30-190 on or before the last day for filing specified in the notice required under G.S. 58-30-125, except that proof of claims for cash surrender values or other investment values in life insurance and annuities need not be filed unless the liquidator expressly so requires.

(b) The liquidator may permit a claimant making a late filing to share in distributions, whether past or future, as if he were not late, to the extent that any such payment will not prejudice the orderly administration of the liquidation, under the following circumstances:

(1) The existence of the claim was not known to the claimant and that he filed his claim as promptly thereafter as reasonably possible after learning of it;

(2) A transfer to a creditor was avoided under G.S. 58-30-140 through 58-30-150, or was voluntarily surrendered under G.S. 58-30-155, and that the filing satisfies the conditions of G.S. 58-30-155; and

(3) The valuation under G.S. 58-30-215, of security held by a secured creditor shows a deficiency, that is filed within 30 days after the valuation.

(c) The liquidator shall permit late filing claims to share in distributions, whether past or future, as if they were not late, if such claims are claims of a guaranty association or foreign guaranty association for reimbursement of covered claims paid or expenses incurred, or both, subsequent to the last day for filing where such payments were made and expenses incurred as provided by law. Claims of domestic and foreign guaranty associations for reimbursement of covered claims paid or expenses incurred shall be deemed to be absolute.

(d) The liquidator may consider any claim filed late that is not covered by subsection (b) of this section, and permit it to receive distributions that are subsequently declared on any claims of the same or lower priority if the payment does not prejudice the orderly administration of the liquidation. The late-filing claimant shall receive, at each distribution, the same percentage of the amount allowed on his claim as is then being paid to claimants of any lower priority. This shall continue until his claim has been paid in full. (1989, c. 452, s. 1.)

§ 58-30-190. Proof of claim.

(a) Proof of claim shall consist of a statement signed by the claimant that includes all of the following that are applicable:

(1) The particulars of the claim, including the consideration given for it;

(2) The identity and amount of the security on the claim;

(3) The payments made on the debt, if any;

(4) That the sum claimed is justly owing and that there is no setoff, counterclaim, or defense to the claim;

(5)   Any right of priority of payment or other specific right asserted by the claimant;

(6)   A copy of the written instrument that is the foundation of the claim; and

(7)   The name and address of the claimant and any attorney who represents him.

(b)   No claim need be considered or allowed if it does not contain all the information in subsection (a) of this section that may be applicable. The liquidator may require that a prescribed form be used, and may require that other information and documents be included.

(c)   At any time the liquidator may request the claimant to present information or evidence supplementary to that required under subsection (a) of this section; and may take testimony under oath, require production of affidavits or depositions, or otherwise obtain additional information or evidence.

(d)   No judgment or order against an insured or the insurer entered after the date of filing of a successful petition for liquidation, and no judgment or order against an insured or the insurer entered at any time by default or by collusion, need be considered as evidence of liability or of amount of damages. No judgment or order against an insured or the insurer entered within four months before the filing of the petition need be considered as evidence of liability or of the amount of damages.

(e)   All claims of a guaranty association or foreign guaranty association shall be in such form and contain such substantiation as may be agreed to by the association and the liquidator; and failing such agreement as ordered by the Court. (1989, c. 452, s. 1.)

§ 58-30-195. Special claims.

(a)   No contingent claim shall share in a distribution of the assets of an insurer that has been adjudicated to be insolvent by an order made pursuant to G.S. 58-30-105; except that such claims shall be considered, if properly presented, and may be allowed to share where:

(1) Such claim becomes absolute against the insurer on or before the last day fixed for filing of proofs of claim against the assets of such insurer, or

(2) There is a surplus and the liquidation is thereafter conducted upon the basis that such insurer is solvent.

(b) Where an insurer has been so adjudicated to be insolvent, any person who has a cause of action against an insured of such insurer under a liability insurance policy issued by such insurer, has the right to file a claim in the liquidation proceedings, regardless of the fact that such claim may be contingent, and such claim may be allowed:

(1) If it may be reasonably inferred from the proof presented upon such claim that such person would be able to obtain a judgment upon such cause of action against such insured; and

(2) If such person furnishes suitable proof, unless the Court for good cause shown otherwise directs, that no further valid claims against such insurer arising out of his cause of action other than those already presented can be made; and

(3) If the total liability of such insurer to all claimants arising out of the same act of its insured is no greater than its total liability would be were it not in liquidation.

No judgment against such an insured taken after the date of the entry of the liquidation order shall be considered in the liquidation proceedings as evidence of liability or of the amount of damages, and no judgment against an insured taken by default, inquest, or by collusion prior to the entry of the liquidation order shall be considered as conclusive evidence in the liquidation proceeding, either of the liability of such insured to such person upon such cause of action or of the amount of damages to which such person is therein entitled.

(c) No claim of any secured claimant shall be allowed at a sum greater than the difference between the value of the claim without security and the value of the security itself as of the date of entry of the order of liquidation or such other date set by the Court for fixation of rights and liabilities as provided in G.S. 58-30-105 unless the claimant surrenders his security to the Commissioner, in which event the claim shall be allowed in the full amount for which it is valued.

(d) Claims that are due but for the passage of time, including any structured settlements or judgments involving periodic payments, shall be treated the same as absolute claims, except that such claims may be discounted at the legal rate of interest.

(e)   Claims made under employment contracts by directors, principal officers, or persons in fact performing similar functions or having similar powers, are limited to payment for services rendered prior to the issuance of any order of rehabilitation or liquidation under this Article. (1989, c. 452, s. 1.)

§ 58-30-200. Special provisions for third party claims.

(a)   Whenever any third party asserts a cause of action against an insured of an insurer in liquidation, the third party may file a claim with the liquidator.

(b)   Whether or not the third party files a claim, the insured may file a claim on his own behalf in the liquidation. If the insured fails to file a claim by the date for filing claims specified in the order of liquidation or within 60 days after mailing of the notice required by G.S. 58-30-125, whichever is later, he is an unexcused late filer.

(c)   The liquidator shall make his recommendations to the Court under G.S. 58-30-225 for the allowance of an insured's claim under subsection (b) of this section after consideration of the probable outcome of any pending action against the insured on which the claim is based, the probable damages recoverable in the action, and the probable costs and expenses of defense. After allowance by the Court, the liquidator shall withhold any dividends payable on the claim, pending the outcome of litigation and negotiation with the insured. Whenever it seems appropriate, he shall reconsider the claim on the basis of additional information and amend his recommendations to the Court. The insured shall be afforded the same notice and opportunity to be heard on all changes in the recommendation as in its initial determination. The Court may amend its allowance as it thinks appropriate. As claims against the insured are settled or barred, the insured shall be paid from the amount withheld the same percentage dividend as was paid on other claims of like property, based on the lesser of (i) the amount actually recovered from the insured by action or paid by agreement plus the reasonable costs and expense of defense, or (ii) the amount allowed on the claims by the Court. After all claims are settled or barred, any sum remaining from the amount withheld shall revert to the undistributed assets of the insurer. Delay in final payment under this subsection shall not be a reason for unreasonable delay of final distribution and discharge of the liquidator.

(d)   No claim may be presented under this section if it is or may be covered by any domestic or foreign guaranty association. (1989, c. 452, s. 1; 2003-221, s. 14.)

§ 58-30-205. Disputed claims.

(a)   When a claim is denied in whole or in part by the liquidator, written notice of the determination shall be given to the claimant or his attorney by first class mail at the address shown in the proof of claim. Within 60 days from the mailing of the notice, the claimant may file his objections with the liquidator. If no such filing is made, the claimant may not further object to the determination.

(b)   Whenever objections are filed with the liquidator and the liquidator does not alter his denial of the claim as a result of the objections, the liquidator shall ask the Court for a hearing as soon as practicable and give notice of the hearing by first class mail to the claimant or his attorney and to any other persons directly affected, not less than 10 nor more than 30 days before the date of the hearing. The matter may be heard by the Court or by a court-appointed referee who shall submit findings of fact along with his recommendation. (1989, c. 452, s. 1.)

§ 58-30-210. Claims of surety.

Whenever a creditor, whose claim against an insurer is secured in whole or in part by the undertaking of another person, fails to prove and file that claim, the other person may do so in the creditor's name and shall be subrogated to the rights of the creditor, whether the claim has been filed by the creditor or by the other person in the creditor's name, to the extent that he discharges the undertaking. In the absence of an agreement with the creditor to the contrary, the other person shall not be entitled to any distribution until the amount paid to the creditor on the undertaking plus the distributions paid on the claim from the insurer's estate to the creditor equals the amount of the entire claim of the creditor. Any excess received by the creditor shall be held by him in trust for such other person. As used in this section, "other person" does not mean a guaranty association or foreign guaranty association. (1989, c. 452, s. 1.)

§ 58-30-215. Secured creditor's claims.

(a) The value of any security held by a secured creditor shall be determined in one of the following ways, as the Court may direct:

(1) By converting the same into money according to the terms of the agreement pursuant to which the security was delivered to such creditors; or

(2) By agreement, arbitration, compromise or litigation between the creditor and the liquidator.

(b) The determination shall be under the supervision and control of the Court with due regard for the recommendation of the liquidator. The amount so determined shall be credited upon the secured claim, and any deficiency shall be treated as an unsecured claim. If the claimant surrenders his security to the liquidator, the entire claim shall be allowed as if unsecured. (1989, c. 452, s. 1; 1991, c. 720, s. 68.)

§ 58-30-220. Priority of distribution.

The priority of distribution of claims from the insurer's estate shall be in accordance with the order in which each class of claims is set forth in this section. Every claim in each class shall be paid in full or adequate funds shall be retained for payment before the members of the next class receive any payment. No subcategories shall be established within the categories in a class. The order of distribution of claims shall be:

(1) The receiver's expenses for the administration and conservation of assets of the insurer.

(2) Claims or portions of claims for benefits under policies and for losses incurred, including claims of third parties under liability policies; claims of HMO enrollees and HMO enrollees' beneficiaries; claims for unearned premiums; claims for funds or consideration held under funding agreements, as defined in G.S. 58-7-16; claims under life insurance and annuity policies, whether for death proceeds, annuity proceeds, or investment values; and claims of domestic and foreign guaranty associations, including claims for the reasonable administrative

expenses of domestic and foreign guaranty associations; but excluding claims of insurance pools, underwriting associations, or those arising out of reinsurance agreements, claims of other insurers for subrogation, and claims of insurers for payments and settlements under uninsured and underinsured motorist coverages.

(2a) For HMOs, claims of providers and participating providers, as defined in G.S. 58-67-5(h) and G.S. 58-67-5(1)[(l)], who are obligated by statute, agreement, or court order to hold enrollees harmless from liability for services provided and covered by an HMO.

(3) Claims of the federal or any state or local government or taxing authority, including claims for taxes.

(4) Compensation actually owing to employees other than officers of the insurer for services rendered within three months before the commencement of a delinquency proceeding against the insurer under this Article, but not exceeding one thousand dollars ($1,000) for each employee. In the discretion of the Commissioner, this compensation may be paid as soon as practicable after the proceeding has been commenced. This priority is in lieu of any other similar priority that may be authorized by law as to wages or compensation of those employees.

(5) Claims of general creditors, including claims of insurance pools, underwriting associations, or those arising out of reinsurance agreements; claims of other insurers for subrogation; and claims of insurers for payments and settlements under uninsured and underinsured motorist coverages. (1989, c. 452, s. 1; 1993 (Reg. Sess., 1994), c. 600, s. 2; 1995, c. 517, s. 14; 1998-211, s. 4.)

§ 58-30-225. Liquidator's recommendations to the Court.

(a) The liquidator shall review all claims duly filed in the liquidation and shall make such further investigation as necessary. He may compound, compromise, or in any other manner negotiate the amount for which claims will be recommended to the Court except where he is required by law to accept claims as settled by any person or organization, including any domestic or foreign guaranty association. Unresolved disputes shall be determined under G.S. 58-30-205. As soon as practicable, the liquidator shall present to the Court a report of the claims against the insurer with his recommendations. The report shall include the name and address of each claimant and the amount of any claim finally recommended. If the insurer has issued annuities or life insurance policies, the liquidator shall report the persons to whom, according to the records of the insurer, amounts are owed as cash surrender values or other investment values and the amounts owed.

(b)   The Court may approve, disapprove, or modify the report on claims by the liquidator. Such reports that are not modified by the Court within a period of 60 days following submission by the liquidator shall be treated by the liquidator as allowed claims, subject thereafter to later modification or to rulings made by the Court pursuant to G.S. 58-30-205. No claim under a policy of insurance shall be allowed for an amount in excess of the applicable policy benefits. (1989, c. 452, s. 1.)

§ 58-30-230. Distribution of assets.

(a)   Under the direction of the Court, the liquidator shall pay distributions in a manner that will assure the proper recognition of priorities and a reasonable balance between the expeditious completion of the liquidation and the protection of unliquidated and undetermined claims, including third party claims. Distribution of assets in kind may be made at valuations set by agreement between the liquidator and the creditor and approved by the Court.

(b)   Interest on claims shall be paid only after all claims have been paid under subsection (a) of this section. This subsection does not apply to interest awarded as part of a judgment. (1989, c. 452, s. 1.)

§ 58-30-235. Unclaimed and withheld funds.

(a)   All unclaimed funds subject to distribution remaining in the liquidator's hands when he is ready to apply to the Court for discharge, including the amount distributable to any creditor, shareholder, member, or other person who is unknown or cannot be found, shall be deposited with the State Treasurer, and shall be paid without interest except in accordance with G.S. 58-30-220 to the person entitled thereto or his legal representative upon proof satisfactory to the State Treasurer of his right thereto. Any amount on deposit not claimed within six years from the discharge of the liquidator shall be considered abandoned and shall be escheated without formal escheat proceedings.

(b)   All funds withheld under G.S. 58-30-195 and not distributed shall upon discharge of the liquidator be deposited with the State Treasurer and paid by him in accordance with G.S. 58-30-220. Any sums remaining that under G.S. 58-30-220 would revert to the undistributed assets of the insurer shall be transferred to the State Treasurer and become the property of the State under subsection (a) of this section, unless the Commissioner in his discretion petitions the Court to reopen the liquidation under G.S. 58-30-245. (1989, c. 452, s. 1.)

§ 58-30-240. Termination of proceedings.

(a)   When all assets justifying the expense of collection and distribution have been collected and distributed under this Article, the liquidator shall apply to the Court for discharge. The Court may grant the discharge and make any other orders, including an order to transfer any remaining funds that are uneconomic to distribute, as may be deemed appropriate.

(b)   Any other person may apply to the Court at any time for an order under subsection (a) of this section. If the application is denied, the applicant shall pay the costs and expenses of the liquidator in resisting the application, including reasonable attorney fees. (1989, c. 452, s. 1.)

§ 58-30-245. Reopening liquidation.

After the liquidation proceeding has been terminated and the liquidator discharged, the Commissioner or other interested party may at any time petition the Court to reopen the proceedings for good cause, including the discovery of additional assets. If the Court is satisfied that there is justification for reopening, it shall so order. (1989, c. 452, s. 1.)

§ 58-30-250. Disposition of records during and after termination of liquidation.

Whenever it appears to the Commissioner that the records of any insurer in process of liquidation or completely liquidated are no longer useful, he may recommend to the Court and the Court shall direct what records should be retained for future reference and what should be destroyed. (1989, c. 452, s. 1.)

§ 58-30-255. External audit of the receiver's books.

The Court may, as it deems to be desirable, cause audits to be made of the books of the Commissioner relating to any receivership established under this Article, and a report of each audit shall be filed with the Commissioner and with the Court. The books, records, and other documents of the receivership shall be made available to any auditor at any time without notice. The expense of each audit shall be considered a cost of administration of the receivership. (1989, c. 452, s. 1.)

§ 58-30-260. Conservation of property of foreign or alien insurers found in this State.

(a) If a domiciliary liquidator has not been appointed, the Commissioner may apply to the Court by verified petition for an order directing him to act as conservator to conserve the property of an alien insurer not domiciled in this State or a foreign insurer on any one or more of the following grounds:

(1) Any of the grounds in G.S. 58-30-75;

(2) That any of its property has been sequestered by official action in its domiciliary state, or in any other state;

(3) That enough of its property has been sequestered in an alien country to give reasonable cause to fear that the insurer is or may become insolvent;

(4) That its license to do business in this State has been revoked or that none was ever issued; and that there are residents of this State with outstanding claims or outstanding policies.

(b) When an order is sought under subsection (a) of this section, the Court shall cause the insurer to be given such notice and time to respond thereto as is reasonable under the circumstances.

(c) The Court may issue the order in whatever terms it shall deem appropriate. The filing or recording of the order with the clerk of court or the register of deeds of the county in which the principal business of the company is located, shall impart the same notice as a deed, bill of sale or other evidence of title duly filed or recorded with that register of deeds would have imparted.

(d) The conservator may at any time petition for and the Court may grant an order under G.S. 58-30-265 to liquidate assets of a foreign or alien insurer under conservation, or, if appropriate, for an order under G.S. 58-30-275, to be appointed ancillary receiver.

(e) The conservator may at any time petition the Court for an order terminating conservation of an insurer. If the Court finds that the conservation is no longer necessary, it shall order that the insurer be restored to possession of its property and the control of its business. The Court may also make such finding and issue such order at any time upon motion of any interested party, but if such motion is denied all costs shall be assessed against such party. (1989, c. 452, s. 1; 1999-132, s. 9.1.)

§ 58-30-265. Liquidation of property of foreign or alien insurers found in this State.

(a) If no domiciliary receiver has been appointed, the Commissioner may apply to the Court by verified petition for an order directing him to liquidate the assets found in this State of a foreign insurer or an alien insurer not domiciled in this State, on any of the following grounds:

(1) Any of the grounds in G.S. 58-30-75 or G.S. 58-30-100; or

(2) Any of the grounds specified in G.S. 58-30-260(a)(2) through (4).

(b) When an order is sought under subsection (a) of this section, the Court shall cause the insurer to be given such notice and time to respond thereto as is reasonable under the circumstances.

(c) If it appears to the Court that the best interests of creditors, policyholders, and the public require, the Court may issue an order to liquidate in whatever terms it deems to be appropriate. The filing or recording of the order with the clerk of the Court or the register of deeds of the county in which the principal business of the insurer is located or the county in which its principal office or place of business is located, shall impart the same notice as a deed, bill of sale, or other evidence of title duly filed or recorded with that register of deeds would have imparted.

(d) If a domiciliary liquidator is appointed in a reciprocal state while a liquidation is proceeding under this section, the liquidator under this section shall thereafter act as ancillary receiver under G.S. 58-30-275. If a domiciliary liquidator is appointed in a nonreciprocal state while a liquidation is proceeding under this section, the liquidator under this section, may petition the court for permission to act as ancillary receiver under G.S. 58-30-275.

(e) On the same grounds as are specified in subsection (a) of this section, the Commissioner may petition any appropriate federal district court to be appointed receiver to liquidate that portion of the insurer's assets and business over which that court will exercise jurisdiction, or any lesser part thereof that the Commissioner considers desirable for the protection of the policyholders and creditors in this State.

(f) The Court may order the Commissioner, when he has liquidated the assets of a foreign or alien insurer under this section, to pay claims of residents of this State against the insurer under such rules as to the liquidation of insurers under this Article as are otherwise compatible with the provisions of this section. (1989, c. 452, s. 1.)

§ 58-30-270. Domiciliary liquidators in other states.

(a) The domiciliary liquidator of an insurer domiciled in a reciprocal state is, except as to special deposits and security on secured claims under G.S. 58-30-275(c), vested by operation of law with the title to all of the assets, property, contracts and rights of action, agents' balances, and all of the books, accounts, and other records of the insurer located in this State. The date of vesting shall be the date of the filing of the petition, if that date is specified by the domiciliary law for the vesting of property in the domiciliary state. Otherwise, the date of vesting shall be the date of entry of the order directing possession to be taken.

The domiciliary liquidator shall have the immediate right to recover the balances due from agents and to obtain possession of the books, accounts, and other records of the insurer located in this State. He also shall have the right to recover all other assets of the insurer located in this State, subject to G.S. 58-30-275.

(b)   If a domiciliary liquidator is appointed for an insurer not domiciled in a reciprocal state, the Commissioner shall be vested by operation of law with the title to all of the property, contracts, and rights of action, and all of the books, accounts and other records of the insurer located in this State, at the same time that the domiciliary liquidator is vested with title in the domicile. The Commissioner may petition for a conservation or liquidation order under G.S. 58-30-260 and G.S. 58-30-265, or for an ancillary receivership under G.S. 58-30-275, or after approval by the Court may transfer title to the domiciliary liquidator, as the interests of justice and the equitable distribution of the assets require.

(c)   Claimants residing in this State may file claims with the liquidator or ancillary receiver, if any, in this State or with the domiciliary liquidator, if the domiciliary law permits. The claims must be filed on or before the last date fixed for the filing of claims in the domiciliary liquidation proceedings. (1989, c. 452, s. 1.)

§ 58-30-275. Ancillary formal proceedings.

(a)   If a domiciliary liquidator has been appointed for an insurer not domiciled in this State, the Commissioner may file a petition with the Court requesting appointment as ancillary receiver in this State:

(1)   If he finds that there are sufficient assets of the insurer located in this State to justify the appointment of an ancillary receiver;

(2)   If the protection of creditors or policyholders in this State so requires.

(b)   The Court may issue an order appointing an ancillary receiver in whatever terms it deems to be appropriate, including provisions for payment of the reasonable and necessary expenses of the proceedings. The filing or recording of the order with a register of deeds in this State imparts the same notice as a deed, bill of sale, or other evidence of title duly filed or recorded with that register of deeds.

(c)   When a domiciliary liquidator has been appointed in a reciprocal state, then the ancillary receiver appointed in this State, may, whenever necessary, aid and assist the domiciliary liquidator in recovering assets of the insurer located in this State. The ancillary receiver shall, as soon as practicable, liquidate from their respective securities those special deposit claims and secured claims which are proved and allowed in the ancillary proceedings in this State, and shall pay the necessary expenses of the proceedings. He shall promptly transfer all remaining assets, books, accounts, and records to the domiciliary liquidator. Subject to this section, the ancillary receiver and his deputies shall have the same powers and be subject to the same duties with respect to the administration of assets as a liquidator of an insurer domiciled in this State.

(d)   When a domiciliary liquidator has been appointed in this State, ancillary receivers appointed in reciprocal states shall have, as to assets and books, accounts, and other records in their respective states, corresponding rights, duties and powers to those provided in subsection (c) of this section for ancillary receivers appointed in this State. (1989, c. 452, s. 1; 1993 (Reg. Sess., 1994), c. 678, s. 17.)

§ 58-30-280. Ancillary summary proceedings.

The Commissioner in his sole discretion may institute proceedings under G.S. 58-30-60 through 58-30-70 at the request of the insurance regulator of the domiciliary state of any foreign or alien insurer having property located in this State. (1989, c. 452, s. 1.)

§ 58-30-285. Claims of nonresidents against insurers domiciled in this State.

(a)   In a liquidation proceeding begun in this State against an insurer domiciled in this State, claimants residing in foreign countries or in states not reciprocal states must file claims in this State, and claimants residing in reciprocal states may file claims either with the ancillary receivers, if any, in their respective states, or with the domiciliary liquidator. Claims must be filed on or before the last date fixed for the filing of claims in the domiciliary liquidation proceeding.

(b) Claims belonging to claimants residing in reciprocal states may be proved either in the liquidation proceeding in this State as provided in this Article, or in ancillary proceedings, if any, in the reciprocal states. If notice of the claims and opportunity to appear and be heard is afforded the domiciliary liquidator of this State as provided in G.S. 58-30-290(b) with respect to ancillary proceedings, the final allowance of claims by the courts in ancillary proceedings in reciprocal states shall be conclusive as to amount and as to priority against special deposits or other security located in such ancillary states, but shall not be conclusive with respect to priorities against general assets under G.S. 58-30-220. (1989, c. 452, s. 1.)

§ 58-30-290. Claims of residents against insurers domiciled in reciprocal states.

(a) In a liquidation proceeding in a reciprocal state against an insurer domiciled in that state, claimants against the insurer who reside within this State may file claims either with the ancillary receiver, if any, in this State, or with the domiciliary liquidator. Claims must be filed on or before the last dates fixed for the filing of claims in the domiciliary proceeding.

(b) Claims belonging to claimants residing in this State may be proved either in the domiciliary state under the law of that state, or in ancillary proceedings, if any, in this State. If a claimant elects to prove his claim in this State, he shall file his claim with the liquidator in the manner provided in G.S. 58-30-185 and G.S. 58-30-190. The ancillary receiver shall make his recommendation to the Court as under G.S. 58-30-225. He shall also arrange a date for hearing if necessary under G.S. 58-30-205 and shall give notice to the liquidator in the domiciliary state, either by certified mail or by personal service at least 40 days prior to the date set for hearing. If the domiciliary liquidator, within 30 days after the giving of such notice, gives notice in writing to the ancillary receiver and to the claimant, either by certified mail or by personal service, of his intention to contest the claim, he shall be entitled to appear or to be represented in any proceedings in this State involving the adjudication of the claim.

(c) The final allowance of the claim by the courts of this State shall be accepted as conclusive as to amount and as to priority against special deposits or other security located in this State. (1989, c. 452, s. 1.)

§ 58-30-295. Attachment, garnishment and levy of execution.

During the pendency in this or any other state of a liquidation proceeding, whether called by that name or not, no action or proceeding in the nature of an attachment, garnishment, or levy of execution shall be commenced or maintained in this State against the delinquent insurer or its assets. (1989, c. 452, s. 1.)

§ 58-30-300. Interstate priorities.

(a) In a liquidation proceeding in this State involving one or more reciprocal states, the order of distribution of the domiciliary state shall control as to all claims of residents of this and reciprocal states. All claims of residents of reciprocal states shall be given equal priority of payment from general assets regardless of where such assets are located.

(b) The owners of special deposit claims against an insurer for which a liquidator is appointed in this or any other state shall be given priority against the special deposits in accordance with the statutes governing the creation and maintenance of the deposits. If there is a deficiency in any deposit, so that the claims secured by it are not fully discharged from it, the claimants may share in the general assets, but the sharing shall be deferred until general creditors, and also claimants against other special deposits who have received smaller percentages from their respective special deposits, have been paid percentages of their claims equal to the percentage paid from the special deposit.

(c) The owner of a secured claim against an insurer for which a liquidator has been appointed in this or any other state may surrender the owner's security and file the claim as a general creditor, or the claim may be discharged by resort to the security in accordance with G.S. 58-30-215 in which case the deficiency, if any, shall be treated as a claim against the general assets of the insurer on the same basis as claims of unsecured creditors. (1989, c. 452, s. 1; 1995, c. 193, s. 32.)

§ 58-30-305. Subordination of claims for noncooperation.

If an ancillary receiver in another state or foreign country, whether called by that name or not, fails to transfer to the domiciliary liquidator in this State any assets within his control other than special deposits, diminished only by the expenses of the ancillary receivership, if any, the claims filed in the ancillary receivership, other than special deposit claims or secured claims shall be placed in the class of claims under G.S. 58-30-220(5). (1989, c. 452, s. 1.)

§ 58-30-310. Exemption from filing fees.

As used in this section, "Commissioner" includes the Commissioner's deputies, employees, or attorneys of record. The Commissioner is not required to pay any fee to any public officer in this State for filing, recording, issuing a transcript or certificate, or authenticating any paper or instrument pertaining to the exercise by the Commissioner of any of the powers or duties conferred upon him under this Article. This section applies whether or not the paper or instrument is connected with the commencement of an action or proceeding by or against the Commissioner or with the subsequent conduct of an action or proceeding. (1989 (Reg. Sess., 1990), c. 1069, s. 15.)

§ 58-31-26. Medical liability insurance for certain physicians and dentists.

(a) The Secretary of the Department of Health and Human Services and the Secretary of the Department of Public Safety may provide medical liability insurance not to exceed one million dollars ($1,000,000) per incident on behalf of employees of these Departments who are licensed to practice medicine or dentistry; on behalf of all licensed physicians who are faculty members of The University of North Carolina who perform work on a contractual basis for the Division of Mental Health, Developmental Disabilities, and Substance Abuse Services for incidents that occur in Division programs; and on behalf of physicians in all residency training programs from The University of North Carolina who are in training at institutions operated by the Department of Health and Human Services. This coverage may include commercial insurance or self-insurance and shall cover these individuals for their acts or omissions only while they are engaged in providing medical and dental services pursuant to their State employment or training.

(b) The coverage provided pursuant to this section shall not cover any individual for any act or omission that the individual knows or reasonably should know constitutes a violation of the applicable criminal laws of any state or the United States, or that arises out of any sexual, fraudulent, criminal, or malicious act or out of any act amounting to willful or wanton negligence.

(c) The coverage provided pursuant to this section shall not require any additional appropriations and, except as provided in subsection (a) of this section, shall not apply to any individual providing contractual service to the Department of Health and Human Services or the Department of Public Safety. (2013-360, s. 12A.7.)

Article 31.

Insuring State Property, Officials and Employees.

§ 58-31-1. State Property Fire Insurance Fund created.

Upon the expiration of all existing policies of fire insurance upon state-owned buildings, fixtures, furniture, and equipment, including all such property the title to which may be in any State department, institution, or agency, the State of North Carolina shall not reinsure any of such properties.

There is hereby created a "State Property Fire Insurance Fund," which shall be as a special fund in the State treasury, for the purpose of providing a reserve against loss from fire at State departments and institutions. The State Treasurer shall be the custodian of the "State Property Fire Insurance Fund" and shall invest its assets in accordance with the provisions of G.S. 147-69.2 and 147-69.3. The unexpended appropriations of State departments and institutions for fire insurance premiums for the fiscal year 1944-1945 and the appropriations for fire insurance premiums made for the biennium 1945-1947 or that may thereafter be made for this purpose shall be transferred to the "State Property

Fire Insurance Fund." (1945, c. 1027, s. 1; 1963, c. 462; 1975, c. 519, s. 1; 1979, c. 467, s. 4.)

§ 58-31-5. Appropriations; fund to pay administrative expenses.

Upon the expiration of the existing fire insurance policies on said properties and in making appropriations for any biennium after the next biennium, the Commissioner shall file with the Department of Administration his estimate of the appropriations which will be necessary in order to set up and maintain an adequate reserve to provide a fund sufficient to protect the State, its departments, institutions, and agencies from loss or damage to any of said properties up to fifty per centum (50%) of the value thereof. Appropriations made for the creating of such fire insurance reserves against property of the Department of Agriculture and Consumer Services, or the Department of Transportation or any special operating fund shall be charged against the funds of such departments.

The State Property Fire Insurance Fund is authorized and empowered to pay all the administrative expenses occasioned by the administration of Article 31 of Chapter 58 of the General Statutes. (1945, c. 1027, s. 2; 1957, c. 65, s. 11; c. 269, s. 1; 1959, c. 182, s. 1; 1973, c. 507, s. 5; 1977, c. 464, s. 34; 1991, c. 720, s. 4; 1997-261, s. 109.)

§ 58-31-10. Payment of losses on basis of actual cost of restoration or replacement; rules; insurance and reinsurance; sprinkler leakage insurance.

(a)   In the case of total or partial loss of any property of any State agency or institution, the Commissioner shall determine the amount of loss and certify that amount to the agency or institution concerned and to the Director of the Budget and Council of State. The Director of the Budget and Council of State may authorize transfers from the Fund to the agency or institution that suffered the loss in amounts that are necessary to pay for the actual cost of restoration or replacement of the property. In the event there is not a sufficient amount in the Fund to pay for the actual cost of restoration or replacement, the Director of the Budget and the Council of State may supplement the Fund by transferring amounts from the Contingency and Emergency Fund.

(b) The Commissioner, with the approval of the Council of State, is authorized to adopt rules necessary to carry out the purpose of this Article, which rules shall be binding on all State agencies and institutions. The Commissioner, with the approval of the Director of the Budget and the Council of State, is authorized to purchase from qualified insurers insurance or reinsurance necessary to protect the Fund against loss on any one building and its contents in excess of fifty thousand dollars ($50,000), and the premiums for this coverage shall be paid from the Fund.

(c) Upon the request of any State agency or institution, sprinkler leakage insurance shall be provided on designated property of the agency or institution that is insured by the Fund. Premiums for this coverage shall be paid by the requesting agency or institution in accordance with rates fixed by the Commissioner. Losses covered by this insurance may be paid out of the Fund in the same manner as other losses. The Commissioner, with the approval of the Director of the Budget and the Council of State, is authorized to purchase from qualified insurers insurance or reinsurance necessary to protect the Fund against loss with respect to sprinkler leakage insurance coverage. (1945, c. 1027, s. 3; 1951, c. 802; 1959, c. 182, s. 2; 1983, c. 913, s. 7; 1985, c. 786.)

§ 58-31-12. Policy forms.

The Commissioner, with the approval of the Council of State, may adopt insurance forms for coverages provided by the State Property Fire Insurance Fund under this Article. (1993, c. 409, s. 13.)

§ 58-31-13. Hazardous conditions in State-owned buildings.

If the Commissioner determines that an undue hazard to life, safety, or property exists because of a condition or the use of a building owned by the State, the Commissioner shall advise the proper agency how to limit or prohibit use of the building until the hazard is abated. (1993, c. 409, s. 13.)

§ 58-31-15. Extended coverage insurance.

Upon request of any State department, agency or institution, extended coverage insurance, and other property insurance, may be provided on designated state-owned property of such department, agency or institution which is insured by the State Property Fire Insurance Fund. Premiums for such insurance coverage shall be paid by each requesting department, agency or institution in accordance with rates fixed by the Commissioner. Losses covered by such insurance may be paid for out of the State Property Fire Insurance Fund in the same manner as fire losses. The Commissioner, with the approval of the Governor and Council of State, is authorized and empowered to purchase from insurers admitted to do business in North Carolina such insurance or reinsurance as may be necessary to protect the State Property Fire Insurance Fund against loss with respect to such insurance coverage. The words "extended coverage insurance," as used in this section, mean insurance against loss or damage caused by windstorm, hail, explosion, riot, riot attending a strike, civil commotion, aircraft, vehicles or smoke. (1957, c. 67; 1975, c. 519, s. 2; 1991, c. 720, s. 4.)

§ 58-31-20. Use and occupancy and business interruption insurance.

Upon request of any State department, agency or institution, use and occupancy and business interruption insurance shall be provided on state-owned property of such department, agency or institution which is insured by the State Property Fire Insurance Fund. Premiums for such insurance coverage shall be paid by each requesting department, agency or institution in accordance with rates fixed by the Commissioner. Losses covered by such insurance may be paid for out of the State Property Fire Insurance Fund in the same manner as fire losses. The Commissioner, with the approval of the Governor and Council of State, is authorized and empowered to purchase from insurers admitted to do business in North Carolina such insurance or reinsurance as may be necessary to protect the State Property Fire Insurance Fund against loss with respect to such insurance coverage. (1957, c. 67; 1991, c. 720, s. 4.)

§ 58-31-25. Professional liability insurance for officials and employees of the State.

The Commissioner may acquire professional liability insurance covering the officers and employees of any State department, institution or agency upon the request of such State department, institution or agency. Premiums for such insurance coverage shall be paid by the requesting department, institution or agency at rates fixed by the Commissioner from funds made available to it for the purpose. The Commissioner, in placing a contract for such insurance is authorized to place such insurance through the Public Officers and Employees' Liability Insurance Commission, and shall exercise all efforts to place such insurance through the said commission prior to attempting to procure such insurance through any other source.

The Commissioner, pursuant to this section, may acquire professional liability insurance covering the officers and employees of a department, institution or agency of State government only if the coverage to be provided by such policy is coverage of claims in excess of the protection provided by Articles 31 and 31A of Chapter 143 of the General Statutes.

The purchase, by any State department, institution or agency of professional liability insurance covering the law-enforcement officers, officers or employees of such department, institution or agency shall not be construed as a waiver of any defense of sovereign immunity by such department, institution or agency. The purchase of such insurance shall not be deemed a waiver by any employee of the defense of sovereign immunity to the extent that such defense may be available to him.

The payment, by any State department, institution or agency of funds as premiums for professional liability insurance through the plan provided herein, covering the law-enforcement officers or officials or employees of such department, institution or agency is hereby declared to be for a public purpose. (1979, c. 206, s. 1; 1987, c. 864, s. 53; 1991, c. 720, s. 4.)

§ 58-31-30: Expired at the end of the 1993-94 fiscal year by its own terms.

§ 58-31-35. Information furnished Commissioner by officers in charge.

It is the duty of the different officers or boards having in their custody any property belonging to the State to inform the Commissioner, giving him in detail a full description of same, and to keep him informed of any changes in such property or its location or surroundings. (1901, c. 710, ss. 1, 2; 1903, c. 771, s. 2; Rev., s. 4828; C.S., s. 6452.)

§ 58-31-40. Commissioner to inspect State property.

(a) The Commissioner shall, as often as is required in the fire code adopted by the North Carolina Building Code Council or more often if the Commissioner considers it necessary, visit, inspect, and thoroughly examine every State property to analyze and determine its protection from fire, including the property's occupants or contents. The Commissioner shall notify in writing the agency or official in charge of the property of any defect noted by the Commissioner or any improvement considered by the Commissioner to be necessary, and a copy of that notice shall be forwarded by the Commissioner to the Department of Administration.

(b) No agency or person authorized or directed by law to select a plan or erect a building comprising 20,000 square feet or more for the use of any county, city, or school district shall receive and approve of the plan until it is submitted to and approved by the Commissioner as to the safety of the proposed building from fire, including the property's occupants or contents.

(c) Repealed by Session Laws 2009-474, s. 1, effective October 1, 2009. (1901, c. 710, ss. 1, 2; 1903, c. 771, s. 3; Rev., s. 4829; 1909, c. 880; 1919, c. 186, s. 3; C.S., s. 6453; 2000-122, s. 10; 2001-487, s. 19; 2001-496, s. 11.1; 2007-303, s. 1; 2009-474, s. 1; 2012-161, s. 2.)

§ 58-31-45. Report required of Commissioner.

The Commissioner must submit to the Governor a full report of his official action under this Article, with such recommendations as commend themselves to the Commissioner. (1901, c. 710, ss. 1, 2; 1903, c. 771, s. 4; Rev., s. 4830; C.S., s. 6454; 1945, c. 386; 1991, c. 720, s. 4; 2013-199, s. 7.)

§ 58-31-50. Liability insurance required for state-owned vehicles.

Every department, agency or institution of the State shall acquire motor vehicle liability insurance on all state-owned motor vehicles under its control. (1959, c. 1248; 1983, c. 717, s. 10.)

§ 58-31-52. State motor vehicle safety program.

(a) Findings, Policy, and Purpose. - Motor vehicle accidents exact a terrible toll of human tragedy and suffering as well as national resources within the United States. The same is true, on a smaller scale, within North Carolina State government. Every year State employees or members of the general public are killed or injured, and a significant portion of the State's financial resources is expended as a direct result of accidents involving State-owned vehicles. Accordingly, it is North Carolina policy that the State-owned motor vehicle fleet and vehicles used on behalf of the State be operated and maintained in such a manner as to minimize deaths, injuries, and costs. The purpose of this section is to direct the Commissioner of Insurance to develop a program to provide policy, requirements, procedures, technical information, and standards for administering a State vehicle safety program which will apply to all State personnel involved in the administration and operation of vehicles on behalf of the State.

(b) The Commissioner shall develop and adopt a State motor vehicle safety program to assure that State-owned motor vehicles are operated and maintained in a safe manner.

(c) In developing the program, the Commissioner shall include the following:

(1) Basic criteria concerning qualifications, screening, and education of drivers.

(2) Required and prohibited driving practices.

(3) Safety maintenance requirements.

(4) Accident reporting and review procedures.

(d) The requirements and procedures established under the program apply to all agencies and persons operating vehicles on behalf of the State, unless specifically exempted by the Commissioner. Agencies may adopt more stringent requirements and procedures than those adopted by the Commissioner under this section. The administration of the program in each agency is the responsibility of each agency head or that person's designee.

(e) The provisions of Chapter 150B of the General Statutes do not apply to the program developed and adopted under this section. (1995, c. 517, s. 15.)

§ 58-31-55. Insurance and official fidelity bonds for State agencies to be placed by Department; exception; costs of placement.

Except as provided in G.S. 58-32-15, all insurance and all official fidelity and surety bonds authorized for State departments, institutions, and agencies shall be effected and placed by the Department, and the cost of such placement shall be paid by the State department, institution, or agency involved upon bills rendered to and approved by the Commissioner. (1975, c. 875, s. 11; 1981, c. 1109, s. 4; 1993, c. 504, s. 21.)

§ 58-31-60. Competitive selection of payroll deduction insurance products paid for by State employees.

(a) Employee Insurance Committee. - The head of each State government employee payroll unit offering payroll deduction insurance products to employees shall appoint an Employee Insurance Committee for the following purposes:

(1) To review insurance products currently offered through payroll deduction to the State employees in the Employee Insurance Committee's payroll unit to determine if those products meet the needs and desires of employees in the Employee Insurance Committee's payroll unit.

(2) To select the types of insurance products that reflect the needs and desires of employees in the Employee Insurance Committee's payroll unit.

(3) To competitively select the best insurance products of the types determined by the Employee Insurance Committee to reflect the needs and desires of the employees of that payroll unit.

As used in this section, "insurance product" includes a prepaid legal services plan registered under G.S. 84-23.1.

(b) Appointment of Employee Insurance Committee Members. - The members of the Employee Insurance Committee shall be appointed by the head of the payroll unit. The Committee shall consist of not less than five or more than nine individuals a majority of whom have been employed in the payroll unit for at least one year. The committee members shall, except where necessary initially to establish the rotation herein prescribed, serve three-year terms with approximately one-third of the terms expiring annually. Committee membership make-up shall fairly represent the work force in the payroll unit and be selected without regard to any political or other affiliations. It shall be the duty of the payroll unit head to assure that the Employee Insurance Committee is completely autonomous in its selection of insurance products and insurance companies and that no member of the Employee Insurance Committee has any conflict of interest in serving on the Committee. A committee on employee benefits elected or appointed by the faculty representative body of a constituent institution of The University of North Carolina shall be deemed constituted and functioning as an employee insurance committee in accordance with this section. Any decision rendered by the Employee Insurance Committee where the autonomy of the Committee or a conflict of interest is questioned shall be subject to appeal pursuant to the Administrative Procedure Act, or in the case of departments, boards and commissions which are specifically exempt from the Administrative Procedure Act, pursuant to the appeals procedure prescribed for such department, board or commission.

(c) Payroll Deduction Slots. - Each payroll unit shall be entitled to not less than four payroll deduction slots to be used for payment of insurance premiums for products selected by the Employee Insurance Committee and offered to the employees of the payroll unit. The Employee Insurance Committee shall select only one company per payroll deduction slot. The Company selected by the Employee Insurance Committee shall be permitted to sell through payroll deduction only the products specifically approved by the Employee Insurance Committee. The assignment by the Employee Insurance Committee of a payroll deduction slot shall be for a period of not less than two years unless the insurance company shall be in violation of the terms of the written agreement specified in this subsection. The insurance company awarded a payroll deduction slot shall, pursuant to a written agreement setting out the rights and duties of the insurance company, be afforded an adequate opportunity to solicit employees of the payroll unit by making such employees aware that a representative of the company will be available at a specified time and at a location convenient to the employees.

Notwithstanding any other provision of the General Statutes, once an employee has selected an insurance product for payroll deduction, that product may not be removed from payroll deduction for that employee without his or her specific written consent.

When an employee retires from State employment and payroll deduction under this section is no longer available, the insurance company may not terminate life insurance products purchased under the payroll deduction plan without the retiree's specific written consent solely because the premium is no longer deducted from payroll.

(c1)   Procedure for Selection of Insurance Product Proposals. - All insurance product proposals shall be sealed. The Committee shall open all proposals in public and record them in the minutes of the Committee, at which time the proposals become public records open to public inspection.

After the public opening, the Committee shall review the proposals, examining the cost and quality of the products, the reputation and capabilities of the insurance companies submitting the proposals, and other appropriate criteria. The Committee shall determine which proposal, if any, would meet the needs and desires of the employees of that Committee's payroll unit and shall award a payroll deduction slot to the company submitting the proposal that meets those needs and desires. The Committee may reject any or all proposals.

A company may seek to modify or withdraw a proposal only after the public opening and only on the basis that the proposal contains an unintentional clerical error as opposed to an error in judgment. A company seeking to modify or withdraw a proposal shall submit to the Committee a written request, with facts and evidence in support of its position, prior to the award of the payroll deduction slot, but not later than two days after the public opening of the proposals. The Committee shall promptly review the request, examine the nature of the error, and determine whether to permit or deny the request.

(d)   Criminal Penalty. - It shall be a Class 3 misdemeanor for any State employee, who has supervisory authority over any member of the Employee Insurance Committee, to attempt to influence the autonomy of any Employee Insurance Committee either in the appointment of members to such Committee or in the operation of such Committee; or for anyone to open a sealed insurance product proposal or disclose or exhibit the contents of a sealed insurance product proposal, prior to the public opening of the proposal. The Commissioner of Insurance shall have the authority to investigate complaints alleging acts subject to the criminal penalty and shall report his findings to the Attorney General of North Carolina. (1985, c. 213, s. 1; 1985 (Reg. Sess., 1986), c. 1013, s. 15; 1987, c. 752, s. 12; c. 864, s. 92; 1989, c. 299; 1991, c. 644, s. 3.1; 1993, c. 539, s. 456; 1994, Ex. Sess., c. 24, s. 14(c); 1995, c. 193, s. 33; 1998-187, s. 1.)

§ 58-31-65. Owner-controlled or wrap-up insurance authorized.

(a) To the extent it is determined necessary and in the best interest of this State, the Department may obtain design and construction insurance or provide for self-insurance against property damage caused by this State, its departments, agencies, boards, and commissions and all officers and employees of this State in connection with the construction of public works projects. Workers' compensation and general liability insurance may be purchased to cover both general contractors and subcontractors doing work on a specific contracted work site. In connection with the construction of public works projects, the Department may also use an owner-controlled or wrap-up insurance program if all of the following conditions are met:

(1) The total cost of the project or group of projects is over fifty million dollars ($50,000,000).

(2) The program maintains completed operations coverage for a term during which coverage is reasonably commercially available as determined by the Commissioner, but in no event for fewer than three years.

(3) Bid specifications clearly specify for all bidders the insurance coverage provided under the program and the minimum safety requirements that shall be met.

(4) The program does not prohibit a contractor or subcontractor from purchasing any additional insurance coverage that a contractor believes is necessary for protection from any liability arising out of the contract. The cost of the additional insurance shall not be passed through to this State on a contract bid.

(5) The program does not include surety insurance.

(6) The State may purchase an owner-controlled or wrap-up policy that has a deductible or self-insured retention as long as the deductible or self-insured retention does not exceed one million dollars ($1,000,000).

(b) For the purposes of subsection (a) of this section:

(1) "Owner-controlled or wrap-up insurance" means a series of insurance policies issued to cover this State and all of the construction managers, contractors, subcontractors, architects, and engineers on a specified contracted work site or work sites for purposes of general liability, property damage, and workers' compensation. A State agency or the State may be a secondary insured under owner-controlled or wrap-up insurance.

(2) "Specific contracted work site" means construction being performed at one site or a series of contiguous sites separated only by a street, roadway, waterway, or railroad right-of-way, or along a continuous system for the provision of water and power. (2001-167, s. 1.)

§ 58-31-66. Public construction contract surety bonds.

(a) Neither the State nor any county, city, or other political subdivision of the State, or any officer, employee, or other person acting on behalf of any such entity shall, with respect to any public building or construction contract, require any contractor, bidder, or proposer to procure a bid bond, payment bond, or performance bond from a particular surety, agent, producer, or broker.

(b) (1) Repealed by Session Laws 2004-203, s. 74(b), effective October 1, 2004.

(2) Repealed by Session Laws 2006-264, s. 7, effective August 27, 2006.

(c) Repealed by Session Laws 2004-203, s. 74(b), effective October 1, 2004. (2003-212, s. 27; 2004-203, s. 74(b); 2006-264, s. 7.)

Article 32.

Public Officers and Employees Liability Insurance Commission.

§ 58-32-1. Commission created; membership.

There is hereby created within the Department a Public Officers and Employees Liability Insurance Commission. The Commission shall consist of 11 members who shall be appointed as follows: the Commissioner shall appoint six members as follows: two members who are members of the insurance industry who may be chosen from a list of six nominees submitted to the Commissioner by the Independent Insurance Agents of North Carolina, Inc.; one member who is employed by a police department who may be chosen from a list of three nominees submitted to the Commissioner jointly by the North Carolina Police Chiefs Association and North Carolina Police Executives Association, and one member who is employed by a sheriff's department who may be chosen from a list of three nominees submitted to the Commissioner by the North Carolina Sheriff's Association; one member representing city government who may be chosen from a list of three nominees submitted to the Commissioner by the North Carolina League of Municipalities; and one member representing county government who may be chosen from a list of three nominees submitted to the Commissioner by the North Carolina Association of County Commissioners; and the General Assembly shall appoint two persons, one upon the recommendation of the Speaker of the House of Representatives, and one upon the recommendation of the President Pro Tempore of the Senate. The Commissioner or the Commissioner's designate shall be an ex officio member. Appointments by the General Assembly shall be made in accordance with G.S. 120-121, and vacancies in those appointments shall be filled in accordance with G.S. 120-122. The terms of the initial appointees by the General Assembly shall expire on June 30, 1983. The Secretary of the Department of Public Safety or the Secretary's designate shall be an ex officio member. The Attorney General or the Attorney General's designate shall be an ex officio member. One insurance industry member appointed by the Commissioner shall be appointed to a term of two years and one insurance industry member shall be appointed to a term of four years. The police department member shall be appointed to a term of two years and the sheriff's department member shall be appointed to a term of four years. The representative of county government shall be appointed to a term of two years and the representative of city government to a term of four years. Beginning July 1, 1983, the appointment made by the General Assembly upon the recommendation of the Speaker shall be for two years, and the appointment made by the General Assembly upon the recommendation of the President Pro Tempore of the Senate shall be for four years. Except as provided in this section, if any vacancy occurs in the membership of the Commission, the appointing authority shall appoint another person to fill the unexpired term of the vacating member. After the initial terms established herein have expired, all appointees to the Commission shall be appointed to terms of four years.

The Commission members shall elect the chair and vice-chair of the Commission. The Commission may, by majority vote, remove any member of the Commission for chronic absenteeism, misfeasance, malfeasance or other good cause. (1979, c. 325, s. 1; 1981 (Reg. Sess., 1982), c. 1191, ss. 24-26; 1983, c. 543, ss. 1, 2; 1985, c. 666, ss. 76, 77, 79; 1991, c. 720, s. 4; 1995, c. 490, s. 41; 1999-132, s. 6.1; 2011-145, s. 19.1(g).)

§ 58-32-5. Meetings of Commission; compensation.

The Commission shall meet at least four times per year, on or about January 15, April 15, July 15, October 15 and upon call of the chairman. The members shall receive no compensation for attendance at meetings, except a per diem expense reimbursement. Members of the Commission who are not officers or employees of the State shall receive reimbursement for subsistence and travel expenses at rates set out in G.S. 138-5 from funds made available to the Commission. Members of the Commission who are officers or employees of the State shall be reimbursed for travel and subsistence at the rates set out in G.S. 138-6 from funds made available to the Commission. (1979, c. 325, s.1; 1981 (Reg. Sess., 1982), c. 1191, s. 27; 1985, c. 666, s. 79.)

§ 58-32-10. Powers and duties of Commission.

The Commission may acquire from an insurance company or insurance companies a group plan of professional liability insurance covering the law-enforcement officers and/or public officers and employees of any political subdivision of the State. The Commission shall have full authority to negotiate with insurance companies submitting bids or proposals and shall award its group plan master contract on the basis of the company or companies found by it to offer maximum coverage at the most reasonable premium. The

Commission is authorized to enter into a master policy contract of such term as it finds to be in the best interests of the law-enforcement officers and/or public officers and employees of the political subdivisions of the State, not to exceed five years. The Commission, in negotiating for such contract, is not authorized to pledge or offer the credit of the State of North Carolina. The insurance premiums shall be paid by the political subdivisions whose employees are covered by the professional liability insurance. Any political subdivision may elect coverage for any or all of its employees on a departmental basis; provided all employees in a department must be covered if coverage is elected for that department. Nothing contained herein shall be construed to require any political subdivision to participate in any group plan of professional liability insurance.

The Commission may, in its discretion, employ professional and clerical staff whose salaries shall be as established by the State Human Resources Commission.

Should the Commission determine that reasonable coverage is not available at a reasonable cost, the Commission may undertake such studies and inquiries into the situation and alternatives, including self insurance and State administered funds, as the Commission deems appropriate. The Commission shall then bring before the General Assembly such recommendations as it deems appropriate.

The Commission may acquire information regarding loss ratios, loss factors, loss experience and other such facts and figures from any agency or company issuing professional liability insurance covering public officers, employees or law-enforcement officers in the State of North Carolina. Such information shall not be deemed a public record within the meaning of Chapter 132 of the General Statutes where it names the company divulging such information, but the Commission may make public such information to show aggregate statistics in respect to the experience of the State as a whole. The information shall be provided to the Commission upon its written demand and shall be submitted to the Commission by such company or companies upon sworn affidavit. If any agency or company shall fail or refuse to supply such information to the Commission within a reasonable time following receipt of the demand, the Commission may apply to the Superior Court sitting in Wake County for appropriate orders to enforce the demand.

For purposes of this section, the term "political subdivision" includes any county, city, town, incorporated village, sanitary district, metropolitan water district, county water and sewer district, water and sewer authority, hospital authority, parking authority, local ABC boards, special airport district, airport authority, soil and water conservation district created pursuant to G.S. 139-5, fire district, volunteer or paid fire department, rescue squads, city or county parks and recreation commissions, area mental health boards, area mental health, mental retardation and substance abuse authority as described in G.S. 122C-117, domiciliary home community advisory committees, county and district boards of health, nursing home advisory committees, county boards of social services, local school administrative units, local boards of education, community colleges, and all other persons, bodies, or agencies authorized or regulated by Chapters 108A, 115C, 115D, 118, 122C, 130A, 131A, 131D, 131E, 153A, 160A, and 160B of the General Statutes. (1979, c. 325, s. 1; 1983, c. 543, s. 3; 1985, c. 666, s. 79; 1985 (Reg. Sess., 1986), c. 1027, s. 30; 1987, c. 564, s. 9; 2013-382, s. 9.1(c).)

§ 58-32-15. Professional liability insurance for State officials.

(a) The Commission may acquire professional liability insurance covering the officers and employees, or any group thereof, of any State department, institution or agency or any community college or technical college. Premiums for such insurance shall be paid by the requesting department, institution, agency, community college or technical college at rates established by the Commission, from funds made available to such department, institution, agency, community college or technical college for the purpose.

(b) The Commission, pursuant to this section, may acquire professional liability insurance covering the officers and employees, or any group thereof, of a department, institution or agency of State government or a community college or technical college only if the coverage to be provided by the insurance policy is in excess of the protection provided by Articles 31 and 31A of Chapter 143 of the General Statutes, other than the protection provided by G.S. 143-300.9.

(c) The purchase, by any State department, institution, agency, community college or technical college of professional liability insurance covering the law-enforcement officers, officers or employees of such department, institution, agency, community college or technical college shall not be construed as a waiver of any defense of sovereign immunity by such department, institution, agency, community college or technical college. The purchase of such insurance shall not be deemed a waiver by any employee of the defense of sovereign immunity to the extent that such defense may be available to him.

(d) The payment, by any State department, institution, agency, community college or technical college of funds as premiums for professional liability insurance through the plan provided herein, covering the law-enforcement officers or officials or employees of such department, institution, agency, community college or technical college is hereby declared to be for a public purpose. (1981, c. 1109, s. 3; 1985, c. 666, s. 79; 1987, c. 301; 1991, c. 674, s. 3.)

§ 58-32-20. Commission to act as liaison; meetings of Commission.

The Commission shall act as liaison between the insurance company or companies with which it contracts, their servicing agent and the insureds. The Commission shall give notice of its meetings to the company or companies and to all insureds. The Commission shall attempt to resolve such difficulties as arise in the servicing and administration of the program of insurance between the company and insureds. (1979, c. 325, s. 1; 1985, c. 666, s. 79.)

§ 58-32-25. Contract conditions.

The Commission, in procuring and negotiating for the contract of insurance herein described shall include in any procurement document the following conditions, which are not subject to negotiation and which are deemed a part of the said contract when entered into:

(1) The master policy shall be issued in the name of the Commission and shall include all governmental entities for which coverage was requested in the procurement document.

(2) The company or companies selected must name a servicing agent resident in North Carolina who shall issue all certificates, collect all premiums, process all claims, and be responsible for all processing, service and administration of the program of insurance provided. (1979, c. 325, s. 1; 1985, c. 666, s. 79.)

§ 58-32-30. Payment a public purpose.

The payment by any county or municipality of funds as premiums for professional liability insurance through the plan provided herein, covering the law-enforcement officers or public officials or employees of such subdivision of government, is declared to be for a public purpose. (1979, c. 325, s. 1; 1985, c. 666, s. 79.)

Article 33.

Licensing of Agents, Brokers, Limited Representatives, and Adjusters.

§ 58-33-1. Scope.

This Article governs the qualifications and procedures for the licensing of agents, brokers, limited representatives, adjusters, and motor vehicle damage appraisers. This Article applies to any and all kinds of insurance and insurers under this Chapter. For purposes of this Article, all references to insurance include annuities, unless the context otherwise requires. (1987, c. 629, s. 1; 2001-203, s. 1.)

§ 58-33-5. License required.

A person shall not sell, solicit, or negotiate insurance in this State unless the person is licensed for that kind of insurance in accordance with this Article. (2001-203, s. 2.)

§ 58-33-10. Definitions.

As used in this Article, the following definitions apply:

(1) "Agent" means a person licensed to solicit applications for, or to negotiate a policy of, insurance. A person not duly licensed who solicits or

negotiates a policy of insurance on behalf of an insurer is an agent within the intent of this Article, and thereby becomes liable for all the duties, requirements, liabilities and penalties to which an agent of such company is subject, and such company by compensating such person through any of its officers, agents or employees for soliciting policies of insurance shall thereby accept and acknowledge such person as its agent in such transaction.

(2) "Adjuster" means any individual who, for salary, fee, commission, or other compensation of any nature, investigates or reports to his principal relative to claims arising under insurance contracts other than life or annuity. An attorney at law who adjusts insurance losses from time to time incidental to the practice of his profession or an adjuster of marine losses is not deemed to be an adjuster for purposes of this Article.

(3) "Broker" means a person who, being a licensed agent, procures insurance for a party other than himself through a duly authorized agent of an insurer that is licensed to do business in this State but for which the broker is not authorized to act as agent. A person not duly licensed who procures insurance for a party other than himself is a broker within the intent of this Article, and thereby becomes liable for all the duties, requirements, liabilities and penalties to which such licensed brokers are subject.

(4) "Business entity" means a corporation, association, partnership, limited liability company, limited liability partnership, or other legal entity. "Business entity" does not mean a sole proprietorship.

(4a) "FINRA" means the Financial Industry Regulatory Authority or any successor entity.

(5) "Home state" means the District of Columbia and any state or territory of the United States in which an insurance producer maintains his or her principal place of residence or principal place of business and is licensed to act as an insurance producer.

(6) "Insurance" means any of the kinds of insurance in G.S. 58-7-15.

(7) "Insurance producer" or "producer" means a person required to be licensed under this Article to sell, solicit, or negotiate insurance. "Insurance producer" or "producer" includes an agent, broker, and limited representative.

(8) "License" means a document issued by the Commissioner authorizing a person to act as an insurance producer for the kinds of insurance specified in the document. The license itself does not create any authority, actual, apparent, or inherent, in the holder to represent or commit an insurance carrier.

(9) "Limited line credit insurance" includes any type of credit insurance written under Article 57 of this Chapter, mortgage life, mortgage guaranty, mortgage disability, automobile dealer gap insurance, and any other form of insurance offered in connection with an extension of credit that is limited to partially or wholly extinguishing that credit obligation and that the Commissioner determines should be designated a form of limited line credit insurance.

(10) "Limited line credit insurance producer" means a person who sells, solicits, or negotiates one or more forms of limited line credit insurance coverage to individuals through a master, corporate, group, or individual policy.

(11) "Limited lines insurance" means motor vehicle physical damage insurance and title insurance, or any other kind of insurance that the Commissioner considers necessary to recognize for the purposes of complying with G.S. 58-33-32(f).

(12) "Limited lines producer" means a person authorized by the Commissioner to sell, solicit, or negotiate limited lines insurance.

(13) "Limited representative" means a person who is authorized by the Commissioner to solicit or negotiate contracts for the particular kinds of insurance identified in G.S. 58-33-26(g) and which kinds of insurance are restricted in the scope of coverage afforded.

(14) "Motor vehicle damage appraiser" means an individual who, for salary, fee, commission, or other compensation of any nature, regularly investigates or advises relative to the nature and amount of damage to motor vehicles located in this State or the amount of money deemed necessary to effect repairs thereto and who is not:

a. An adjuster licensed to adjust insurance claims in this State;

b. An agent for an insurance company who is not required by law to be licensed as an adjuster;

c. An attorney at law who is not required by law to be licensed as an adjuster; or

d. An individual who, incident to his regular employment in the business of repairing defective or damaged motor vehicles, investigates and advises relative to the nature and amount of motor vehicle damage or the amount of money deemed necessary to effect repairs thereto.

(15) "Negotiate" means the act of conferring directly with, or offering advice directly to, a purchaser or prospective purchaser of a particular contract of insurance concerning any of the substantive benefits, terms, or conditions of the contract, only if the person engaged in that act either sells insurance or obtains insurance from insurers for purchasers. "Negotiate" does not mean a referral to a licensed insurance agent or broker that does not include a discussion of specific insurance policy terms and conditions.

(16) "Person" means an individual or a business entity, but does not mean a county, city, or other political subdivision of the State of North Carolina.

(17) "Sell" means to exchange a contract of insurance by any means, for money or its equivalent, on behalf of an insurance company. "Sell" does not mean a referral to a licensed insurance agent or broker that does not include a discussion of specific insurance policy terms and conditions.

(18) "Solicit" means attempting to sell insurance or asking or urging a person to apply for a particular kind of insurance from a particular company. "Solicit" does not mean a referral to a licensed insurance agent or broker that does not include a discussion of specific insurance policy terms and conditions.

(19) "Terminate" means the cancellation of the relationship between an insurance producer and the insurer or the termination of a producer's authority to transact insurance.

(20) "Uniform Business Entity Application" means the current version of the NAIC Uniform Business Entity Application for resident and nonresident business entities.

(21) "Uniform Application" means the current version of the NAIC Uniform Application for resident and nonresident producer licensing. (1987, c. 629, s. 1; c. 864, ss. 76, 77; 1987 (Reg. Sess., 1988), c. 975, s. 8; 2001-203, s. 3; 2007-507, s. 2; 2009-566, s. 1.)

§ 58-33-15. Restricted license for overseas military agents.

Notwithstanding any other provision of this Article, an individual may be licensed by the Commissioner as a foreign military sales agent to represent a life insurance company domiciled in this State, provided the agent represents the insurance company only in a foreign country or territory and either on a United States military installation or with United States military personnel. The Commissioner may, upon request of the insurance company on application forms furnished by the Commissioner and upon payment of the fee specified in G.S. 58-33-125, issue to the applicant a restricted license which will be valid only for the representation of the insurance company in a foreign country or territory and either on a United States military installation or with United States military personnel. The insurance company shall certify to the Commissioner that the applicant has the necessary training to hold himself out as a life insurance agent, and that the insurance company is willing to be bound by the acts of the applicant within the scope of his employment. A restricted license issued under this section shall be renewed annually as provided in G.S. 58-33-25(n). (1987, c. 629, s. 1; 1987 (Reg. Sess., 1988), c. 975, s. 9.)

§ 58-33-17. Limited license for rental car companies.

(a) As used in this section:

(1) "Limited licensee" means a person authorized to sell certain coverages relating to the rental of motor vehicles pursuant to the provisions of this section and Article 28 of Chapter 66 of the General Statutes.

(2) "Rental agreement" means any written agreement setting forth the terms and conditions governing the use of a vehicle provided by the rental car company.

(3) "Rental car company" means any person in the business of providing vehicles to the public.

(4) "Renter" means any person obtaining the use of a vehicle from a rental car company under the terms of a rental agreement.

(5) "Vehicle" means a motor vehicle of the private passenger type including passenger vans and minivans that are primarily intended for the transport of persons.

(b) The Commissioner may issue to a rental car company, or to a franchisee of a rental car company, that has complied with the requirements of this section, a limited license authorizing the licensee, known as a "limited licensee" for the purpose of this Article, to act as agent, with reference to the kinds of insurance specified in this section, of any insurer authorized to write such kinds of insurance in this State.

(c) The prerequisites for issuance of a limited license under this section are the filing with the Commissioner of the following:

(1) A written application, signed by an officer of the applicant, for the limited license in such form or forms, and supplements thereto, and containing such information, as the Commissioner may prescribe; and

(2) A certificate by the insurer that is to be named in such limited license, stating that it has satisfied itself that the named applicant is trustworthy and competent to act as its insurance agent for this limited purpose and that the insurer will appoint such applicant to act as the agent in reference to the doing of such kind or kinds of insurance as are permitted by this section, if the limited license applied for is issued by the Commissioner. Such certificate shall be subscribed by an officer or managing agent of such insurer and affirmed as true under the penalties of perjury.

(d) In the event that any provision of this section is violated by a limited licensee, the Commissioner may:

(1) Revoke or suspend a limited license issued under this section in accordance with the provisions of G.S. 58-33-46; or

(2) After notice and hearing, impose such other penalties, including suspending the transaction of insurance at specific rental locations where violations of this Article have occurred, as the Commissioner deems to be necessary or convenient to carry out the purposes of this section.

(e) The rental car company or franchisee licensed pursuant to subsection (b) of this section may act as agent for an authorized insurer only in connection with the rental of vehicles and only with respect to the following kinds of insurance:

(1) Excess liability insurance that provides coverage to the rental car company or franchisee and renters and other authorized drivers of rental vehicles, in excess of the standard liability limits provided by the rental car company in its rental agreement, for liability arising from the negligent operation of the rental vehicle;

(2) Accident and health insurance that provides coverage to renters and other vehicle occupants for accidental death or dismemberment and for medical expenses resulting from an accident that occurs during the rental period;

(3) Personal effects insurance that provides coverage to renters and other vehicle occupants for the loss of, or damage to, personal effects that occurs during the rental period; or

(4) Any other coverage that the Commissioner may approve as meaningful and appropriate in connection with the rental of vehicles.

(f) No insurance may be issued pursuant to this section unless:

(1) The rental period of the rental agreement does not exceed 30 consecutive days; and

(2) At every rental car location where rental car agreements are executed, brochures or other written materials are readily available to the prospective renter that:

a. Summarize, clearly and correctly, the material terms of insurance coverage, including the identity of the insurer, offered to renters;

b. Disclose that these policies offered by the rental car company may provide a duplication of coverage already provided by a renter's personal automobile insurance policy, homeowner's insurance policy, personal liability insurance policy, or other source of coverage;

c. State that the purchase by the renter of the kinds of insurance specified in this section is not required in order to rent a vehicle;

d. Describe the process for filing a claim in the event the renter elects to purchase coverage and in the event of a claim; and

e. Contain any additional information on the price, benefits, exclusions, conditions or other limitations of such policies as the Commissioner may by regulation prescribe; and

(3) Evidence of coverage is provided to every renter who elects to purchase such coverage.

(g) Any limited license issued under this section shall also authorize any salaried employee of the licensee who, pursuant to subsection (h) of this section, is trained to act individually on behalf, and under the supervision, of the licensee with respect to the kinds of insurance specified in this section.

(h) Each rental car company or franchisee licensed pursuant to this section shall conduct a training program which shall be submitted to the commissioner for approval prior to use and which shall meet the following minimum standards:

(1) Each trainee shall receive basic instruction about the kinds of insurance specified in this section offered for purchase by prospective renters of rental vehicles;

(2) Each trainee shall be instructed to acknowledge to a prospective renter of a rental vehicle that purchase of any such insurance specified in this section is not required in order for the renter to rent a vehicle; and

(3) Each trainee shall be instructed to acknowledge to a prospective renter of a rental vehicle that the renter may have insurance policies that already provide the coverage being offered by the rental car company pursuant to this section.

(i) Limited licensees acting pursuant to and under the authority of this section shall comply with all applicable provisions of this Article, except that notwithstanding any other provision of this Article, or any rule adopted by the Commissioner, a limited licensee pursuant to this section shall not be required to treat premiums collected from renters purchasing such insurance when renting vehicles as funds received in a fiduciary capacity, provided that:

(1) The insurer represented by the limited licensee has consented in writing, signed by the insurer's officer, that premiums need not be segregated from funds received by the rental car company on account of vehicle rental; and

(2) The charges for insurance coverage are itemized but not billed to the renter separately from the charges for rental vehicles.

(j) No limited licensee under this section shall advertise, represent, or otherwise hold itself or any of its employees themselves out as licensed insurance agents or brokers. (1991, c. 139, s. 1; 2001-203, s. 4.)

§ 58-33-18. Limited license for self-service storage companies.

(a) As used in this section:

(1) "Limited licensee" means a person authorized to sell certain coverages relating to the rental of self-service storage units pursuant to the provisions of this section and Article 39 of Chapter 66 of the General Statutes.

(2) "Rental agreement" means any written agreement setting forth the terms and conditions governing the use of a storage unit provided by the owner of a self-service storage facility company.

(3) "Self-service storage company" means any person in the business of renting storage units to the public.

(4) "Renter" or "occupant" means any person obtaining the use of a storage unit from a self-service storage company under the terms of a rental agreement.

(5) "Storage unit" means a semienclosed or fully enclosed area, room, or space that is primarily intended for the storage of personal property and which shall be accessible by the renter of the unit pursuant to the terms of the rental agreement.

(b) The Commissioner may issue to a self-service storage company, or to a franchisee of a self-service storage company, that has complied with the requirements of this section a limited license authorizing the licensee, known as a "limited licensee" for the purpose of this Article, to act as agent, with reference to the kinds of insurance specified in this section of any insurer authorized to write such kinds of insurance in this State.

(c) The prerequisites for issuance of a limited license under this section are the filing with the Commissioner of the following:

(1) A written application, signed by an officer of the applicant, for the limited license in such form or forms, and supplements thereto, and containing such information as the Commissioner may prescribe; and

(2) A certificate by the insurer that is to be named in such limited license, stating that it has satisfied itself that the named applicant is trustworthy and competent to act as its insurance agent for this limited purpose and that the insurer will appoint such applicant to act as the agent in reference to the doing of such kind or kinds of insurance as are permitted by this section if the limited license applied for is issued by the Commissioner. Such certificate shall be subscribed by an officer or managing agent of such insurer and affirmed as true under the penalties of perjury.

(d) In the event that any provision of this section is violated by a limited licensee, the Commissioner may:

(1) Revoke or suspend a limited license issued under this section in accordance with the provisions of G.S. 58-33-46; or

(2) After notice and hearing, impose such other penalties, including suspending the transaction of insurance at specific rental locations where violations of this Article have occurred, as the Commissioner deems to be necessary or convenient to carry out the purposes of this section.

(e) The self-service storage company or franchisee licensed pursuant to subsection (b) of this section may act as agent for an authorized insurer only in connection with the rental of storage units and only with respect to the following kinds of insurance:

(1) Personal effects insurance that provides coverage to renters of storage units at the same facility for the loss of, or damage to, personal effects that occurs at the same facility during the rental period; or

(2) Any other coverage that the Commissioner may approve as meaningful and appropriate in connection with the rental of storage units.

(f) No insurance may be issued pursuant to this section unless:

(1) The rental period of the rental agreement does not exceed two years; and

(2) At every self-service storage location where self-service storage agreements are executed, brochures or other written materials are readily available to the prospective renter that:

a. Summarize, clearly and correctly, the material terms of insurance coverage, including the identity of the insurer, offered to renters;

b. Disclose that these policies offered by the self-service storage company may provide a duplication of coverage already provided by a renter's homeowners' insurance policy, personal liability insurance policy, or other source of coverage;

c. State that the purchase by the renter of the kinds of insurance specified in this section is not required in order to rent a storage unit;

d. Describe the process for filing a claim in the event the renter elects to purchase coverage and in the event of a claim; and

e. Contain any additional information on the price, benefits, exclusions, conditions, or other limitations of such policies as the Commissioner may by regulation prescribe; and

(3) Evidence of coverage is provided to every renter who elects to purchase such coverage.

(g) Any limited license issued under this section shall also authorize any employee of the licensee who is trained, pursuant to subsection (h) of this section, to act individually on behalf, and under the supervision, of the licensee with respect to the kinds of insurance specified in this section.

(h) Each self-service storage company or franchisee licensed pursuant to this section shall conduct a training program which shall be submitted to the Commissioner for approval prior to use and which shall meet the following minimum standards:

(1) Each trainee shall receive basic instruction about the kinds of insurance specified in this section offered for purchase by prospective renters of storage units;

(2) Each trainee shall be instructed to acknowledge to a prospective renter of a storage unit that purchase of any such insurance specified in this section is not required in order for the renter to rent a storage unit; and

(3) Each trainee shall be instructed to acknowledge to a prospective renter of a storage unit that the renter may have insurance policies that already provide the coverage being offered by the self-service storage company pursuant to this section.

(i) Limited licensees acting pursuant to and under the authority of this section shall comply with all applicable provisions of this Article, except that notwithstanding any other provision of this Article, or any rule adopted by the Commissioner, a limited licensee pursuant to this section shall not be required to treat premiums collected from renters purchasing such insurance when renting storage units as funds received in a fiduciary capacity, provided that:

(1) The insurer represented by the limited licensee has consented in writing, signed by the insurer's officer, that premiums need not be segregated from funds received by the self-service storage company on account of storage unit rental; and

(2) The charges for insurance coverage are itemized but not billed to the renter separately from the charges for storage units.

(j) No limited licensee under this section shall advertise, represent, or otherwise hold itself or any of its employees out as licensed insurance agents or brokers. No renter or occupant may be required to obtain insurance under this section as a condition of obtaining a rental agreement for a storage unit. The renter shall be informed that the insurance offered under this section is not required as a condition for obtaining a rental agreement for a storage unit. (2003-290, s. 5.)

§ 58-33-19. Limited lines travel insurance.

(a) As used in this Article, the following definitions apply:

(1) Limited lines travel insurance producer. - Any of the following:

a. A licensed managing general underwriter.

b. A licensed managing general agent or third-party administrator.

c. A licensed insurance producer as defined by G.S. 58-33-10(7), including:

1. A limited lines producer designated by an insurer as the travel insurance supervising entity, as set forth in subsection (h) of this section.

2. A limited lines producer appointed by an insurer, as set forth in G.S. 58-33-40, who acts as a landlord or real estate broker engaged in the rental or management of residential property for vacation rental as defined in Chapter 42A of the General Statutes.

(2) Offer and disseminate. - Providing general information, including a description of the coverage and price, as well as processing the application, collecting premiums, and performing other activities that do not require a license and are permitted by the Department.

(3) Travel insurance. - Insurance coverage for the personal risks incident to planned travel that includes, but is not limited to, the coverages listed in sub-subdivisions a. through d. of this subdivision. Travel insurance does not include major medical plans that provide comprehensive medical protection for travelers with trips lasting six months or longer, including deployed military personnel or those U.S. citizens working overseas as expatriates. [Travel insurance includes:]

a. Interruption or cancellation of trip or event.

b. Loss of baggage or personal effects.

c. Damages to accommodations or rental vehicles.

d. Sickness, accident, disability, or death occurring during travel.

(4) Travel retailer. - A business entity that makes, arranges, or offers travel services and may offer and disseminate travel insurance as a service to its

customers on behalf of and under the direction of a limited lines travel insurance producer.

(b)   An individual or business entity may apply for a limited lines travel insurance producer license by filing with the Department an application in a form and manner prescribed by the Commissioner. If issued, the license authorizes the limited lines travel insurance producer to sell, solicit, or negotiate travel insurance through a licensed insurer.

(c)   A travel retailer may offer and disseminate travel insurance under a limited lines travel insurance producer business entity license only if the following conditions are met:

(1)   The limited lines producer or travel retailer provides all of the following to purchasers of travel insurance:

a.   A description of the material terms or the actual material terms of the insurance coverage.

b.   A description of the process for filing a claim.

c.   A description of the review or cancellation process for the travel insurance policy.

d.   The identity and contact information of the insurer and limited lines travel insurance producer.

(2)   At the time of licensure, the limited lines travel insurance producer shall establish and maintain a register on a form prescribed by the Commissioner of each travel retailer that offers travel insurance on the limited lines travel insurance producer's behalf. The register shall be maintained and updated annually by the limited lines travel insurance producer and shall include the name, address, and contact information of the travel retailer and an officer or person who directs or controls the travel retailer's operations, and the travel retailer's federal Tax Identification Number. The limited lines travel insurance producer shall submit the register to the Department upon request. The limited lines producer shall also certify that the travel retailer register complies with 18 U.S.C. § 1033.

(3)   The limited lines travel insurance producer has designated one of its employees who is a licensed individual producer as the person responsible for

the limited lines travel insurance producer's compliance with this Chapter and administrative rules adopted by the Commissioner.

(4)   The person designated in subdivision (3) of this subsection and the president, secretary, treasurer, and any other officer or person who directs or controls the limited lines travel insurance producer's insurance operations comply with the fingerprinting requirements applicable to insurance producers in the resident state of the limited lines travel insurance producer.

(5)   The limited lines travel insurance producer has paid all applicable insurance producer licensing fees as set forth in applicable State law.

(6)   The limited lines travel insurance producer requires each employee and authorized representative of the travel retailer whose duties include offering and disseminating travel insurance to receive a program of instruction or training, which may be subject to review by the Commissioner. The training material shall, at a minimum, contain instructions on the types of insurance offered, ethical sales practices, and required disclosures to prospective customers.

(7)   Limited lines travel insurance producers, and those registered under its license, are exempt from the examination and continuing education requirements under G.S. 58-33-30, 58-33-32, and 58-33-130.

(d)   Any travel retailer offering or disseminating travel insurance shall make available to prospective purchasers brochures or other written materials that include all of the following:

(1)   The identity and contact information of the insurer and the limited lines travel insurance producer.

(2)   An explanation that the purchase of travel insurance is not required in order to purchase any other product or service from the travel retailer.

(3)   A disclaimer that an unlicensed travel retailer is permitted to provide general information about the insurance offered by the travel retailer, including a description of the coverage and price, but is not qualified or authorized to answer technical questions about the terms and conditions of the insurance offered by the travel retailer or to evaluate the adequacy of the customer's existing insurance coverage.

(e)   A travel retailer's employee or authorized representative who is not licensed as a limited lines travel insurance producer shall not do any of the following:

(1)   Evaluate or interpret the technical terms, benefits, and conditions of the offered travel insurance coverage.

(2)   Evaluate or provide advice concerning a prospective purchaser's existing insurance coverage.

(3)   Hold himself or herself out as a licensed insurer, licensed producer, or insurance expert.

(f)   A travel retailer, whose insurance-related activities and the activities of its employees and authorized representatives are limited to offering or disseminating travel insurance on behalf of and under the direction of a limited lines travel insurance producer meeting the conditions stated in this section, is authorized to do so and receive related compensation upon compliance with subdivision (c)(2) of this section by the limited lines travel insurance producer.

(g)   Travel insurance may be provided under an individual policy or under a group or master policy.

(h)   As the travel insurance supervising entity, the limited lines travel insurance producer is responsible for the acts of the travel retailer and shall use reasonable means to ensure compliance by the travel retailer with this section.

(i)   The limited lines travel insurance producer and any travel retailer offering or disseminating travel insurance under the limited lines travel insurance producer license shall be subject to the provisions of Article 63 of this Chapter and to the full enforcement powers of the Commissioner granted by Article 2 of this Chapter. (2013-285, s. 1.)

§ 58-33-20. Representation.

(a)   Every agent or limited representative who solicits or negotiates an application for insurance of any kind, in any controversy between the insured or his beneficiary and the insurer, is regarded as representing the insurer and not the insured or his beneficiary. This provision does not affect the apparent authority of an agent.

(b)   Every broker who solicits an application for insurance of any kind, in any controversy between the insured or his beneficiary and the insurer issuing any policy upon such application, is regarded as representing the insured or his beneficiary and not the insurer; except any insurer that directly or through its agents delivers in this State to any insurance broker a policy of insurance pursuant to the application or request of such broker, acting for an insured other than himself, is deemed to have authorized such broker to receive on its behalf payment of any premium that is due on such policy of insurance at the time of its issuance or delivery. (1987, c. 629, s. 1.)

§ 58-33-25: Repealed by Session Laws 2001-203, s. 5, effective July 1, 2002.

§ 58-33-26. General license requirements.

(a)   No person shall act as or hold himself or herself out to be an agent, broker, limited representative, adjuster, or motor vehicle damage appraiser unless duly licensed.

(b)   No agent, broker, or limited representative shall make application for, procure, negotiate for, or place for others, any policies for any kinds of insurance as to which that person is not then qualified and duly licensed.

(c)   Effective for new licenses issued before January 1, 2008, an agent or broker may be licensed for the following kinds of insurance:

(1)   Life and health insurance, meaning:

a.   Life-insurance coverage on human lives, including benefits of endowment and annuities, and may include benefits in the event of death or dismemberment by accident and benefits for disability income.

b.   Variable life and variable annuity products-insurance coverage provided under variable life insurance contracts and variable annuities.

c. Accident and health or sickness-insurance coverage for sickness, bodily injury, or accidental death and may include benefits for disability income.

(2) Property and liability insurance, meaning:

a. Coverage for the direct or consequential loss or damage to property of every kind.

b. Coverage against legal liability, including that for death, injury, or disability or damage to real or personal property.

(3) Personal lines, meaning property and liability insurance coverage sold to individuals and families for primarily noncommercial purposes.

(4) Medicare supplement insurance and long-term care insurance, as a supplement to a license for the kinds of insurance listed in subdivision (1) of this subsection.

These lines of authority shall remain applicable for holders of these licenses until the Commissioner provides applicable replacement licenses under the new lines that will go into effect for new licenses on January 1, 2008. Replacement licenses shall grant authority comparable to the licenses being replaced.

(c1) Effective for licenses issued on or after January 1, 2008, an agent or broker may be licensed for the following kinds of insurance:

(1) Accident and health or sickness. - Insurance coverage for sickness, bodily injury, or accidental death and may include benefits for disability income.

(2) Casualty. - Insurance coverage against legal liability, including that for death, injury, or disability, or damage to real or personal property.

(3) Limited line insurance.

(4) Life. - Insurance coverage on human lives, including benefits in the event of death or dismemberment by accident and benefits for disability income.

(5) Medicare supplement insurance and long-term care insurance, as a supplement to a license for the kinds of insurance listed in subdivision (1) of this subsection.

(6) Personal lines. - Property and casualty insurance coverage sold to individuals and families for primarily noncommercial purposes.

(7) Property. - Insurance coverage for the direct or consequential loss or damage to property of every kind.

(8) Variable life and variable annuity products. - Insurance coverage provided under variable life insurance contracts and variable annuities.

(9) Any other kind of insurance permitted under State laws or administrative rules.

(d) A person holding a license or licenses for the kind or kinds of insurance specified in subsection (c1) of this section may sell, solicit, or negotiate only the kind or kinds of insurance for which that person is licensed.

(e) A variable life and variable annuity products license authorizes a resident agent to sell, solicit, or negotiate variable contracts if the agent satisfies the Commissioner that the agent has met the FINRA requirements of the Secretary of State of North Carolina.

(f) An accident and health or sickness license authorizes a resident agent to sell, solicit, or negotiate Medicare supplement and long-term care insurance policies as defined respectively in Articles 54 and 55 of this Chapter, provided that the licensee takes and passes a supplemental written examination for the insurance as provided in G.S. 58-33-30(e) and pays the supplemental registration fee provided in G.S. 58-33-125(c).

(g) The Commissioner may issue one or more licenses without examination to individuals for limited lines insurance per qualifications and application procedures defined in the administrative rules.

(h) No licensed agent, broker, or limited representative shall sell, solicit, or negotiate anywhere in the boundaries of this State, or receive or transmit an application or premium of insurance, for a company not licensed to do business in this State, except as provided in G.S. 58-28-5 and Article 21 of this Chapter.

(i) No agent shall place a policy of insurance with any insurer unless the agent has a current appointment as agent for the insurer in accordance with G.S. 58-33-40 or has a valid temporary license issued in accordance with G.S. 58-33-66.

(j) A business entity that sells, solicits, or negotiates insurance shall be licensed in accordance with G.S. 58-33-31(b). Every member of the partnership and every officer, director, stockholder, and employee of the business entity personally engaged in this State in selling, soliciting, or negotiating policies of insurance shall qualify as an individual licensee. A business entity license shall expire on March 31 of each year unless the business entity pays the renewal fee.

(k) The license shall state the name and an identifying number of the licensee, date of issue, kind or kinds of insurance covered by the license, and any other information as the Commissioner deems to be proper.

(l) A license issued to an agent authorizes him to act until his license is otherwise suspended or revoked. Upon the suspension or revocation of a license, the licensee or any person having possession of such license shall return it to the Commissioner.

(m) A license of a broker, limited representative, adjuster, or motor vehicle damage appraiser shall be renewed on April 1 each year, and renewal fees shall be paid. The Commissioner is not required to print licenses for the purpose of renewing licenses. The Commissioner may establish for licenses "staggered" license renewal dates that will apportion renewals throughout each calendar year. If the system of staggered licensing is adopted, the Commissioner may extend the licensure period for some licensees. License renewal fees prescribed by G.S. 58-33-125 shall be prorated to the extent they are commensurate with extensions.

(n) A license as an insurance producer is not required of the following:

(1) An officer, director, or employee of an insurer or of an insurance producer, provided that the officer, director, or employee does not receive any commission on policies written or sold to insure risks residing, located, or to be performed in this State, except for indirect receipt of proceeds of commissions in the form of salary, benefits, or distributions, and:

a. The officer, director, or employee's activities are executive, administrative, managerial, clerical, or a combination of these, and are only indirectly related to the sale, solicitation, or negotiation of insurance; or

b. The officer, director, or employee's function relates to underwriting, loss control, inspection, or the processing, adjusting, investigating, or settling of a claim on a contract of insurance; or

c. The officer, director, or employee is acting in the capacity of a special agent or agency supervisor assisting insurance producers where the person's activities are limited to providing technical advice and assistance to licensed insurance producers and do not include the sale, solicitation, or negotiation of insurance.

(2) A person who secures and furnishes information for the purpose of group life insurance, group property and casualty insurance, group annuities, group or blanket accident and health insurance; or for the purpose of enrolling individuals under plans; issuing certificates under plans or otherwise assisting in administering plans; or performs administrative services related to mass-marketed property and casualty insurance; where no commission is paid to the person for the service.

(3) An employer or association or its officers, directors, employees, or the trustees of an employee trust plan, to the extent that the employers, officers, employees, director, or trustees are engaged in the administration or operation of a program of employee benefits for the employer's or association's own employees or the employees of its subsidiaries or affiliates, which program involves the use of insurance issued by an insurer, as long as the employers, associations, officers, directors, employees, or trustees are not in any manner compensated, directly or indirectly, by the company issuing the contracts.

(4) Employees of insurers or organizations employed by insurers who are engaging in the inspection, rating, or classification of risks, or in the supervision of the training of insurance producers and who are not individually engaged in the sale, solicitation, or negotiation of insurance.

(5) A person whose activities in this State are limited to advertising without the intent to solicit insurance in this State through communications in printed publications or other forms of electronic mass media whose distribution is not limited to residents of this State, provided that the person does not sell, solicit, or negotiate insurance that would insure risks residing, located, or to be performed in this State.

(6) A person who is not a resident of this State who sells, solicits, or negotiates a contract of insurance for commercial property and casualty risks to

an insured with risks located in more than one state insured under that contract, provided that that person is otherwise licensed as an insurance producer to sell, solicit, or negotiate that insurance in the state where the insured maintains its principal place of business and the contract of insurance insures risks located in that state.

(7) A salaried full-time employee who counsels or advises his or her employer relative to the insurance interests of the employer or of the subsidiaries or business affiliates of the employer provided that the employee does not sell or solicit insurance or receive a commission.

(8) Licensed insurers authorized to write the kinds of insurance described in G.S. 58-7-15(1) through G.S. 58-7-15(3) that do business without the involvement of a licensed agent.

(9) A person indirectly receiving proceeds of commissions as part of the transfer of insurance business or in the form of retirement or similar benefits.

(o) Nothing in this Article requires an insurer to obtain an insurance producer license. In this subsection, "insurer" does not include an insurer's officers, directors, employees, subsidiaries, or affiliates.

(p) An individual shall not simultaneously hold a property, casualty, or personal lines insurance license and an adjuster's license in this State. An individual who holds a property, casualty, or personal lines insurance license may apply for an adjuster license without having to take the adjuster examination in G.S. 58-33-30(e) if the individual applies for the adjuster license within 60 days after surrendering the property, casualty, or personal lines insurance license. An individual who holds an adjuster license may apply for a property and liability insurance license without having to take the property and liability insurance agent examination in G.S. 58-33-30(e) if the individual applies for the property, casualty, or personal lines insurance license within 60 days after surrendering the adjuster license. (2001-203, s. 6; 2007-507, s. 1; 2009-383, s. 1; 2009-566, ss. 2, 3.)

§ 58-33-27. Claims handling for portable consumer electronic devices.

(a) As used in this section, the following definitions apply:

(1) "Automated claims adjudication system" means a preprogrammed computer system designed for the collection, data entry, calculation, and system-generated final resolution of claims on insurance policies that cover only portable consumer electronic devices, which system shall meet the following criteria:

a. Be utilized only by a licensed adjuster, licensed agent, or supervised individuals operating pursuant to this section.

b. Comply with all claims payment requirements of this Chapter.

c. Be certified as compliant with this section by a licensed adjuster who is an officer of a licensed business entity under this Chapter.

(2) "Portable consumer electronic devices" include the following, which must be easily carried or conveyed by hand: smartphones, navigation devices, cellular phones, personal digital assistants, iPads, iPhones, Androids, video games, wireless reading devices, laptops, tablets, netbooks, MP3 players, digital cameras, and other electronic devices that are portable in nature, their accessories, and services related to the use of the device.

(b) No adjuster license is required for an individual who, in connection with insurance covering only portable consumer electronic devices as defined in subdivision (a)(2) of this section, collects claim information from or furnishes claim information to insureds, who conducts data entry, including entering data into an automated claims adjudication system, and who does not exercise any discretion in the disposition of the portable consumer electronic device claim; provided that the individual is supervised by a licensed adjuster or licensed agent and there are no more than 25 individuals who may adjust claims under the supervision of the licensed adjuster or licensed agent. No agent acting as a supervisor pursuant to this section is required to be licensed as an adjuster.

(c) If other property losses occur in conjunction with the loss associated with the portable consumer electronic device, the individual who performs duties as described in G.S. 58-33-10(2) on the total loss, including the loss associated with the portable consumer electronic device, must hold an adjuster's license. (2011-196, s. 8.)

§ 58-33-30. License requirements.

The Commissioner shall not issue or continue any license of an agent, broker, limited representative, adjuster, or motor vehicle damage appraiser except as follows:

(a) Application. - The applicable license application requirements of G.S. 58-33-31 shall be satisfied.

(b), (c) Repealed by Session Laws 2001-203, s. 7, effective July 1, 2002.

(d) Education and Training. -

(1) Each applicant must have had special education, training, or experience of sufficient duration and extent reasonably to satisfy the Commissioner that the applicant possesses the competence necessary to fulfill the responsibilities of an agent, broker, limited representative, adjuster, or motor vehicle damage appraiser.

(2) All individual applicants for licensing as agents under G.S. 58-33-26(c1)(1), (2), (4), (6), or (7) shall furnish evidence satisfactory to the Commissioner of successful completion of at least 20 hours of instruction for each license, which shall in all cases include the general principles of insurance and any other topics relevant to the license that the Commissioner establishes by administrative rules. Any applicant who submits satisfactory evidence of having successfully completed an agent training course that has been approved by the Commissioner and that is offered by or under the auspices of a property or liability or life or health insurance company admitted to do business in this State or a professional insurance association shall be deemed to have satisfied the educational requirements of this subdivision.

(3) Each resident applicant for a Medicare supplement and long-term care insurance license shall furnish evidence satisfactory to the Commissioner of successful completion of 10 hours of instruction, which shall in all cases include the principles of Medicare supplement and long-term care insurance and federal and North Carolina law relating to such insurance. A resident applicant who submits satisfactory evidence of having successfully completed an agent training course that has been approved by the Commissioner and that is offered by or under the auspices of a licensed life or health insurer or a professional insurance association satisfies the educational requirements of this subdivision.

(e) Examination. -

(1) After completion and filing of the application with the Commissioner, the Commissioner shall require each applicant for license as an agent or an adjuster to take an examination as to the applicant's competence to be licensed. The applicant must take and pass the examination according to requirements prescribed by the Commissioner. This subsection shall not apply to adjusters who adjust only federal crop insurance claims and are certified in accordance with subdivision (2a) of this subsection.

(2) The Commissioner may require any licensed agent, adjuster, or motor vehicle damage appraiser to take and successfully pass an examination in writing, testing his competence and qualifications as a condition to the continuance or renewal of his license, if the licensee has been found guilty of any violation of any provision of this Chapter. If an individual fails to pass such an examination, the Commissioner shall revoke all licenses issued in his name and no license shall be issued until such individual has passed an examination as provided in this Article.

(2a) Adjusters who adjust federal crop insurance claims shall be certified as having passed a proficiency examination approved by the federal Risk Management Agency (RMA) as a condition of obtaining an adjuster's license under this Chapter or another proficiency examination approved by the Commissioner. An adjuster who intends to adjust crop insurance claims shall furnish the Commissioner proof that the adjuster is certified as having passed the required examination pursuant to this section.

(3) Each examination shall be as the Commissioner prescribes and shall be of sufficient scope to test the applicant's knowledge of:

a. The terms and provisions of the policies or contracts of insurance the applicant proposes to effect; or

b. The types of claims or losses the applicant proposes to adjust; and

c. The duties and responsibilities of the license; and

d. The current laws of this State applicable to the license.

(4) The answers of the applicant to the examination shall be provided by the applicant under the Commissioner's supervision. The Commissioner shall give examinations at such times and places within this State as the Commissioner

considers necessary reasonably to serve the convenience of both the Commissioner and applicants: Provided that the Commissioner may contract directly with persons for the processing of examination application forms and for the administration and grading of the examinations required by this section; the Commissioner may charge a reasonable fee in addition to the registration fee charged under G.S. 58-33-125, to offset the cost of the examination contract authorized by this subsection; and such contracts shall not be subject to Article 3 of Chapter 143 of the General Statutes. However, the Commissioner shall: (i) submit all proposed agreements or contracts for supplies, materials, printing, equipment, and contractual services that exceed one million dollars ($1,000,000) authorized by this subdivision to the Attorney General or the Attorney General's designee for review as provided in G.S. 114-8.3; and (ii) include in all contracts to be awarded by the Commissioner under this subdivision a standard clause which provides that the State Auditor and internal auditors of the Commissioner may audit the records of the contractor during and after the term of the contract to verify accounts and data affecting fees and performance. The Commissioner shall not award a cost plus percentage of cost contract for any purpose.

(5) The Commissioner shall collect in advance the examination and registration fees provided in G.S. 58-33-125 and in subsection (4) of this section. The Commissioner shall make or cause to be made available to all applicants, for a reasonable fee to offset the costs of production, materials that he considers necessary for the applicants' proper preparation for examinations. The Commissioner may contract directly with publishers and other suppliers for the production of the preparatory materials, and contracts so let by the Commissioner shall not be subject to Article 3 of Chapter 143 of the General Statutes. However, the Commissioner shall: (i) submit all proposed contracts for supplies, materials, printing, equipment, and contractual services that exceed one million dollars ($1,000,000) authorized by this subdivision to the Attorney General or the Attorney General's designee for review as provided in G.S. 114-8.3; and (ii) include in all contracts to be awarded by the Commissioner under this subdivision a standard clause which provides that the State Auditor and internal auditors of the Commissioner may audit the records of the contractor during and after the term of the contract to verify accounts and data affecting fees and performance. The Commissioner shall not award a cost plus percentage of cost contract for any purpose.

(6) In addition to the examinations for the kinds of insurance specified in G.S. 58-33-25(c)(1) and (2), before any resident may sell Medicare supplement or long-term care insurance policies defined respectively in Articles 54 and 55 of

this Chapter, the resident must take and pass a supplemental written examination according to requirements prescribed by the Commissioner.

(7)   An individual who fails to appear for the examination as scheduled or fails to pass the examination shall reapply for an examination and remit all required fees and forms before being rescheduled for another examination.

(f)   Brokers. -

(1)   Bond. - Prior to issuance of a license as a broker, the applicant shall file with the Commissioner and thereafter, for as long as the license remains in effect, shall keep in force a bond in favor of the State of North Carolina for the use of aggrieved parties in the sum of not less than fifteen thousand dollars ($15,000), executed by an authorized corporate surety approved by the Commissioner. The aggregate liability of the surety for any and all claims on any such bond shall in no event exceed the sum thereof. The bond shall be conditioned on the accounting by the broker (i) to any person requesting the broker to obtain insurance for moneys or premiums collected in connection therewith, (ii) to any licensed insurer or agent who provides coverage for such person with respect to any such moneys or premiums, and (iii) to any premium finance company or to any association of insurers under any plan or plans for the placement of insurance under the laws of North Carolina which afforded coverage for such person with respect to any such moneys or premiums. No such bond shall be terminated unless at least 30 days' prior written notice thereof is given by the surety to the licensee and the Commissioner. Upon termination of the license for which the bond was in effect, the Commissioner shall notify the surety within 10 business days. A person required by this subdivision to maintain a bond may, in lieu of that bond, deposit with the Commissioner the equivalent amount in cash, in certificates of deposit issued by banks organized under the laws of the State of North Carolina, or any national bank having its principal office in North Carolina, or securities, which shall be held in accordance with Article 5 of this Chapter. Securities may only be obligations of the United States or of federal agencies listed in G.S. 147-69.1(c)(2) guaranteed by the United States, obligations of the State of North Carolina, or obligations of a city or county of this State. Any proposed deposit of an obligation of a city or county of this State is subject to the prior approval of the Commissioner.

(2)   Other Requirements. - An applicant must hold a valid agent's license at the time of application for the broker's license and throughout the duration of the broker's license. A broker's license shall be issued to cover only those kinds of

insurance authorized by his agent's license. Suspension or revocation of the agent's license shall cause immediate revocation of the broker's license.

(g) Denial of License. - If the Commissioner finds that the applicant has not fully met the requirements for licensing, the Commissioner shall refuse to issue the license and shall notify in writing the applicant and the appointing insurer, if any, of the denial, stating the grounds for the denial. The application may also be denied for any reason for which a license may be suspended or revoked or not renewed under G.S. 58-33-46. In order for an applicant to be entitled to a review of the Commissioner's action to determine the reasonableness of the action, the applicant must make a written demand upon the Commissioner for a review no later than 30 days after service of the notification upon the applicant. The review shall be completed without undue delay, and the applicant shall be notified promptly in writing of the outcome of the review. In order for an applicant who disagrees with the outcome of the review to be entitled to a hearing under Article 3A of Chapter 150B of the General Statutes, the applicant must make a written demand upon the Commissioner for a hearing no later than 30 days after service upon the applicant of the notification of the outcome.

(h) Resident-Nonresident Licenses. - The Commissioner shall issue a resident or nonresident license to an agent, broker, limited representative, adjuster, or motor vehicle damage appraiser as follows:

(1) Resident.

An individual may qualify for a license as a resident if he resides in this State. Any license issued pursuant to an application claiming residency in this State shall be void if the licensee, while holding a resident license in this State, also holds or makes application for a resident license in, or thereafter claims to be a resident of, any other state, or ceases to be a resident of this State; provided, however, if the applicant is a resident of a county in another state, the border of which county is contiguous with the state line of this State, the applicant may qualify as a resident for licensing purposes in this State.

(2) Nonresident.

a. An individual may qualify for a license under this Article as a nonresident if he holds a like license in another state or territory of the United States. An individual may qualify for a license as a nonresident motor vehicle damage appraiser or a nonresident adjuster if the applicant's state of residency does not offer such licenses and such applicant meets all other requirements for licensure of a resident. A license issued to a nonresident of this State shall grant the same rights and privileges afforded a resident licensee, except as provided in subsection (i) of this section.

b.   Except as provided in G.S. 58-33-32, a nonresident of this State may be licensed without taking an otherwise required written examination if the insurance regulator of the state of the applicant's residence certifies that the applicant has passed a similar written examination or has been a continuous holder, prior to the time such written examination was required, of a license like the license being applied for in this State.

c.   Notwithstanding other provisions of this Article, no new bond shall be required for a nonresident broker if the Commissioner is satisfied that an existing bond covers his insurance business in this State.

d.   Process Against Nonresident Licensees.

1.   Each licensed nonresident agent, broker, adjuster, limited representative, or motor vehicle damage appraiser shall by the act of acquiring such license be deemed to appoint the Commissioner as his attorney to receive service of legal process issued against the agent, broker, adjuster, limited representative, or motor vehicle damage appraiser in this State upon causes of action arising within this State.

2.   The appointment shall be irrevocable for as long as there could be any cause of action against the nonresident arising out of his insurance transactions in this State.

3.   Duplicate copies of such legal process against such nonresident licensee shall be served upon the Commissioner either by a person competent to serve a summons, or through certified or registered mail. At the time of such service the plaintiff shall pay to the Commissioner a fee in the amount set in G.S. 58-16-30, taxable as costs in the action to defray the expense of such service.

4.   Upon receiving such service, the Commissioner or his duly appointed deputy shall within three business days send one of the copies of the process, by registered or certified mail, to the defendant nonresident licensee at his last address of record as filed with the Commissioner.

5. The Commissioner shall keep a record of the day and hour of service upon him of all such legal process. No proceedings shall be had against the defendant nonresident licensee, and such defendant shall not be required to appear, plead or answer until the expiration of 40 days after the date of service upon the Commissioner.

e. If the Commissioner revokes or suspends any nonresident's license through a formal proceeding under this Article, he shall promptly notify the appropriate Commissioner of the licensee's residence of such action and of the particulars thereof.

(i) Retaliatory Provision. - Whenever, by the laws or regulations of any other state or jurisdiction, any limitation of rights and privileges, conditions precedent, or any other requirements are imposed upon residents of this State who are nonresident applicants or licensees of such other state or jurisdiction in addition to, or in excess of, those imposed on nonresidents under this Article, the same such requirements shall be imposed upon such residents of such other state or jurisdiction. This subsection does not apply to fees charged to insurance producers.

(j) Reciprocity Provision. - To the extent that other states that provide for the licensing and regulation of and payment of commissions to agents, limited representatives, or brokers, waive restrictions on the basis of reciprocity with respect to North Carolina licensees applying for or holding nonresident licenses in those states, the same restrictions on licensees from those states applying for or holding North Carolina nonresident licenses shall be waived. (1987, c. 629, s. 1; c. 864, ss. 80, 86; 1987 (Reg. Sess., 1988), c. 975, s. 30; 1989, c. 485, s. 21; c. 645, s. 5; c. 657, s. 1.1; 1989 (Reg. Sess., 1990), c. 941, ss. 3, 7; 1991, c. 212, s. 2; c. 476, s. 3; 1993, c. 409, s. 2; c. 504, ss. 26, 37; 1998-211, s. 18; 2000-122, s. 3; 2001-203, ss. 7, 8, 9, 10, 11, 29; 2005-240, s. 1; 2007-507, s. 3; 2009-566, s. 6(b); 2010-194, s. 7; 2011-196, s. 9; 2011-326, s. 15(g).)

§ 58-33-31. Application for license.

(a) A person applying for a resident insurance producer license shall make application to the Commissioner on the Uniform Application and declare under penalty of denial, suspension, or revocation of the license that the statements made in the application are true, correct, and complete to the best of the individual's knowledge and belief. Before approving the application, the Commissioner shall find that the individual:

(1)   Is at least 18 years of age.

(2)   Has not committed any act that is a ground for probation, suspension, nonrenewal, or revocation set forth in G.S. 58-33-46.

(3)   Has satisfied any applicable requirements of G.S. 58-33-30(d).

(4)   Has paid the applicable fees set forth in G.S. 58-33-125.

(5)   Has successfully passed any examinations required by G.S. 58-33-30(e).

(b)   A business entity selling, soliciting, or negotiating insurance shall obtain an insurance producer license. Application shall be made using the Uniform Business Entity Application. Before approving the application, the Commissioner shall find that:

(1)   The business entity has paid the applicable fees set forth in G.S. 58-33-125.

(2)   The business entity has designated a licensed producer, who is a natural person, responsible for the business entity's compliance with the insurance laws and administrative rules of this State and orders of the Commissioner.

(c)   The Commissioner may require any documents reasonably necessary to verify the information contained in an application. (2001-203, s. 12.)

§ 58-33-32. Interstate reciprocity in producer licensing.

(a)   The purpose of this section is to make North Carolina insurance producer licensing comply with the reciprocity requirements in the federal Gramm-Leach-Bliley Act, Public Law 106-102. This section does not apply to surplus lines licensees in Article 21 of this Chapter, except as provided in subsections (c) and (d) of this section.

(b)   Repealed by Session Laws 2001-203, s. 13, effective July 1, 2002.

(c) Unless denied licensure under G.S. 58-33-30 or G.S. 58-33-50, a nonresident person shall receive a nonresident producer license if:

(1) The person is currently licensed as a resident and in good standing in that person's home state;

(2) The person has submitted the request for licensure in the form prescribed by the Commissioner and has paid the applicable fees required by G.S. 58-33-125;

(3) The person has submitted or transmitted to the Commissioner a copy of the application for licensure that the person submitted to that person's home state, or in lieu of the same, a completed Uniform Application or Uniform Business Entity Application; and

(4) The person's home state awards nonresident producer licenses to residents of this State on a reciprocal basis.

The Commissioner may verify the producer's licensing status through the producer database maintained by the NAIC or affiliates or subsidiaries of the NAIC.

(d) A person licensed as a surplus lines producer in that person's home state shall receive a nonresident surplus lines license under subsection (c) of this section. Except for the licensure provisions of this section, nothing in this section otherwise amends or supersedes any provision of Article 21 of this Chapter.

(e) A person licensed or registered as a viatical settlement broker or provider, as defined in G.S. 58-58-205, in that person's home state shall receive a nonresident viatical settlement broker or provider license under subsection (c) of this section. Except for the licensure provisions of this section, nothing in this section otherwise amends or supersedes any provision of Part 5 of Article 58 of this Chapter.

(f) A person licensed as a limited line credit insurance producer or other type of limited lines producer in that person's home state may, under subsection (c) of this section, receive a nonresident limited lines producer license granting the same scope of authority as granted under the license issued by the producer's home state. For the purposes of this subsection, limited lines insurance is any authority granted by the home state that restricts the authority of the license to less than the total authority prescribed in the associated major lines under G.S. 58-33-26(c)(1), 58-33-26(c)(2), 58-33-26(c)(3), and 58-33-26(c)(4).

(g) An individual who applies for an insurance producer license in this State who was previously licensed for the same kinds of insurance in that individual's home state shall not be required to complete any prelicensing education or examination. This exemption is available only if:

(1) The applicant is currently licensed in the applicant's home state; or

(2) The application is received within 90 days after the cancellation of the applicant's previous license and the applicant's home state issues a certification that, at the time of cancellation, the applicant was in good standing in that state; or

(3) The home state's producer database records, maintained by the NAIC or affiliates or subsidiaries of the NAIC, indicate that the producer is or was licensed in good standing for the kind of insurance requested.

A person licensed as an insurance producer in another state who moves to this State and who wants to be licensed as a resident under G.S. 58-33-31 shall apply within 90 days after establishing legal residence.

(h) The Commissioner shall not assess a greater fee for an insurance license or related service to a nonresident producer based solely on the fact that the producer does not reside in this State.

(i) The Commissioner shall waive any license application requirements for a nonresident license applicant with a valid license from the applicant's home state, except the requirements imposed by subsection (c) of this section, if the applicant's home state awards nonresident licenses to residents of this State on the same basis.

(j) A nonresident producer's satisfaction of the nonresident producer's home state's continuing education requirements for licensed insurance producers shall constitute satisfaction of this State's continuing education requirements if the nonresident producer's home state recognizes the satisfaction of its continuing education requirements imposed upon producers from this State on the same basis.

(k) A producer shall report to the Commissioner any administrative action taken against the producer in another state or by another governmental agency in this State within 30 days after the final disposition of the matter. As used in this subsection, "administrative action" includes enforcement action taken against the producer by the FINRA. This report shall include a copy of the order or consent order and other information or documents filed in the proceeding necessary to describe the action.

(l) Within 30 days after the initial pretrial hearing date or similar proceeding, a producer shall report to the Commissioner any criminal prosecution of the producer. The report shall include a copy of the initial complaint filed, the order resulting from the hearing or similar proceeding, and any other information or documents filed in the proceeding necessary to describe the prosecution. (2000-122, s. 2; 2001-203, s. 13; 2001-436, s. 4; 2007-507, s. 4; 2009-566, s. 5.)

§ 58-33-35: Repealed by Session Laws 2009-566, s. 6(a), effective August 28, 2009.

§ 58-33-40. Appointment of agents.

(a) Except as provided in subsection (b) of this section, no individual who holds a valid insurance agent's license issued by the Commissioner shall, either directly or for an insurance agency, solicit, negotiate, or otherwise act as an agent for an insurer by which the individual has not been appointed.

(b) Any insurer authorized to transact business in this State may appoint as its agent any individual who holds a valid agent's license issued by the Commissioner. To appoint an individual as its agent, the appointing insurer shall file, in a format approved by the Commissioner, a notice of appointment within 15 days after the date the first insurance application is submitted. The individual shall be authorized to act as an agent for the appointing insurer for the kinds of insurance for which the insurer is authorized in this State and for which the appointed agent is licensed in this State, unless specifically limited. For purposes of determining the number of appointments for an agent, there shall be one appointment for each kind of insurance for which the appointed agent is licensed in this State, unless specifically limited.

(c)   Repealed by Session Laws 2009-566, s. 9, effective August 28, 2009.

(d)   Every insurer shall remit in a manner prescribed by the Commissioner the appointment fee specified in G.S. 58-33-125 for each appointed agent.

(e)   An appointment shall continue in effect as long as the appointed agent is properly licensed and the appointing insurer is authorized to transact business in this State, unless the appointment is cancelled.

(f)   Prior to April 1 of each year, every insurer shall remit in a manner prescribed by the Commissioner the renewal appointment fee specified in G.S. 58-33-125.

(g)   Any agent license in effect on February 1, 1988, shall be deemed to be an appointment for the unexpired term of that license.

(h)   Repealed by Session Laws 2009-566, s. 9, effective August 28, 2009. (1987, c. 629, s. 1; 2001-203, s. 14; 2009-383, s. 3; 2009-566, ss. 7-9.)

§ 58-33-45: Repealed by Session Laws 2001-203, s. 15.

§ 58-33-46. Suspension, probation, revocation, or nonrenewal of licenses.

(a)   The Commissioner may place on probation, suspend, revoke, or refuse to renew any license issued under this Article, in accordance with the provisions of Article 3A of Chapter 150B of the General Statutes, for any one or more of the following causes:

(1)   Providing materially incorrect, misleading, incomplete, or materially untrue information in the license application.

(2)   Violating any insurance law of this or any other state, violating any administrative rule, subpoena, or order of the Commissioner or of another state's insurance regulator, or violating any rule of the FINRA.

(3) Obtaining or attempting to obtain a license through misrepresentation or fraud.

(4) Improperly withholding, misappropriating, or converting any monies or properties received in the course of doing insurance business.

(5) Intentionally misrepresenting the terms of an actual or proposed insurance contract or application for insurance.

(6) Having been convicted of a felony or a misdemeanor involving dishonesty, a breach of trust, or moral turpitude.

(7) Having admitted or been found to have committed any insurance unfair trade practice or fraud.

(8) Using fraudulent, coercive, or dishonest practices, or demonstrating incompetence, untrustworthiness, or financial irresponsibility in the conduct of business in this State or elsewhere.

(9) Having an insurance producer license, or its equivalent, denied, suspended, or revoked in any other jurisdiction for reasons substantially similar to those listed in this subsection.

(10) Forging another's name to an application for insurance or to any document related to an insurance transaction.

(11) Willfully failing to provide the notification required by subsection (c) of this section.

(12) Knowingly accepting brokered insurance business from an individual who is not licensed to broker that kind of insurance.

(12a) Soliciting, negotiating, or selling insurance in this State for an unauthorized insurer, regardless of whether the licensee or applicant knew that the insurer was unauthorized. As used in this section, the terms "soliciting", "negotiating", and "selling" shall have the meaning of "solicit", "negotiate", and "sell", respectively, set forth in G.S. 58-33-10.

(13) Failing to comply with an administrative or court order imposing a child support obligation, after entry of a final judgment or order finding the violation to have been willful.

(14) Failing to pay State income tax or comply with any administrative or court order directing payment of State income tax, after entry of a final judgment or order finding the violation to have been willful.

(15) Cheating on an examination for an insurance license or for a prelicensing or continuing education course, including improperly using notes or any other reference material to complete an examination for an insurance license or for a prelicensing or continuing education course.

(16) Willfully overinsuring property.

(17) Any cause for which issuance of the license could have been refused had it then existed and been known to the Commissioner at the time of issuance.

(b) G.S. 58-2-50 applies to any investigation under this section. G.S. 58-2-70 applies to any person subject to licensure under this Article.

(c) Any person licensed under this Article shall notify the Commissioner of the commencement of any bankruptcy, insolvency, or receivership proceeding affecting the person licensed, or upon making an assignment for the benefit of creditors of the person licensed. Each owner, manager, or officer of a business entity that is a licensed person shall be responsible for providing this notification. Any person responsible for notifying the Commissioner shall provide the notice within three business days after the commencement of the proceeding or the making of the assignment.

(d) If the Commissioner refuses to grant a license, or suspends or revokes a license, any appointment of the applicant or licensee shall likewise be revoked. No individual whose license is revoked shall be issued another license without first complying with all requirements of this Article.

(e) No person shall be issued a license or appointment to enter the employment of any other person, which other person is at that time found by the Commissioner to be in violation of any of the insurance laws of this State, or which other person has been in any manner disqualified under any state or federal law to engage in the insurance business.

(f) The Commissioner shall retain the authority to enforce the provisions of, and impose any penalty or remedy authorized by, this Chapter against any person who is under investigation for or charged with a violation of this Chapter even if the person's license or registration has been surrendered or has lapsed by operation of law. (2001-203, s. 16; 2004-166, s. 2; 2007-507, ss. 5, 6; 2009-566, s. 10.)

§ 58-33-48. Criminal history record checks.

(a)   An applicant for an insurance producer license under this Article shall furnish the Commissioner with a complete set of the applicant's fingerprints in a manner prescribed by the Commissioner. The applicant's fingerprints shall be certified by an authorized law enforcement officer. The fingerprints of every applicant shall be forwarded to the State Bureau of Investigation for a search of the applicant's criminal history record file, if any. If warranted, the State Bureau of Investigation shall forward a set of the fingerprints to the Federal Bureau of Investigation for a national criminal history record check. An applicant shall pay the cost of the State and any national criminal history record check of the applicant.

(b)   The Commissioner shall keep all information pursuant to this section privileged, in accordance with applicable State law and federal guidelines, and the information shall be confidential and shall not be a public record under Chapter 132 of the General Statutes.

(c)   This section does not apply to a person applying for renewal or continuation of a home state insurance producer license or a nonresident insurance producer license. (2009-566, s. 4.)

§ 58-33-50. Notices; loss of residency; duplicate licenses.

(a)   The Commissioner shall notify every appointing insurer about any suspension, revocation, or nonrenewal of a license by the Commissioner and about any surrender of a license by a licensee, whether by consent order or otherwise.

(b)   Upon suspension, revocation, nonrenewal, surrender, or reinstatement of any license, the Commissioner shall notify the Central Office of the NAIC.

(c) Any licensee who ceases to maintain his residency in this State shall deliver his insurance license or licenses to the Commissioner by personal delivery or by mail within 30 days after terminating residency.

(d) The Commissioner may issue a duplicate license for any lost, stolen, or destroyed license issued pursuant to this Article upon a written request from the licensee and payment of appropriate fees. (1987, c. 629, s. 1; 1993, c. 504, s. 29.)

§ 58-33-55: Repealed by Session Laws 2001-203, s. 17.

§ 58-33-56. Notification to Commissioner of termination.

(a) An insurer or authorized representative of the insurer that terminates the appointment, employment, contract, or other insurance business relationship with a producer shall notify the Commissioner within 30 days after the effective date of the termination, using a form prescribed by the Commissioner, if the reason for termination is for or related to one of the causes listed in G.S. 58-33-46(a) or the insurer has knowledge the producer was found by a court, government body, or self-regulatory organization authorized by law to have engaged in any of the activities in G.S. 58-33-46(a). Upon the written request of the Commissioner, the insurer shall provide additional information, documents, records, or other data pertaining to the termination or activity of the producer.

(b) An insurer or authorized representative of the insurer that terminates the appointment, employment, or contract with a producer for any reason that is not for or related to one of the causes listed in G.S. 58-33-46(a) shall notify the Commissioner within 30 days after the effective date of the termination, using a form prescribed by the Commissioner. Upon written request of the Commissioner, the insurer shall provide additional information, documents, records, or other data pertaining to the termination.

(c) The insurer or the authorized representative of the insurer shall promptly notify the Commissioner in a form acceptable to the Commissioner if, upon further review or investigation, the insurer discovers additional information that would have been reportable to the Commissioner in accordance with subsection (a) of this section had the insurer then known of its existence.

(d)   Within 15 days after making the notification required by subsections (a), (b), and (c) of this section, the insurer shall mail a copy of the notification to the producer at the producer's last known address. If the producer is terminated for cause for any of the reasons listed in G.S. 58-33-46(a), the insurer shall provide a copy of the notification to the producer at the producer's last known address by certified mail, return receipt requested, postage prepaid, or by overnight delivery using a nationally recognized carrier.

(e)   Within 30 days after the producer has received the original or additional notification, the producer may file written comments concerning the substance of the notification with the Commissioner. The producer shall, by the same means, simultaneously send a copy of the comments to the reporting insurer, and the comments shall become a part of the Commissioner's file and accompany every copy of a report distributed or disclosed for any reason about the producer as permitted under subsection (h) of this section.

(f)   In the absence of actual malice, neither an insurer, the authorized representative of the insurer, a producer, the Commissioner, an organization of which the Commissioner is a member, nor the respective employees and agents of such persons acting on behalf of such persons shall be subject to civil liability as a result of any statement or information provided pursuant to this section.

(g)   In any action brought against a person that may have immunity under subsection (f) of this section for making any statement required by this section or for providing any information relating to any statement that may be requested by the Commissioner, the party bringing the action shall plead specifically in any allegation that subsection (f) of this section does not apply because the person making the statement or providing the information did so with actual malice. Subsections (f) and (g) of this section do not abrogate or modify any existing statutory or common law privileges or immunities.

(h)   Notwithstanding any other provision of this Chapter, any documents, materials, or other information in the control or possession of the Commissioner or any organization of which the Commissioner is a member that is (i) furnished by an insurer, producer, or an employee or agent thereof acting on behalf of the insurer or producer under this section, or (ii) obtained by the Commissioner in an investigation under this section shall be confidential by law and privileged, shall not be subject to or public records under G.S. 58-2-100 or Chapter 132 of the General Statutes, shall not be subject to subpoena, and shall not be subject to discovery in any civil action other than a proceeding brought by the

Commissioner against a person to whom such documents, materials, or other information relate. However, the Commissioner is authorized to use the documents, materials, or other information in the furtherance of any regulatory or legal action brought as a part of the Commissioner's duties. Neither the Commissioner nor any person who received documents, materials, or other information while acting under the authority of the Commissioner shall be permitted or required to testify in any civil action other than a proceeding brought by the Commissioner against a person to whom such documents, materials, or other information relate concerning any such documents, materials, or information.

(i) In order to assist in the performance of the Commissioner's duties under this Article, the Commissioner may:

(1) Share documents, materials, or other information, including the confidential documents, materials, or information described in this section, with other state, federal, and international regulatory agencies, with the NAIC, its affiliates or subsidiaries, and with state, federal, and international law enforcement authorities. The Commissioner may condition such sharing on an agreement by the recipient to maintain the confidentiality and privileged status of the document, material, or other information;

(2) Receive documents, materials, or information, including otherwise confidential and privileged documents, materials, or information from other state, federal, and international regulatory agencies, from the NAIC, its affiliates or subsidiaries, and from state, federal, and international law enforcement authorities, and may agree to maintain the confidential and privileged status of the document, material, or other information received under the laws of the jurisdiction that is the source of the document, material, or information; and

(3) Enter into agreements governing sharing and use of information consistent with this subsection.

(j) No waiver of any applicable privilege or claim of confidentiality in the documents, materials, or information shall occur as a result of disclosure to the Commissioner under this section or as a result of sharing as authorized in subsection (i) of this section.

(k) Nothing in this Article prohibits the Commissioner from releasing final, adjudicated actions including for cause terminations that are open to public inspection under G.S. 58-2-100, to a database or other clearinghouse service maintained by the NAIC, its affiliates, or subsidiaries of the NAIC.

(l) An insurer, the authorized representative of the insurer, or producer that fails to report as required under this section or that is found to have reported with actual malice by a court of competent jurisdiction may, after notice and hearing, have its license suspended or revoked and may be fined in accordance with G.S. 58-2-70. (2001-203, s. 18.)

§ 58-33-60. Countersignature and related laws.

Subject to the retaliatory provisions of G.S. 58-33-30(i), there shall be no requirement that a licensed resident agent or broker must countersign, solicit, transact, take, accept, deliver, record, or process in any manner an application, policy, contract, or any other form of insurance on behalf of a nonresident agent or broker or an authorized insurer; or share in the payment of commissions, if any, related to such business. (1987, c. 629, s. 1.)

§ 58-33-65: Repealed by Session Laws 2001-203, s. 19.

§ 58-33-66. Temporary licensing.

(a) The Commissioner may issue a temporary insurance producer license for a period not to exceed 180 days or longer, for good cause, without requiring an examination if the Commissioner deems that the temporary license is necessary for the servicing of an insurance business in any of the following cases:

(1) To the spouse or surviving spouse or court-appointed personal representative or guardian of a licensed insurance producer who dies or becomes mentally or physically disabled to allow adequate time for the transfer of the insurance business owned by the producer, for the recovery or return of the producer to the business, or for the training and licensing of new personnel to operate the producer's business.

(2) To a member or employee of a business entity licensed as an insurance producer, upon the death or disability of an individual designated in the business entity application or the license.

(3) To the designee of a licensed insurance producer entering active service in the Armed Forces of the United States.

(4) In any other circumstance where the Commissioner deems that the public interest will be served best by the issuance of this license.

(b) The Commissioner may by order limit the authority of any temporary licensee in any way deemed necessary to protect insureds and the public. The Commissioner may require the temporary licensee to have a suitable sponsor who is a licensed producer or insurer and who assumes responsibility for all acts of the temporary licensee and may impose other similar requirements designed to protect insureds and the public. The Commissioner may by order revoke a temporary license if the interest of insureds or the public are endangered. A temporary license terminates upon the transfer of the business.

(c) An individual requesting a temporary license on account of death or disability of an agent or broker shall be licensed to represent only those insurers that had appointed such agent at the time of death or commencement of disability. (2001-203, s. 20; 2011-183, s. 42.)

§ 58-33-70. Special provisions for adjusters and motor vehicle damage appraisers.

(a) It shall be unlawful and cause for revocation of license for a licensed adjuster to engage in the practice of law.

(b) On behalf and on request of an insurer by which an agent or limited representative is appointed, the agent or limited representative may from time to time act as an adjuster and investigate and report upon claims without being licensed as an adjuster. No agent or limited representative shall adjust any losses where the agent's or representative's remuneration for the sale of insurance is in any way dependent upon the adjustment of those losses.

(c) Upon the filing of the application for an adjuster's license, the advance payment of the examination fee, and the filing with the Commissioner of a certificate signed by the applicant's employer, the Commissioner may issue a learner's permit authorizing the applicant to act as an adjuster for a learning period of 90 days without a requirement of any other license. Not more than one learner's permit shall ever be issued to one individual. The employer's certificate required by this subsection shall certify that:

(1) The applicant is an individual of good character.

(2) The applicant is employed by the signer of the certificate.

(3) The applicant will operate as a student or learner under the instruction and general supervision of a licensed adjuster.

(4) The employer will be responsible for the adjustment acts of the applicant during the learning period.

(d) Repealed by Session Laws 1998-211, s. 19, effective November 1, 1998.

(e) The Commissioner may permit an experienced adjuster, who regularly adjusts in another state and who is licensed in the other state (if that state requires a license), to act as an adjuster in this State without a North Carolina license only for an insurance company authorized to do business in this State, for emergency insurance adjustment work, for a period to be determined by the Commissioner, done for an employer who is an adjuster licensed by this State or who is a regular employer of one or more adjusters licensed by this State; provided that the employer shall furnish to the Commissioner a notice in writing immediately upon the beginning of any such emergency insurance adjustment work. As used in this subsection, "emergency insurance adjustment work" includes, but is not limited to, (i) adjusting of a single loss or losses arising out of an event or catastrophe common to all of those losses or (ii) adjusting losses in any area declared to be a state of emergency or disaster by the Governor under G.S. 166A-19.20 or G.S. 166A-19.21 or by the President of the United States under applicable federal law.

(f) The Commissioner may permit an experienced motor vehicle damage appraiser who is regularly appraising in another state and who is licensed in such other state (if that state requires a license) to act as a motor vehicle damage appraiser in this State without a North Carolina license for emergency motor vehicle damage appraisal work for a period not exceeding 30 days done for an employer who notifies the Commissioner, in writing, at the beginning of the period of emergency appraisal work and who is:

(1)   An insurance adjuster licensed by this State;

(2)   A motor vehicle damage appraiser licensed by this State;

(3)   A regular employer of one or more insurance adjusters licensed by this State; or

(4)   A regular employer of one or more motor vehicle damage appraisers licensed by this State. (1987, c. 629, s. 1; 1998-211, s. 19; 2012-12, s. 2(l); 2013-199, s. 22(c).)

§ 58-33-75. Twisting with respect to insurance policies; penalties.

No licensee shall make or issue, or cause to be issued, any written or oral statement that willfully misrepresents or willfully makes an incomplete comparison as to the terms, conditions, or benefits contained in any policy of insurance for the purpose of inducing or attempting to induce a policyholder in any way to terminate or surrender, exchange, or convert any insurance policy. Any person who violates this section is subject to the provisions of G.S. 58-2-70 and G.S. 58-33-46. (1987, c. 629, s. 1; c. 864, s. 75; 2001-203, s. 21.)

§ 58-33-76. Referral of business to repair source; prohibitions.

(a)   No insurance company, agent, adjuster or appraiser or any person employed to perform their service shall recommend the use of a particular service or source for the repair of property damage without clearly informing the claimant that the claimant is under no obligation to use the recommended repair service.

(b)   No insurance company, agent, adjuster or appraiser or any person employed to perform their service shall accept any gratuity or other form of remuneration from a repair service for recommending that repair service to a claimant. Provided, however, discounts agreed to by repair services shall not violate this section.

(c) Any person who violates this section is subject to the provisions of G.S. 58-2-70 and G.S. 58-33-46. (1991, c. 386, s. 1; 1993, c. 525, s. 1; 2001-203, s. 22.)

§ 58-33-80. Discrimination forbidden.

No agent or representative of any company doing the business of insurance as defined in G.S. 58-7-15 shall make any discrimination in favor of any person. (1987, c. 629, s. 1.)

§ 58-33-82. Commissions.

(a) An insurance company or insurance producer shall not pay a commission, service fee, or other valuable consideration to a person for selling, soliciting, or negotiating insurance in this State if that person is required to be licensed under this Article and is not so licensed.

(b) A person shall not accept a commission, service fee, brokerage, or other valuable consideration for selling, soliciting, or negotiating insurance in this State if that person is required to be licensed under this Article and is not so licensed.

(c) Renewal or other deferred commissions may be paid to a person for selling, soliciting, or negotiating insurance in this State if the person was required to be licensed under this Article at the time of the sale, solicitation, or negotiation and was so licensed at that time.

(d) Except as provided in subsection (e) of this section, only agents who are duly licensed with appropriate company appointments, licensed brokers, licensed limited lines producers, or licensed limited representatives may accept, directly or indirectly, any commission, fee, or other valuable consideration for the sale, solicitation, or negotiation of insurance.

(e) Commissions, fees, or other valuable consideration for the sale, solicitation, or negotiation of insurance may be assigned or directed to be paid in the following circumstances:

(1) To a business entity by a person who is an owner, shareholder, member, partner, director, employee, or agent of that business entity.

(2) To a producer in connection with renewals of insurance business originally sold by or through the licensed person or for other deferred commissions.

(3) In connection with the indirect receipt of commissions in circumstances in which a license is not required under G.S. 58-33-26(n). (2001-203, s. 23; 2004-199, s. 20(e).)

§ 58-33-83. Assumed names.

An insurance producer doing business under any name other than the producer's legal name shall notify the Commissioner before using the assumed name. (2001-203, s. 24; 2003-221, s. 13.)

§ 58-33-85. Rebates and charges in excess of premium prohibited; exceptions.

(a) No insurer, agent, broker or limited representative shall knowingly charge, demand or receive a premium for any policy of insurance except in accordance with the applicable filing approved by the Commissioner. No insurer, agent, broker or limited representative shall pay, allow, or give, or offer to pay, allow, or give, directly or indirectly, as an inducement to insurance, or after insurance has been effected, any rebate, discount, abatement, credit, or reduction of the premium named in a policy of insurance, or any special favor or advantage in the dividends or other benefits to accrue thereon, or any valuable consideration or inducement whatever, not specified in the policy of insurance. No insured named in a policy of insurance, nor any employee of such insured, shall knowingly receive or accept, directly or indirectly, any such rebate, discount, abatement or reduction of premium, or any special favor or advantage or valuable consideration or inducement. Nothing herein contained shall be construed as prohibiting the payment of commissions or other compensation to duly licensed agents, brokers and limited representatives, nor as prohibiting any participating insurer from distributing to its policyholders dividends, savings or the unused or unabsorbed portion of premiums and premium deposits. As used in this section the word "insurance" includes suretyship and the word "policy" includes bond.

(b)   No insurer, agent, broker, or limited representative shall knowingly charge to or demand or receive from an applicant for insurance any money or other consideration in return for the processing of applications or other forms or for the rendering of services associated with a contract of insurance, which money or other consideration is in addition to the premium for such contract, unless the applicant consents in writing before any services are rendered. This subsection does not apply to the charging or collection of any fees otherwise provided for by law. (1987, c. 629, s. 1; c. 864, ss. 49, 89; 1989, c. 485, s. 52; 1991, c. 720, s. 4; 2001-203, s. 25.)

§ 58-33-90. Rebate of premiums on credit life and credit accident and health insurance; retention of funds by agent.

It shall be unlawful for any insurance carrier, or officer, agent or representative of an insurance company writing credit life and credit accident and health insurance, as defined in G.S. 58-58-10 and G.S. 58-51-100, or combination credit life, accident and health, hospitalization and disability insurance in connection with loans, to permit any agent or representative of such company to retain any portion of funds received for the payment of losses incurred, or to be incurred, under such policies of insurance issued by such company, or to pay, allow, permit, give or offer to pay, allow, permit or give, directly, or indirectly, as an inducement to insurance, or after insurance has been effected, any rebate, discount, abatement, credit or reduction of the premium, to any loan agency, insurance agency or broker, or to any creditor of the debtor on whose account the insurance was issued, or to any person, firm or corporation which received a commission or fee in connection with the issuance of such insurance: Provided, that this section shall not prohibit the payment of commissions to a licensed insurance agent or agency or limited representative on the sale of a policy of credit life and credit accident and health insurance, or combination credit life, accident and health, hospitalization and disability insurance in connection with loans.

It shall be unlawful for any agent, agency, broker, limited representative, or insured named in any such policy, or for any loan agency or broker, or any agent, officer or employee of any loan agency or broker to receive or accept, directly or indirectly, any such rebate, discount, abatement, credit or reduction of the premium as set out in this section. (1987, c. 629, s. 1.)

§ 58-33-95. Agents personally liable; representing unlicensed company prohibited; penalty.

(a) Any person or entity who solicits, negotiates, or sells insurance or acts as a third-party administrator in this State for an unauthorized insurer:

(1) Is the representative of that insurer and shall be strictly liable for any losses or unpaid claims if an unauthorized insurer fails to pay in full or in part any claim or loss within the provisions of any insurance contract sold, directly or indirectly, by or through that person or entity on behalf of the unauthorized insurer. The liability imposed by this subsection shall be joint and several if more than one person violates this section.

(2) Shall be guilty of a Class 1 misdemeanor if the person or entity does not know that the insurer is an unauthorized insurer. Each solicitation, negotiation, or sale shall constitute a separate offense.

(3) Shall be guilty of a Class H felony if the person or entity knew or should have known that the insurer is an unauthorized insurer. Each solicitation, negotiation, or sale shall constitute a separate offense.

(b) A civil action may be filed or a license revocation proceeding may be initiated under this section regardless of whether a criminal action is brought or a criminal conviction is obtained for the act alleged in the civil action or revocation proceeding.

(c) For the purposes of this section, the status of an entity or person as an "unauthorized insurer" shall be determined in accordance with Article 28 of this Chapter and, if applicable, Article 49 of this Chapter.

(d) As used in this section, "third-party administrator" means a person who performs administrative functions, including claims administration and payment, marketing, premium accounting, premium billing, coverage verification, underwriting authority, or certificate issuance in regard to any kind of insurance; but does not include the persons specified in G.S. 58-56-2(5)a. through (5)l.

(1987, c. 629, s. 1; 1993, c. 539, s. 457; 1994, Ex. Sess., c. 24, s. 14(c); 2004-166, s. 1; 2006-105, s. 2.8; 2007-305, s. 5.)

§ 58-33-100. Payment of premium to agent valid; obtaining by fraud a crime.

(a) Any agent, broker or limited representative who acts for a person other than himself negotiating a contract of insurance is, for the purpose of receiving the premium therefor, the company's agent, whatever conditions or stipulations may be contained in the policy or contract. This subsection does not apply to the Insurance Underwriting Association established under Article 45 of this Chapter or the Joint Underwriting Association established under Article 46 of this Chapter.

(b) Any agent, broker or limited representative knowingly procuring by fraudulent representations payment, or the obligation for the payment, of a premium of insurance, shall be guilty of a Class 1 misdemeanor. (1987, c. 629, s. 1; 1993, c. 539, s. 458; 1994, Ex. Sess., c. 24, s. 14(c); 1997-498, s. 4.)

§ 58-33-105. False statements in applications for insurance.

If any agent, examining physician, applicant, or other person shall knowingly or willfully make any false or fraudulent statement or representation in or with reference to any application for insurance, or shall make any such statement for the purpose of obtaining any fee, commission, money or benefit from any company engaged in the business of insurance in this State, he shall be guilty of a Class 1 misdemeanor. This section shall also apply to contracts and certificates issued under Articles 65 through 67 of this Chapter. (1987, c. 629, s. 1; 1993, c. 539, s. 459; 1994, Ex. Sess., c. 24, s. 14(c).)

§ 58-33-110. Agents signing certain blank policies.

Any agent or limited representative who signs any blank contract or policy of insurance is guilty of a Class 3 misdemeanor and, upon conviction, shall be punished only by a fine of not less than one thousand dollars ($1,000) nor more than five thousand dollars ($5,000); provided, however, that transportation ticket policies of accident insurance and baggage insurance policies may be countersigned in blank for issuance only through coin-operated machines, subject to regulations prescribed by the Commissioner. (1987, c. 629, s. 1; 1993, c. 539, s. 460; 1994, Ex. Sess., c. 24, s. 14(c).)

§ 58-33-115. Adjuster acting for unauthorized company.

If any person shall act as adjuster on a contract made otherwise than as authorized by the laws of this State, or by any insurance company or other person not regularly licensed to do business in this State, or shall adjust or aid in the adjustment, either directly or indirectly, of a claim arising under a contract of insurance not authorized by the laws of the State, he shall be deemed guilty of a Class 1 misdemeanor. (1987, c. 629, s. 1; 1993, c. 539, s. 461; 1994, Ex. Sess., c. 24, s. 14(c).)

§ 58-33-120. Agent, adjuster, etc., acting without a license or violating insurance law.

If any person shall assume to act either as principal, agent, broker, limited representative, adjuster or motor vehicle damage appraiser without license as is required by law or pretending to be a principal, agent, broker, limited representative, adjuster or licensed motor vehicle damage appraiser, shall solicit, examine or inspect any risk, or shall examine into, adjust, or aid in adjusting any loss, investigate or advise relative to the nature and amount of damages to motor vehicles or the amount necessary to effect repairs thereto, or shall receive, collect, or transmit any premium of insurance, or shall do any other act in the soliciting, making or executing any contract of insurance of any kind otherwise than the law permits, or as principal or agent shall violate any provision of law contained in Articles 1 through 64 of this Chapter, the punishment for which is not elsewhere provided for, he shall be deemed guilty of a Class 1 misdemeanor. (1987, c. 629, s. 1; 1987 (Reg. Sess., 1988), c. 975, s. 11; 1993, c. 539, s. 462; 1994, Ex. Sess., c. 24, s. 14(c).)

§ 58-33-125. Fees.

(a) The following table indicates the annual fees that are required for the respective licenses issued, renewed, or cancelled under this Article and Article 21 of this Chapter:

Adjuster	$75.00
Adjuster, crop hail only	20.00
Agent appointment cancellation (paid by insurer)	10.00
Agent appointment, individual	10.00
Agent appointment, Medicare supplement and long-term care, individual	10.00
Agent, overseas military	20.00
Broker, nonresident	50.00
Broker, resident	50.00
Business entity	100.00
Limited representative	20.00
Limited representative cancellation (paid by insurer)	10.00
Motor vehicle damage appraiser	75.00
Surplus lines licensee, corporate	100.00
Surplus lines licensee, individual	50.00

(b) Whenever a temporary license is issued under this Article, the fee shall be at the same rate as provided in subsection (a) of this section; and any amounts so paid for a temporary license may be credited against the fee required for an appointment by the sponsoring company.

(c) Any person who is not licensed and who is required by law or administrative rule to secure a license shall, upon application for licensing, pay to the Commissioner a fee of fifty dollars ($50.00). If additional licensing for other kinds of insurance is requested, a fee of fifty dollars ($50.00) shall be paid to the Commissioner upon application for licensing for each additional kind of insurance.

In addition to the fees prescribed by this subsection, any person applying for a supplemental license to sell Medicare supplement and long-term care insurance policies shall pay an additional fee of fifty dollars ($50.00) upon application for licensing for those kinds of insurance.

(d) The requirement for an examination, prelicensing education, continuing education, or a registration fee does not apply to agents for domestic farmers' mutual assessment fire insurance companies or associations who solicit and sell only those kinds of insurance specified in G.S. 58-7-75(5)d for those companies or associations.

(e) A resident licensee may obtain a duplicate photo-bearing license at times and places within this State that the Commissioner considers necessary and reasonable to serve the convenience of both the Commissioner and the licensee. The Commissioner may contract directly with persons for processing of duplicate photo-bearing licenses, and the contract shall not be subject to Article 3 of Chapter 143 of the General Statutes. The Commissioner may charge a reasonable fee for duplicating a photo-bearing license in an amount that offsets the costs to the Department of duplicating the license, including costs associated with any contract entered into pursuant to this subsection. However, the Commissioner shall: (i) submit all proposed contracts for supplies, materials, printing, equipment, and contractual services that exceed one million dollars ($1,000,000) authorized by this subsection to the Attorney General or the Attorney General's designee for review as provided in G.S. 114-8.3; and (ii) include in all contracts to be awarded by the Commissioner under this subsection a standard clause which provides that the State Auditor and internal auditors of the Commissioner may audit the records of the contractor during and after the term of the contract to verify accounts and data affecting fees and performance. The Commissioner shall not award a cost plus percentage of cost agreement or contract for any purpose.

(f) Repealed by Session Laws 2007-507, s. 7, effective January 1, 2008, and applicable to fees or charges due, and actions occurring, on or after that date.

(g) All fees prescribed by this section are nonrefundable. The fees in subsection (a) of this section are in lieu of any other license fees. The fee for an individual agent appointment under subsection (a) of this section applies to each license.

(h)   Fees paid by an insurer on behalf of a person who is licensed or appointed to represent the insurer are payable to the Commissioner when billed. Billing of insurers for renewal fees must be on an annual basis. The frequency for billing insurers for other licensing and appointment fees is determined by the Commissioner and may be daily, monthly, or quarterly. An electronic payment made through the NAIC or an affiliate of NAIC is considered a payment to the Commissioner. (1987, c. 629, s. 1; c. 864, ss. 84, 85; 1989 (Reg. Sess., 1990), c. 941, ss. 4-5; c. 1021, s. 9; c. 1069, s. 14; 1991, c. 476, s. 3; c. 721, s. 7; 1991 (Reg. Sess., 1992), c. 837, s. 3; 2000-122, s. 1; 2007-507, s. 7; 2008-107, s. 29.10(a); 2010-194, s. 8; 2011-326, s. 15(h).)

§ 58-33-130. Continuing education program for licensees.

(a)   The Commissioner may adopt rules to provide for a program of continuing education requirements for the purpose of enhancing the professional competence and professional responsibility of adjusters and motor vehicle damage appraisers. The rules may include criteria for:

(1)   The content of continuing education courses;

(2)   Accreditation of continuing education sponsors and programs;

(3)   Accreditation of videotape or other audiovisual programs;

(4)   Computation of credit;

(5)   Special cases and exemptions;

(6)   General compliance procedures; and

(7)   Sanctions for noncompliance.

The Commissioner may contract directly with persons for the administration of the program provided for by this section, and those contracts shall not be subject to Article 3 of Chapter 143 of the General Statutes. However, the Commissioner shall: (i) submit all proposed contracts for supplies, materials, printing, equipment, and contractual services that exceed one million dollars ($1,000,000) authorized by this subsection to the Attorney General or the Attorney General's designee for review as provided in G.S. 114-8.3; and (ii) include in all contracts to be awarded by the Commissioner under this subsection a standard clause which provides that the State Auditor and internal auditors of the Commissioner may audit the records of the contractor during and after the term of the contract to verify accounts and data affecting fees and performance. The Commissioner shall not award a cost plus percentage of cost agreement or contract for any purpose. The Commissioner may charge a reasonable fee to course providers to offset the cost of the program, including costs associated with contracts authorized by this subsection. The fee authorized by this subsection shall be in addition to the fees specified in G.S. 58-33-133. As used in this section and in G.S. 58-33-132, "administrator" means any person with whom the Commissioner has contracted under this subsection.

(b) The Commissioner may adopt rules to provide for the continuing professional education of all agents and brokers who are licensed to sell, solicit, and negotiate the kinds of insurance specified in G.S. 58-33-26(c1)(1), (2), (4), (6), (7), or (8). In adopting the rules, the Commissioner may use the same criteria as specified in subsection (a) of this section.

(c) The license of any person who fails to comply with the continuing education requirements under this section shall lapse except that the Commissioner or administrator may either grant an extension of time for good cause shown or charge an administrative fee of seventy-five dollars ($75.00), or both, in lieu of having the person's license lapse.

(d) Biennial continuing professional education hour requirements shall be determined by the Commissioner, but shall not be more than 24 credit hours. The Commissioner may by rule establish a staggered system in which the credit hour compliance period is based on the month and year of birth of each individual licensee.

(e) Repealed by Session Laws 2007-507, s. 8, effective January 1, 2008, and applicable to fees or charges due, and actions occurring, on or after that date.

(f) Repealed by Session Laws 1993 (Reg. Sess., 1994), c. 678, s. 18, effective July 5, 1994.

(g)   Repealed by Session Laws 2007-507, s. 8, effective January 1, 2008, and applicable to fees or charges due, and actions occurring, on or after that date.

(h)   Any licensee who, after obtaining an extension under subsection (c) of this section, offers evidence satisfactory to the Commissioner or administrator that the licensee has satisfactorily completed the required continuing professional education courses is in compliance with this section.

(i)   The Commissioner is authorized to approve continuing professional education courses.

(j)   Repealed by Session Laws 2002-144, s. 3, as amended by Session Laws 2003-284, s. 22.2, and as amended by Session Laws 2004-124, s. 21.1, effective July 1, 2002.

(k)   Repealed by Session Laws 1993, c. 409, s. 4, effective July 1, 1993. (1989, c. 657, s. 1; 1989 (Reg. Sess., 1990), c. 941, s. 6; 1991, c. 476, s. 2; c. 554, s. 1; c. 720, s. 22; 1993, c. 409, s. 4; 1993 (Reg. Sess., 1994), c. 678, s. 18; 1998-211, ss. 20, 21; 2002-144, s. 3; 2003-284, s. 22.2; 2004-124, s. 21.1; 2007-507, s. 8; 2010-194, s. 9; 2011-326, s. 15(i).)

§ 58-33-132. Qualifications of instructors.

(a)   The Commissioner may adopt rules to establish requisite qualifications for and issuance, renewal, summary suspension, and termination of provider, presenter, and instructor authority for prelicensing and continuing insurance education courses. During any suspension, the instructor shall not engage in any instruction of prelicensing or continuing insurance education courses prior to an administrative review. No person shall provide, present, or instruct any course unless that person has been qualified and possesses a license from the Commissioner or administrator.

(b)   The Commissioner or administrator may summarily suspend or terminate the authority of an instructor, course provider, or presenter if the course presentation:

(1)   Is determined to be inaccurate; or

(2) Receives an evaluation of poor from any Department monitor and a majority of attendees responding to Department questionnaires about the presentation. (1995, c. 517, s. 17; 1999-132, s. 9.1; 2007-507, s. 9.)

§ 58-33-133. Continuing education course provider fees.

(a) Each course provider shall pay to the Commissioner a fee of one dollar ($1.00) per approved credit hour per individual who successfully completes a course under G.S. 58-33-130.

(b) At the time a course provider submits an application to the Commissioner for approval of a course under G.S. 58-33-130, the provider shall pay to the Commissioner a filing fee of one hundred dollars ($100.00) per course up to a two thousand five hundred dollars ($2,500) per calendar year maximum.

(b1) Licensees who are required to comply with G.S. 58-33-130 shall pay to the Commissioner a fee of one dollar ($1.00) per credit hour earned. These fees also apply to national designation courses and other courses approved by the Commissioner from other State or federal programs.

(c) Fees collected by the Commissioner under this section and under G.S. 58-33-130 shall be credited to the Insurance Regulatory Fund created under G.S. 58-6-25 for the purpose of offsetting the cost of administering the program authorized by G.S. 58-33-130. (2002-144, s. 2; 2003-221, s. 5; 2003-284, s. 22.2; 2004-124, s. 21.1; 2007-507, s. 10.)

§ 58-33-135. Continuing education advisory committee.

(a) The Commissioner shall appoint, in accordance with G.S. 58-2-30, one advisory committee for fire and casualty insurance licensees and one advisory committee for life and health insurance licensees. The advisory committees shall recommend reasonable rules to the Commissioner for promulgation under G.S. 58-33-130. The Commissioner may adopt, reject, or modify such recommendations. After the promulgation of rules under G.S. 58-33-130, the committees may from time to time make further recommendations to the Commissioner for additional rules or changes in existing rules.

(b) The property and liability advisory committee shall comprise:

(1) Two employees of the Department of Insurance;

(2) Two representatives from a list of four nominees submitted by the Independent Insurance Agents of North Carolina;

(3) Repealed by Session Laws 1999-132, s. 6.3.

(4) One representative of a licensed property and liability insurance company writing business in this State that operates through an exclusive agency force;

(5) One representative from a list of two nominees submitted by the North Carolina Adjusters Association;

(6) One representative of property and liability insurers from a list of two nominees submitted by the Association of North Carolina Property and Casualty Insurance Companies; and

(7) One representative from a list of two nominees submitted by the Community Colleges System Office.

(c) The life and health advisory committee shall comprise:

(1) Two employees of the Department of Insurance, which may be the same persons appointed under the subsection (b) of this section;

(2) One representative from a list of two nominees submitted by the North Carolina Association of Life Underwriters;

(3) One representative of life and health insurers from a list of two nominees submitted by the Association of North Carolina Life Insurance Companies;

(4) One representative from a list of two nominees submitted by the General Agents and Managers Conference;

(5) One representative from a licensed medical or hospital service corporation;

(6) One licensed health insurance agent from a list of two nominees submitted by the North Carolina Association of Health Underwriters;

(7) One representative of a licensed life or health insurer writing business in this State that operates through an exclusive agency force;

(8) One representative from a list of two nominees submitted by the North Carolina Fraternal Congress; and

(9) One representative from a list of two nominees submitted by the Community Colleges System Office. (1989, c. 657, s. 1; 1999-84, ss. 17, 18; 1999-132, s. 6.3.)

Article 33A.

Public Adjusters.

§ 58-33A-1. Purpose and scope.

This Article governs the qualifications and procedures for the licensing of public adjusters. It specifies the duties of and restrictions on public adjusters, which include limiting their licensure to assisting insureds in first-party claims. (2009-565, s. 1.)

§ 58-33A-5. Definitions.

(1) Business entity. - A corporation, association, partnership, limited liability company, limited liability partnership, or other legal entity.

(2) Catastrophic incident. - As defined in the National Response Framework, any natural or man-made incident, including terrorism, that results in extraordinary levels of mass casualties, damage, or disruption severely affecting the population, infrastructure, environment, economy, national morale, and/or government functions. A catastrophic incident shall be declared by the

President of the United States or the Governor of the state or district in which the disaster occurred. If state and local resources are insufficient, the Governor may ask the President of the United States to make such a declaration.

(3)   Fingerprints. - An impression of the lines on the finger taken for purpose of identification. The impression may be electronic or in ink converted to electronic format.

(4)   Home state. - The District of Columbia and any state or territory of the United States in which the public adjuster's principal place of residence or principal place of business is located. If neither the state in which the public adjuster maintains the principal place of residence nor the state in which the public adjuster maintains the principal place of business has a substantially similar law governing public adjusters, the public adjuster may declare another state in which it becomes licensed and acts as a public adjuster to be the home state.

(5)   Individual. - A natural person.

(6)   Person. - An individual or a business entity.

(7)   Public adjuster. - Any person who, for compensation or any other thing of value on behalf of the insured, does any of the following:

a.   Acts or aids, solely in relation to first-party claims arising under insurance contracts that insure the real or personal property of the insured, on behalf of an insured in negotiating for, or effecting the settlement of, a claim for loss or damage covered by an insurance contract.

b.   Advertises for employment as a public adjuster of insurance claims or solicits business or represents himself or herself to the public as a public adjuster of first-party insurance claims for losses or damages arising out of policies of insurance that insure real or personal property.

c.   Directly or indirectly solicits business, investigates or adjusts losses, or advises an insured about first-party claims for losses or damages arising out of policies of insurance that insure real or personal property for another person engaged in the business of adjusting losses or damages covered by an insurance policy for the insured.

(8) Uniform business entity application. - The current version of the NAIC Uniform Business Entity Application for resident and nonresident business entities.

(9) Uniform individual application. - The current version of the NAIC Uniform Individual Application for resident and nonresident individuals. (2009-565, s. 1.)

§ 58-33A-10. License required.

(a) A person shall not act or hold himself or herself out as a public adjuster in this State unless the person is licensed as a public adjuster in accordance with this Article.

(b) A person licensed as a public adjuster shall not misrepresent to a claimant that he or she is an adjuster representing an insurer in any capacity, including acting as an employee of the insurer or acting as an independent adjuster unless so appointed by an insurer in writing to act on the insurer's behalf for that specific claim or purpose. A licensed public adjuster is prohibited from charging that specific claimant a fee when appointed by the insurer and the appointment is accepted by the public adjuster.

(c) A business entity acting as a public adjuster is required to obtain a public adjuster license. Application shall be made using the uniform business entity application. Before approving the application, the Commissioner shall find all of the following:

(1) The business entity has paid the fees set forth in G.S. 58-33-125.

(2) The business entity has designated a licensed public adjuster responsible for the business entity's compliance with the insurance laws and regulations of this State.

(d) Notwithstanding subsections (a) through (c) of this section, a license as a public adjuster shall not be required of any of the following:

(1) An attorney-at-law admitted to practice in this State, when acting in his or her professional capacity as an attorney.

(2) A person who negotiates or settles claims arising under a life or health insurance policy or an annuity contract.

(3) A person employed only for the purpose of obtaining facts surrounding a loss or furnishing technical assistance to a licensed public adjuster, including photographers, estimators, private investigators, engineers, and handwriting experts.

(4) A licensed health care provider, or employee of a licensed health care provider, who prepares or files a health claim form on behalf of a patient.

(5) A person who settles subrogation claims between insurers. (2009-565, s. 1.)

§ 58-33A-15. Application for license.

(a) A person applying for a public adjuster license shall apply to the Commissioner on the appropriate uniform application or other application prescribed by the Commissioner.

(b) The applicant shall declare under penalty of perjury and under penalty of refusal, suspension, or revocation of the license that the statements made in the application are true, correct, and complete to the best of the applicant's knowledge and belief.

(c) An applicant for a license under this Article shall furnish the Commissioner with a complete set of the applicant's fingerprints in a manner prescribed by the Commissioner and a recent passport size full-face photograph of the applicant. The applicant's fingerprints shall be certified by an authorized law enforcement officer. The fingerprints of every applicant shall be forwarded to the State Bureau of Investigation for a search of the applicant's criminal history record file, if any. If warranted, the State Bureau of Investigation shall forward a set of the fingerprints to the Federal Bureau of Investigation for a national criminal history record check. An applicant shall pay the cost of the State and any national criminal history record check of the applicant. This subsection does not apply to a person applying for renewal or continuation of a home state public adjuster license or a nonresident public adjuster license.

(d) In addition, if an applicant described in subsection (b) of this section is a business entity, each key person must furnish the Commissioner a complete set of the key person's fingerprints and a recent passport size full-face photograph of the applicant. The key person's fingerprints shall be certified by an authorized law enforcement officer. The fingerprints of every key person shall be forwarded to the State Bureau of Investigation for a search of the applicant's criminal history record file, if any. If warranted, the State Bureau of Investigation shall forward a set of the fingerprints to the Federal Bureau of Investigation for a national criminal history record check. Each key person shall pay the cost of the State and any national criminal history record check of the key person. As used in this subsection, "key person" means a proposed officer, director, or any other individual who will be in a position to influence the operating decisions of the business entity. This subsection does not apply to a person applying for renewal or continuation of a home state public adjuster license or a nonresident public adjuster license.

(e) The Commissioner shall keep all information received pursuant to subsections (c) and (d) of this section privileged, in accordance with applicable State and federal law, and the information shall be confidential and shall not be a public record under Chapter 132 of the General Statutes. (2009-565, s. 1.)

§ 58-33A-20. Resident license.

(a) Before issuing a public adjuster license to an applicant under this section, the Commissioner shall find that the applicant meets all of the following criteria:

(1) Is eligible to designate this State as his or her home state or is a nonresident who is not eligible for a license under G.S. 58-33A-35.

(2) Has not committed any act that is a ground for denial, suspension, or revocation of a license as set forth in G.S. 58-33A-45.

(3) Is trustworthy, reliable, and of good reputation, evidence of which may be determined by the Commissioner.

(4) Is financially responsible to exercise the license and has provided proof of financial responsibility as required in G.S. 58-33A-50.

(5) Has paid the fees set forth in G.S. 58-33-125.

(6) Maintains an office in the home state of residence with public access by reasonable appointment and/or regular business hours. This includes a designated office within a home state of residence.

(b) In addition to satisfying the requirements of subsection (a) of this section, an individual shall:

(1) Be at least 18 years of age; and

(2) Have successfully passed the public adjuster examination.

(c) The Commissioner may require any documents reasonably necessary to verify the information contained in the application. (2009-565, s. 1.)

§ 58-33A-25. Examination.

(a) An individual applying for a public adjuster license under this act shall pass a written examination unless exempt pursuant to G.S. 58-33A-30. The examination shall test the knowledge of the individual concerning the duties and responsibilities of a public adjuster and the insurance laws and regulations of this State. Examinations required by this section shall be developed and conducted under rules and regulations prescribed by the Commissioner.

(b) The Commissioner may make arrangements, including contracting with an outside testing service, for administering examinations and collecting the nonrefundable fee set forth in G.S. 58-33-125.

(c) Each individual applying for an examination shall remit a nonrefundable fee as prescribed by the Commissioner as set forth in G.S. 58-33-125.

(d) An individual who fails to appear for the examination as scheduled or fails to pass the examination shall reapply for an examination and remit all required fees and forms before being rescheduled for another examination. (2009-565, s. 1.)

§ 58-33A-30. Exemptions from examination.

(a) An individual who applies for a public adjuster license in this State who was previously licensed as a public adjuster in another state based on a public adjuster examination shall not be required to complete any prelicensing examination. This exemption is only available if the person is currently licensed in that state or if the application is received within 12 months of the cancellation of the applicant's previous license and if the prior state issues a certification that, at the time of cancellation, the applicant was in good standing in that state or the state's producer database records or records maintained by the NAIC, its affiliates, or subsidiaries indicate that the public adjuster is or was licensed in good standing.

(b) A person licensed as a public adjuster in another state based on a public adjuster examination who moves to this State shall apply within 90 days after establishing legal residence to become a resident licensee pursuant to G.S. 58-33A-20. No prelicensing examination shall be required of that person to obtain a public adjuster license.

(c) An individual who applies for a public adjuster license in this State who was previously licensed as a public adjuster in this State shall not be required to complete any prelicensing examination. This exemption is only available if the application is received within 12 months after the cancellation of the applicant's previous license in this State and if, at the time of cancellation, the applicant was in good standing in this State. (2009-565, s. 1.)

§ 58-33A-35. Nonresident license reciprocity.

(a) Unless denied licensure pursuant to G.S. 58-33A-45, a nonresident person shall receive a nonresident public adjuster license if the person meets all of the following criteria:

(1) The person is currently licensed as a resident public adjuster and in good standing in his or her home state.

(2) The person has submitted the proper request for licensure, has paid the fees required by G.S. 58-33-125, and has provided proof of financial responsibility as required in G.S. 58-33A-50.

(3) The person has submitted or transmitted to the Commissioner the appropriate completed application for licensure.

(4) The person's home state awards nonresident public adjuster licenses to residents of this State on the same basis.

(b) The Commissioner may verify the public adjuster's licensing status through the producer database maintained by the NAIC, its affiliates, or subsidiaries.

(c) As a condition to continuation of a public adjuster license issued under this section, the licensee shall maintain a resident public adjuster license in his or her home state. The nonresident public adjuster license issued under this section shall terminate and be surrendered immediately to the Commissioner if the home state public adjuster license terminates for any reason, unless the public adjuster has been issued a license as a resident public adjuster in his or her new home state. Notification to the state or states where nonresident license is issued must be made as soon as possible, yet no later than 30 days after change in new state resident license. Licensee shall include new and old address. A new state resident license is required for nonresident licenses to remain valid. The new state resident license must have reciprocity with the licensing nonresident state(s) for the nonresident license not to terminate. (2009-565, s. 1.)

§ 58-33A-40. License.

(a) Unless denied licensure under this Article, persons who have met the requirements of this Article shall be issued a public adjuster license.

(b) A public adjuster license shall remain in effect unless revoked, terminated, or suspended as long as the request for renewal and fee set forth in G.S. 58-33-125 is paid and any other requirements for license renewal are met by the due date.

(c) The licensee shall inform the Commissioner by any means acceptable to the Commissioner of a change of address, change of legal name, or change of information submitted on the application within 30 days after the change.

(d) A licensed public adjuster shall be subject to Article 63 of this Chapter.

(e) A public adjuster who allows his or her license to lapse may, within 12 months from the due date of the renewal, be issued a new public adjuster license upon the Commissioner's receipt of the request for renewal. However, an administrative fee in the amount of double the unpaid renewal fee shall be required for the issuance of the new public adjuster license. The new public adjuster license shall be effective the date the Commissioner receives the request for renewal and the late payment penalty.

(f) Any public adjuster licensee that fails to apply for renewal of a license before expiration of the current license shall pay a lapsed license fee of twice the license fee and be subject to other penalties as provided by law before the license will be renewed. If the Department receives the request for reinstatement and the required lapsed license fee within 60 days after the date the license lapsed, the Department shall reinstate the license retroactively to the date the license lapsed. If the Department receives the request for reinstatement and the required lapsed license fee after 60 days but within one year of the date the license lapsed, the Department shall reinstate the license prospectively with the date the license is reinstated. If the person applies for reinstatement more than one year from the date of lapse, the person shall reapply for the license under this Article.

(g) A licensed public adjuster who is unable to comply with license renewal procedures because of military service, a long-term medical disability, or some other extenuating circumstance may request a waiver of those procedures. The public adjuster may also request a waiver of any examination requirement, fine, or other sanction imposed for failure to comply with renewal procedures.

(h) The license shall contain the licensee's name, city and state of business address, personal identification number, the date of issuance, the expiration date, and any other information the Commissioner deems necessary.

(i) In order to assist in the performance of the Commissioner's duties, the Commissioner may contract with nongovernmental entities, including the NAIC or any affiliates or subsidiaries that the NAIC oversees, to perform any ministerial functions related to licensing, including the collection of fees and data, that the Commissioner may deem appropriate. (2009-565, s. 1.)

Vision Books Order Form

Fax Orders: 1-980-299-5965

Phone Orders: 1-704-898-0770

E-mail Orders: www.visionbooks.org

Mail Orders: Vision Books, LLC
P.O. Box 42406
Charlotte, NC 28215

Shipp To:
Name_____
Address_____
City_____State_____Zip_____
Phone_____Fax_____
Email_____@_____

Bill To: We can bill a third party on your behalf.
Name_____
Address_____
City_____State_____Zip_____
Phone____(_____)_____Fax_____
Email_____@_____

Pamphlet Number ($15.00 Each)	Qty	Total Cost
_____	_____	_____
_____	_____	_____
_____	_____	_____
_____	_____	_____
_____	_____	_____
_____	_____	_____
_____	_____	_____
_____	_____	_____
<u>Full Volume Set 1-92</u>	<u>92 Pamphlets</u>	<u>1,380.00</u>

Free Shipping Shipping & Handling on Full Volume Orders
Add $1.00 Shipping & Handling per pamphlet $_____

Total Cost $_____

Thank you for your support. Management!

DID YOU ENJOY THIS BOOK?

Vision Books, LLC would like to hear from you! If you or someone you know has been fasely imprisoned, we would like to hear your story. If the 'North Carolina Criminal Law and Procedure' has had an effect in your life or if you have suggestions, we would like to hear from you. Send your letters to:

Vision Books, LLC
Attn: Staff Writers
P.O. Box 42406
Charlotte, NC 28215
Email: staff@visionbooks.org

Order Additional Copies:

Fax Orders:	1-980-299-5965
Phone Orders:	1-704-898-0770
E-mail Orders:	www.visionbooks.org
Mail Orders:	Vision Books, LLC P.O. Box 42406 Charlotte, NC 28215

www.ingramcontent.com/pod-product-compliance
Lightning Source LLC
Chambersburg PA
CBHW051628170526
45167CB00001B/104